THE COMPLETE CATALOGUE
OF
BRITISH TANKS

THE COMPLETE CATALOGUE
OF
BRITISH TANKS

James Taylor

H&S
Herridge & Sons

Published 2022 by
Herridge & Sons Ltd
Lower Forda
Shebbear
Beaworthy EX21 5SY
England

© Copyright James Taylor 2022
ISBN: 978-1-914929-03-8

Layout by Chris Fayers
Printed in Great Britain
by Short Run Press, Exeter, Devon

CONTENTS

INTRODUCTION

It is always dangerous to describe any book as a Complete Catalogue, because almost inevitably something will have been missed out through oversight. There is also bound to be somebody, somewhere, who can correct what is in print and at least offer a plausible explanation of why it is not exactly correct. For that reason, if you, reading this book, can fill in any gaps, please do not hesitate to get in touch through the publishers. I never mind being proved wrong or shown where my information is inadequate.

This attempt to fit the whole story of the British tank between two covers deliberately takes a few risks: not everybody would accept that the members of the CVR(T) family include vehicles that can be classified as tanks. Whether the Vijayanta that Vickers sold to India qualifies as a British tank (especially when it was built abroad) and whether the Sherman and other tanks of US origin that were used by British forces during the Second World War deserve the places they have in this book is another potential bone of contention. Self-propelled guns are listed if they are derived from a tank (the Archer for example) but not when purpose-built (such as the Abbott). There is zero chance of pleasing everybody!

I make no claims that this book is definitive; it is simply a ready reference source which gives basic information about its subject-matter. For readers who want more information about individual catalogue entries, I have offered suggestions for further reading. Some of the books I have suggested set very high standards indeed, and I am very happy to acknowledge that they and many others, as well as multiple on-line sources of information, have contributed to the material in the present volume.

The selection of photographs for this book combines historical material from museum collections with contemporary pictures (many submitted for general use on the web) and others from my own collection. Wherever possible, I have shown the source of photographs, but if there are incorrect attributions here, I apologise.

James Taylor
Oxfordshire, August 2022

The earliest tanks were designed to operate alongside the Infantry. This a Mk I "male" tank, number C19 Clan Leslie, pictured in France in 1916. The steering "tail" seen here soon proved unnecessary. (National Army Museum – out of Copyright)

Chapter 1
A HISTORY OF BRITISH TANKS

It was the fighting conditions that faced British troops during the Great War of 1914-1918 that led to the creation of the tank. By 1916, the combat had reached a stalemate as both sides dug-in to lines of trenches. Traditional infantry and cavalry tactics, backed up by heavy artillery, failed to make significant progress: gains made on one day were likely to be lost the next and the terrible cost in human terms was made glaringly apparent by the infamous battles on the Somme.

In these circumstances, the Army's thinkers believed that the only way to make progress on the battlefield was to use mobile armoured machines. None yet existed, and the War Office established a committee to look at proposals. Its work was fruitless, and the Royal Naval Air Service now joined in, reasoning that its armoured car squadrons could at least contribute their experience of armoured warfare to the debate. Then Winston Churchill, First Lord of the Admiralty, established a new Landships Committee to investigate further.

After various abortive experiments, work focused on an armoured box mounted on caterpillar tracks, and this showed promise. A first prototype, somewhat derisively known as Little Willie, was running by late 1915, and an improved design with tracks that ran all round its lozenge- or rhomboid-shaped armoured hull gained War Office approval in January 1916. The Landships Committee became the Tank Supply Committee ("tank" coming from the cover name for these new creations) and an order for the first 100 tanks was placed in February.

The first tanks were conceived as armoured support for the infantry, and needed to move no more quickly than an infantryman could walk in battle. Their main purpose was to break through fixed defences impeding the infantry advance, and then to follow on until needed

Vickers developed the Medium Mk II tank in the 1920s and sold examples both to the British Army and overseas. By this stage, the need to mount the primary weapon in a revolving turret had been more or less universally accepted. This example survives as an exhibit at the Bovington Tank Museum.

Britain also bought a number of Light tanks for Colonial peace-keeping duties, and was forced to press them into service for more serious fighting in the early years of the Second World War. These MK VIB types were pictured on patrol in North Africa in August 1940. (Imperial War Museum E443.2, Public Domain)

Britain learned a great deal about tank warfare very quickly in the Western Desert, where tanks like these Crusaders proved no match for the latest German designs in 1941. (Imperial War Museum, Public Domain)

Once the need for tanks in quantity became apparent, several British heavy engineering firms were co-opted to build them. This picture shows Matilda II tanks under construction at the Vulcan works in Lancashire.

again. Considerable scepticism among infantry commanders meant that there was little training in co-ordinating infantry activities with those of the tanks, and the first use of tanks during the Battle of the Somme on 15 September 1916 had mixed results. Many tanks broke down, but nearly a third achieved their breakthrough objectives, which was an impressive achievement. Tanks would continue to be used, though sparingly, for the rest of the war.

As the British Army gained more experience from the use of tanks, it became clear that these original lumbering giants were not the complete answer; there was an additional need for a lighter and faster type that could exploit breaches in the enemy front in the manner traditionally associated with the cavalry. Lightly armed and less heavily armoured, the Whippet tank of 1917 was developed to fit the bill.

Britain emerged from the Great War with technical leadership in tank design, although

other countries had begun to catch up and the Germans, French and Americans were among them. Nevertheless, in the immediate post-war years the British General Staff had little appetite for new tank designs. The trench warfare that had created the need for tanks in the first place was to some extent seen as an aberration, and old-school tactical thinking made a return. The cost of tanks was also undoubtedly a deterrent. The biggest problem, perhaps, was that there was no clearly identifiable threat, and therefore no clearly identifiable need to develop tanks to counter it. In 1923, Britain actually closed its Department of Tank Design.

Fortunately, British commercial interests created the momentum even if military tacticians had for the most part lost it. Heavy engineering firm Vickers Armstrongs had recognised that the use of tanks in the recent conflict had aroused the interest of armies around the world and had created a lucrative export market. With a certain amount of encouragement from the British Government, Vickers accordingly developed a number of Medium tanks that were primarily intended for export, and its Mark E or Six-ton type became probably the most influential design of the late 1920s. While the General Staff focused on other issues, Vickers developed the tank concept by adding features such as sprung suspension, more powerful engines, and a rotating turret with a useful gun. In fairness, the British Army did examine some of the Vickers designs, but adopted few of them.

Despite the indifference of the General Staff, there were those in Britain who could see the tank's potential. Thinkers like Col JFC Fuller, the assistant to the Chief of the Imperial General Staff, and Captain Basil Liddell Hart were behind late 1920s experiments with an All-Mechanised Force (which Fuller famously declined to lead when he was denied the staff he needed). In these experiments lay the origins of the later German Blitzkrieg tactics, but Britain failed to follow through. Although the Vickers Armstrong efforts helped Britain to retain its technical dominance of tank design into the early 1930s, that lead gradually dwindled. Where Germany, Russia and the USA were moving to welded tank hulls, Britain still used the riveted construction of its Great War tanks.

Even though peacetime financial restrictions limited the development and further procurement of tanks in this inter-war period, there was no shortage of new designs. Different types of tanks began to appear, to meet different military requirements, and as a result the tank concept was being pulled in several different directions at once. On the one hand, small, light tanks (some actually called "tankettes") were developed for what might be called Colonial policing duties – taking over some of the functions of the older armoured car. There were experiments with multi-turreted tanks, borrowing their basic concept from the Navy's warships to develop the idea of an armoured infantry support vehicle further. Meanwhile, cavalry officers were interested in developing the tank's mobility to enable it to take on some of the roles traditionally assigned to the cavalry.

Things began to change by the middle of the 1930s. Britain embarked on a rearmament programme in 1936 to counter the threat of another war with Germany, and inevitably many military thinkers fell back on their experience of the Great War and expected the next one to be similar. The new tank designs that were commissioned in this period followed the entrenched doctrine of separate Infantry and Cavalry designs, and would prove woefully inadequate when war actually came a few years later. The Matilda and Valentine cruiser tanks drawn up in this period are best viewed in hindsight as stop-gap designs. They suffered from being put into service too quickly before their teething troubles had all

been eliminated, and they had mechanical problems as well as design limitations.

WORLD WAR II

The second war with Germany led not only to a demand for more tanks but to a very rapid appraisal of the merits of those that were already in service. Almost without exception, they were found lacking. Lessons from desert warfare in North Africa in 1941 fed into the plans for new tanks, but in the early stages the General Staff approved so many new designs (not all of which

Under Lend-Lease arrangements with the USA, British forces were provided with large quantities of tanks designed and built in America. The stand-out design was the M4 Sherman, which the British further adapted by fitting their own 17pdr gun to create the Sherman Firefly.

TANK TYPES

As soon as the first "rhomboid" tanks were joined by the lighter and faster Whippet tanks, it became clear that there could and should be more than one type of tank. The Whippet was the first Medium tank, and other names followed.

In the 1930s, British tank doctrine identified three major types of tank and named them after their intended roles.

Light tanks, as their name suggested, were usually small and relatively agile, with a minimum of armour and perhaps only machine-guns for armament. They were typically used for reconnaissance work, or for general peacekeeping duties in the Colonies.

Infantry tanks continued the line begun by the slow-moving rhomboid designs of the Great War. Their purpose was to support infantry troops and to travel alongside them at walking speed. They had to be heavily armoured to withstand attack by anti-tank guns, and they had to have armament that could deal with enemy positions and sometimes with enemy tanks as well.

Cruiser tanks took over from the unsatisfactory Medium

tanks in the 1930s. Their purpose was not only to exploit breakthroughs but also to penetrate behind enemy lines and act independently of the infantry to disrupt communications and supply lines. They had to have greater speed, and as a result tended to lack the heavy armour of the Infantry types. Their main armament had to be capable of tackling threats from other tanks.

The early campaigns of the Second World War made clear that the Light tank had very limited value. They also showed that the Infantry tanks were hampered by their lack of speed and that the Cruisers lacked sufficient armour when faced with enemy tanks. These limitations gradually led to the realisation that the ideal solution was a multi-purpose or universal tank, and since the late 1940s the concept of the Main Battle Tank (MBT) has predominated.

Nevertheless, not every British tank since the Second World War has been an MBT. It has been necessary to create Heavy Gun Tanks to meet specific threats, and also to create light and nimble reconnaissance types. In addition, many tanks have been adapted and converted for special roles, such as bridge-laying and combat engineer duties.

Needs must: the Rotatrailer was a wartime British invention that allowed a tank to tow additional supplies of ammunition and fuel on a quick-release coupling. Tank crews hated it.

With the A34 Comet in 1944, Britain finally delivered a tank that combined reliability, speed and firepower. This running survivor was pictured at one of the regular demonstrations of historic tanks that are now held at the Tank Museum in Bovington. (Alan Wilson/Wiki Media Commons)

reached production) that it is difficult not to get a strong impression of desperation. This was certainly compounded by the loss of so much British armour in France when the BEF was evacuated from Dunkirk in 1940.

Nevertheless, by 1943 the position was improving. New and more powerful guns were available, the Rolls-Royce Meteor solved the problem of inadequate engine performance, and the new A27 tank family promised to provide British troops with the fighting machines they needed. In addition, Lease-Lend was delivering American-made tanks in quantity to provide the

numbers required, and with them came inspirational technology such as the dual-purpose 75mm gun that could fire both armour-piercing and high-explosive rounds.

Most important among the British tanks in the later years of the Second World War were the A22 Churchill, the A27M Cromwell, and the A34 Comet. Infantry tanks gained speed and Cruiser tanks gained better armour, with the result that the differences between them became less marked. By the end of the war, and as exemplified by the new Centurion tank that was then under development, the time was right for the all-round capabilities of the Main Battle Tank. The Churchill had been designed as the last of the old-style Infantry tanks, but by the end of the war it had been extensively improved to become one of Britain's most successful designs.

COLD WAR

As the new world order settled into place after the end of the Second World War, it became clear that the two opposing forces in Europe were those of NATO (the North Atlantic Treaty Organisation, to which Britain belonged) and those of the Warsaw Pact, led by the Soviet Union. Britain was committed to maintaining a force in the now divided Germany as a first line

Too late for the Second World War, the A41 Centurion became Britain's first all-purpose or universal tank. It was a tremendously capable all-rounder that was further developed during the 1950s and had a long service life both in the British Army and with friendly overseas forces. This one is now an exhibit at the RAF Museum in Cosford. (Tony Hisgett, CC 2.0)

of defence in case of attack from the east, and to that end it needed a strong tank force. Like other NATO countries with similar commitments, it was dismayed to see the Russian IS-3 heavy tank appear in victory celebrations during 1945, and the need to counter both this and Russia's vast armada of ever-more threatening tanks prompted some important changes to tank design and policy in the years that followed.

While the Warsaw Pact forces were largely dependent on Russian designs and were in effect standardised around a small number of types, the main NATO countries preferred to develop their own individual designs while the smaller countries generally took one or the other of these. Britain still had large numbers of wartime tanks in service, but even its latest Centurion could not match the Soviet IS-3. The solution was to develop an additional heavy gun tank to support the front-line Centurions. Designed in something of a hurry, the Conqueror was a compromise that lasted for a relatively brief period until

the Centurion could be up-gunned with a new and more powerful main gun. In this guise, the Centurion was considered to be an excellent tank and wholly suitable for its intended role against the forces of the Warsaw Pact.

Meanwhile, new developments in both gunnery and drivetrains made it possible to design a single tank that would combine the mobility of the Centurion with the firepower of the heavy

The Chieftain was designed to counter the threat from Warsaw Pact forces in Europe and entered service in 1965. Two of them were pictured here on BAOR exercises in Germany. (MoD/BAOR)

Conqueror. Development went ahead during the second half of the 1950s, and the result was the Chieftain. This modern design was one of the most heavily armed and armoured tanks of its time, and yet its weakness was unreliability: in order to comply with a NATO call for multi-fuel engines, it had been designed around a new power pack that was prone to endless troubles. Its real significance, however, was that it finally banished the need for separate cruiser and heavy gun tanks. The Chieftain was Britain's first real Main Battle Tank, and used a US-designed main gun with the 120mm calibre standardised for NATO tanks.

An improved Chieftain developed for export was cancelled for political reasons in 1979, but it was swiftly redeveloped as the Challenger and now incorporated the latest British tank development – the world-leading Chobham armour, precise details of which remain secret to this day. Challenger entered service in 1983 and proved to be an excellent tank in most respects, with an automated fire control system that delivered great accuracy for its main gun. Even so, Britain rapidly embarked on a new joint project with Germany that aimed to deliver a new MBT in the late 1980s. When that project fell apart, a number of the ideas developed for it were diverted to create the Challenger 2 that entered service in mid-1994 and again proved to be an excellent tank. An upgrade programme announced in 2021 planned to convert a number of these tanks into Challenger 3 types to extend their service life beyond 2030.

The Challenger tank entered service in the early 1980s. One is seen here during Exercise Highland Monarch in Germany, held by BAOR. (MoD/BAOR)

Life Extension Programmes are expected to keep the Challenger in service into the 2030s. This publicity picture of the Challenger 3 upgrade was issued in 2021. (RBSL)

NAMES AND CODES

The A prefix Codes

Between the early 1920s and 1945, British tank designs were given identifying numbers by the General Staff, in a numerical sequence preceded by the letter A. The first of these was the A1 Independent. Each number referred to a specification that had been issued as a requirement by the General Staff.

Not every paper specification with an A number led to a production tank. Tanks developed for export as private ventures (notably by Vickers) were not allocated A numbers. There might be variations within a specification that led to two related codes: thus the A27L had a Liberty engine while the A27M had a Meteor engine built by Rolls-Royce. Lastly, General Staff numbers could change after a major redesign. The 1944 upgrade of the A22 Churchill tank initially attracted the General Staff designation A22F but was later redesignated A42.

The FV Codes

After the Second World War, a new identification system was put in place. All military vehicles were given codes beginning with FV (Fighting Vehicle), and the FV4000 series was allocated to tanks. The Centurion tank, which had started life as an A41, became an FV4007, while later variants included the FV4011. The later Chieftain tank became an FV4201.

Type Name and Mark

Like all British Army equipment, tanks were given a descriptive name according to a prescribed formula. Typical of these was the "Tank, Medium, Mark D."

As this example makes clear, the descriptive name incorporated a variant descriptor, or Mark number. Mark B came after Mark A, and so on; Mark III likewise came after Mark II. These variants might include sub-variants; an A might be added ("Mark IIA") to indicate a change of armament, or an asterisk ("star") might be added to indicate some other change. In some cases, more than one star might be added; the Mk V tank of 1917, for example, gave rise to Mk V* and Mk V** variants.

Service Name

Before 1941, some tanks gained names that had been applied at the project stage. The Whippet, for example, was so called by its creator, and the Valentine was probably called that when under development at Vickers.

In June 1941, Prime Minister Winston Churchill asked for all tanks to be named. Like most people, he probably found the A codes and descriptive type names impenetrable and confusing. For reasons that are no longer clear, names beginning with C were allocated to tanks, and among the first allocated were Cavalier and Cromwell. Roman numerals were used to indicate new variants, such as a Crusader II. The tradition remains intact today, as the current British Main Battle Tank is called the Challenger, although the British Army now prefers Roman numerals and the upgraded Challenger will be called a Challenger 3.

Chapter 2
A-Z OF BRITISH TANKS

The prototype A1 Independent tank was completed in 1926 and was the first of the multi-turreted tanks.

A1 INDEPENDENT

The Vickers A1 Independent tank was built only in prototype form but was the first multi-turreted tank and exerted a major influence on tank design globally in the inter-war years. In Britain, it influenced other multi-turreted designs from Vickers such as the Medium Mk III and the Cruiser Mk I.

In late 1921, the General Staff invited Vickers to design a new Heavy Tank, and provided a set of guidelines. By March 1923, Vickers had a preliminary design ready, but it also had an alternative of its own, much of it designed by WG Wilson. The General Staff preferred the Vickers design, which probably led to the "Independent" name it later acquired.

The A1 had the length of the existing rhomboid "heavies" but with lower track runs and turrets instead of sponsons for maximum firepower and self-defence capability. The main gun was a 3pdr, mounted in the central turret, and each of the four subsidiary turrets mounted a .303 Vickers heavy machine gun. One gun was installed with enough elevation to provide anti-aircraft cover.

The engine was an air-cooled Armstrong-Siddeley Puma V12 with 370bhp at 1500rpm and an 18.8-litre swept volume, which drove through a lorry-type gearbox to give a maximum speed of 20mph. The suspension consisted of four coil-sprung double bogies on each side, plus a single bogie fore and aft, and the tank had a specially developed new hydraulic braking system. It was designed for a crew of eight, and the commander communicated with them by means of an intercom.

The prototype was delivered in 1926 and was displayed to leaders of the Dominions later that year. It also took part in the Salisbury Plain exercises in the later 1920s. However, it always remained an experimental model and was withdrawn in 1935. In the mean time, a British officer had been court-martialled in 1933 for providing plans of the Independent and other documents to a German contact; the plans reached the Soviet Union where they may have influenced the design of the T-28 and T-33 tanks.

The single prototype of the A1 tank, numbered A1E1, still survives, at the Bovington Tank Museum.

DIMENSIONS AND WEIGHT:
Length 24ft 11in, width 8ft 9in, height 8ft 11in. Weight 32 tons.

FURTHER READING:
The Vickers Tanks, from Landships to Challenger 2, Christopher Foss & Peter McKenzie.

A2 TANK
See Vickers Medium Mark I.

A3 TANK
See Three-man Light Tank.

A4 TANK
The A4 designation was given to the early versions of the family of Vickers Light Tanks accepted into service by the British Army. These ran from the Mk I to the Mk IV, and are listed here under Light Tank Mk I (etc).

A5 TANK
The later versions of the Vickers Light Tank, the Mk V and Mk VI, were given the new designation of A5. They are described here under the headings of Light Tank Mk V and Light Tank Mk VI.

A6 "SIXTEEN-TON" TANK
The A6 tank was built by Vickers as a series of three prototypes in 1928-1929 to meet a War Office requirement for a tank to replace its existing Medium Mark II types. It was unsuccessful but did lead on to the Medium Mark III design.

The War Office specification was drawn up in July 1926 and called for a weight no greater than 15.5 tons (which led to the "16-ton" nickname for these models). Crew protection and comfort were addressed by the requirement for 16mm frontal armour and 9mm armour elsewhere, and by the insistence on a separate engine compartment.

The order for a prototype went to Vickers, and unsurprisingly their first proposal in September shared features with the A1E1 Independent that was in design at the time. So what was now called the A6 was a multi-turreted design, with its fighting compartment at the front and its engine at the rear. The central two-man turret would have a 3pdr main gun and a co-axial machine gun, and there would be no fewer than three machine-gun turrets. The front two were planned with a pair of Vickers machine guns each and the rear turret was to have an anti-aircraft weapon. There would be a seven-man crew and Vickers offered the options of a 120bhp engine that promised a top speed of 14mph or a 180bhp engine that would give 20mph.

Two prototypes (A6E1 and A6E2) had been built by June 1928 and a third (A6E3) had been ordered. All would have the 180bhp Armstrong-Siddeley Puma engine that exceeded expectations by giving a 26mph maximum speed. Further development included trials of a 180bhp Ricardo C1 six-cylinder diesel engine in A6E2. Testing during 1928 made clear that there were shortcomings with the proposed machine-gun arrangement as well as with the suspension. The third prototype was completed in mild steel with a simplified gun arrangement, and in 1929 Vickers submitted three alternative suspension designs, one of which was tried on each prototype. However, none provided the stable gun platform that the Army wanted and the project was brought to an end.

The A6 project was superseded by the Vickers Medium Mark III, but the three prototypes were relegated to mechanical trials duties, where they remained until 1938. A plan to fit twin Rolls-Royce Phantom car engines to A6E1 was rejected on cost grounds, and A6E3 was tried with a 500bhp Thornycroft RY12 marine engine.

None of the A6 prototypes survives today.

DIMENSIONS AND WEIGHT:
Length 21ft 6in, width 8ft 9in, height 9ft 2in. Weight 17.4 tons.

FURTHER READING:
The Vickers Tanks, from Landships to Challenger 2, Christopher Foss & Peter McKenzie.

A7 MEDIUM TANK
The A7 was an unsuccessful late-1920s design for a Medium tank. Just three prototypes were built, the first two in 1929 and the third in 1934. Although the A7 did not enter production, it was influential on several later designs, and especially on the Matilda, for which the prototypes were used as development "mules".

The tank was conceived as an alternative to the Vickers-designed A6 and was designed at ROF Woolwich. Inevitably, armour and armament were similar, but to keep weight down to 14 tons the machine-gun turrets were replaced by a hull gunner with a Vickers machine gun. The hull was flat-topped, while the turret was rectangular with sloped sides and a commander's cupola, and accommodated three of the five crew members.

Two mild steel prototypes (A7E1 and A7E2) were ready in May 1929, both powered by an

The A7 was one of the many ideas that did not prosper. The project lasted from 1929 to 1937, but produced just three prototypes.

15

First of the Cruiser tanks was the A9 of 1936, officially a "Cruiser Mark I". Its powered turret traverse was a first for British tanks, but the multi-turret configuration had been largely discredited by the time it was built.

air-cooled 120bhp Armstrong-Siddeley engine; A7E1 had the four-speed gearbox from the Medium Mark III project and A7E2 had a Wilson hydraulic planetary type. Suspension was derived from the Birch Gun variant of the Medium Mark II, with leaf springs on A7E1 but there was a different design with coils on A7E2.

Trials in 1931 revealed the A7 tanks to be slower than expected, and unreliable as well. Although A7E2 remained on test until 1936, attention had switched elsewhere. Following a January 1934 requirement for a modernised A7, a third prototype appeared in May that year. This time power came from a pair of AEC 7.7-litre six-cylinder diesel bus engines. The suspension was radically redesigned with a coil spring for each road wheel, and a new turret on a widened hull was among the multiple improvements. The main gun was now a 2pdr. A7E3 proceeded to trials in 1936 but again proved unreliable despite its improved speed. Suggestions for further improvement included a Vickers-Hortsmann suspension and a Liberty engine, but work on the project stopped in 1937.

DIMENSIONS AND WEIGHT:
Length 22ft 6in (A7E3), width 8ft 11.5in (A7E3), height 9ft 1in (A7E3). Weight 14 tons (A7E3 18.2 tons).

FURTHER READING:
Forgotten Tanks and Guns of the 1920s, 1930s and 1940s, David Lister.

A8 MEDIUM TANK

The A8 was planned as a Medium tank and the project to develop it lasted from 1933 to 1937. However, only a wooden mock-up was ever built.

Conceptually, the A8 followed on from the unsuccessful third prototype of the A7, and it drew on the experience gained with the two earlier A7 prototypes. The design by Vickers-Armstrongs incorporated some A7 elements, including the later turret with the 2pdr gun, and the tank was expected to weigh 17.5 tons. The plan was to install a pair of Rolls-Royce Phantom II six-cylinder engines driving through a Wilson gearbox and giving around 240bhp between them.

DIMENSIONS AND WEIGHT:
Length, Width and Height not known.
Weight 17.5 tons.

FURTHER READING:
Forgotten Tanks and Guns of the 1920s, 1930s and 1940s, David Lister. [?]

A9 CRUISER TANK

The A9 or Cruiser Mark I tank was pressed into service as a cruiser in pursuit of changing tank warfare doctrine in the late 1930s. However, it had originally been designed as a 12-ton Medium tank to fill the gap left by the failure of the Medium Mark III project.

In its original form, the A9 design was approved in late 1935, and a development contract was placed with Vickers. The project was initially headed by Sir John Carden, but after his death in an air accident in December 1935 the job passed to Leslie Little. A first prototype was completed in April 1936. The A9 followed Vickers practice in having multiple turrets, the main turret being based on that of the third A7 prototype but with a sloping rear and a new high-velocity 2pdr gun. More significantly, this turret was the first one in a British tank to have a powered traverse, using a system similar to that developed for the Vickers Wellington bomber aircraft. There were two smaller turrets, one either side of the driver's compartment, and each with a Vickers machine gun and a distinctive conical roof. There was no separation between the driving and fighting compartments in the hull, and the A9 had a six-man crew of commander, driver, gunner, loader, and two machine-gunners.

Vickers chose a new suspension system similar to the one on their own light tanks that allowed easy replacement of assemblies in the field. They also decided to use the 120bhp six-cylinder Rolls-Royce car engine, driving through a five-speed Meadows gearbox. A notably compact transmission layout allowed a shorter hull and lower overall height. Although Vickers did not quite meet the 12-ton target, the final weight of 12.5 tons was close.

The new tank was generally successful in trials at Farnborough, but the engine was considered weak. Little solved the problem by replacing it with a new six-cylinder diesel engine that AEC had developed for buses. Although the War Office was not keen on the idea of a diesel engine, the A9 was accepted as an interim buy and an order was placed for 125 in 1937. Vickers built 50 at Elswick, and the remaining 75 were constructed by Harland & Wolff in Belfast. In the mean time, tank doctrine had been changing and the War Office had begun to think in terms of Cruiser tanks. As the A9 was the only design in prospect that even remotely satisfied the criteria, it was redesignated as the Cruiser, Mark I.

Production models were quite extensively modified from the prototype, with changes to the hull and turrets, a new cupola that gave better visibility, and provision for a radio. But the A9 lacked the mobility and armour to be a genuine cruiser tank, and as a result the last 36 from Harland & Wolff were diverted to close-support work and were built with a 3.7in howitzer, becoming the Cruiser Tank Mk I CS.

Deliveries of the A9 began in January 1939 and continued through to July 1940.

The first 24 tanks were sent to France but all were lost to the Germans after Dunkirk. A few went to North Africa with the 7th Armoured Division in February 1940. Crews had difficulties with the diesel engine, with the narrow tracks, the suspension and the clutch, and the A9's thin armour made it very vulnerable to anti-tank weapons. Machine-gun turrets were often modified for anti-aircraft defence or removed altogether, but the 2pdr main gun did prove effective even though no HE shells were available.

Nevertheless, by the autumn of 1941, it was clear that the A9 was obsolete. Although a few remained on active service, most were withdrawn and used for training.

Two A9 tanks still survive. One is at the Tank Museum in Bovington, and the other is at the Indian Cavalry Tank Museum in Ahmednagar.

DIMENSIONS AND WEIGHT:
Length 19ft, width 8ft 4in, height 8ft 8in.
Weight 12.8 tons.

FURTHER READING:
British Cruiser Tanks, A9 & A10, Peter Brown.

A10 CRUISER TANK

The A10 was designed by Sir John Carden at Vickers alongside the A9 and was originally intended to be an Infantry Support version of it. As tank doctrine changed in the mid-1930s, it was repurposed as a Cruiser tank but was far from ideally suited to that role. The tank was in production between 1938 and 1940 but was soon replaced by newer designs.

The A10 had essentially the same hull as the A9 but without the twin machine-gun turrets and with 25mm armour that was twice as thick as on the A9. This was the main reason why the tank was over two tons heavier than an A9 and, with the same 150bhp AEC A179 engine, it had a top speed of only 16mph. Range was 100 miles, and the suspension featured a pair of coil-sprung triple-wheel bogies on each side.

As on the A9, there was no separation between the driving and fighting compartments; the five-man crew consisted of commander, gunner, loader, driver and hull machine gunner. The main gun was a QF 2pdr; there was a coaxial Vickers .303 machine gun, and the first variants had a 7.92mm Besa machine gun in a barbette to the driver's right.

The A10 or Cruiser Mk II was very similar to the A9 and was originally planned as an Infantry version of it. This close-support variant at Bovington is a rare survivor. (Hohum/ WikiMedia Commons)

The first A10 prototype was completed in 1936, a few months after the first A9. In 1937 it was dropped from its original role of Infantry support tank but was repurposed as a Heavy Cruiser, eventually gaining the designation of Tank, Cruiser, Mk II. The first order was placed for 100 tanks in July 1938, BRCW and Metropolitan being allocated 45 each and Vickers the remaining ten. A further order for 75 went to BRCW in late 1939, making 175 in all.

The first A10s entered service in December 1939 and unsurprisingly several went with the BEF to France. Here, they revealed track problems and poor cross-country performance. Those sent to North Africa nevertheless did well in the desert conditions alongside the A9s also sent there. Sixty examples were subsequently sent to Greece with 3RTR, but most were eventually lost to mechanical breakdowns, of which a large proportion were the result of lost tracks.

Narrow escape hatches proved a problem, compromising crew safety from the beginning, and the A10 was too slow to be a true cruiser tank. Nevertheless, its lower hull and suspension went on to become the basis of the much more successful Valentine tank.

There were two variants of the A10 design. The first was the A10 Mk IA (or Cruiser Mark IIA), in which a Besa machine gun replaced the co-axial Vickers to standardise ammunition, and an armoured radio housing was added. The second was a batch of 30 designated A10 Mk IA CS (or Cruiser Mark IIA CS), where the main gun was replaced by a 3.7in howitzer for close-support (mainly smoke) roles.

The only complete survivor of the A10 is a close-support example at the Tank Museum in Bovington, but an early example was found on a firing range in the early 2000s and was under long-term restoration at the time of writing.

DIMENSIONS AND WEIGHT:
Length 18ft 4in, width 8ft 4in, height 8ft 8in. Weight 14.3 tons.

FURTHER READING:
British Cruiser Tanks, A9 & A10, Peter Brown.

A11 INFANTRY TANK
See Matilda I.

A12 TANK
See Matilda II.

A13 TANK
There were three tanks designated A13, which was the 1936 General Staff specification for a Cruiser type. The A13 Mk I was the Cruiser

Tank Mk III, the Mk II was the Cruiser Tank Mk IV, and the MkIII was the Covenanter or Cruiser Tank Mk V. Each of these tanks has its own separate entry.

A14 TANK

The A14 was a heavy Cruiser tank drawn up to a modified General Staff specification, and the project was entrusted to the London Midland and Scottish Railway in 1939. The specification included Horstmann suspension and a Thornycroft V12 engine driving through a new Wilson compound epicyclic gearbox, while the overall layout of the superstructure and turret was similar to that of the A9 and A10 tanks. During trials, the first pilot model proved noisy and mechanically complicated, and the project was abandoned in late 1939 before a second tank had been completed.

A15

The A15 designation was initially applied to a specification for the 1938 Class Medium tank, a heavy cruiser with Christie suspension. This specification was later redesignated A16, and the A15 designation was re-used for the tank that became the Crusader.

A16 CRUISER

In 1936, Lt Col Giffard le Q. Martel, Assistant Director of Mechanisation at the War Office, visited Russia, where he saw the BT tank, a fast tank that used Christie suspension. Convinced that a Christie tank would outperform the A9 Cruiser Tank Mk I that was then being developed, he persuaded the General Staff to look into creating a heavier cruiser tank with the new suspension and 30mm armour.

Two specifications were developed, as A14 and A15. Completion of the A15 specification lagged behind that of the A14 and when finally ready it was redesignated A16 and was given to Nuffield Mechanisation and Aero for development. Unsurprisingly, the new A16 had some visual similarities to other Nuffield designs, not least the A13 Cruiser Mk III, and was designed to use the Liberty engine that Nuffield were then building under licence. Like the later A15 Crusader, it had five road wheels on each side to spread its weight evenly. The hull had a flat top surface and the turret was rectangular with gently sloping sides.

At an April 1939 review of the heavy cruiser designs then under consideration, the General Staff decided that the A16 would be too expensive, and the project was shelved. Nuffield had built one prototype, which was designed to use the 2pdr gun as its main armament and had provision for three machine guns, two in the hull and one in the turret.

A17 TANK

See Tetrarch.

A18 TANK

The A18 was a 1939 proposal for a cruiser tank based on the A17 Tetrarch. Although the proposal was abandoned, the turret design was used for later cruiser tanks.

A19 HEAVY CRUISER

The General Staff gave the A19 designation to a proposal for a heavy cruiser tank that was put forward in December 1938. Its key characteristics were a transversely-mounted engine (which was presumably intended to reduce length) and a main turret which had smaller subsidiary turrets mounted on top of it. The engine itself was intended to be a shortened version of the Thornycroft RY12, which put out 650bhp in its original marine form. However, it took so long to agree on a detailed specification that the whole project was cancelled in May 1940 without leaving the drawing-board.

A20 TANK

The War Office drew up the A20 specification in 1939 in the expectation that battle conditions would prove to be similar to those of the First World War. When it became clear during 1940

The first prototype of the A16 tank was pictured before its main armament had been installed. This heavy Cruiser was a pioneer of Christie suspension but did not enter production.

This mild-steel pilot model of the A20 tank was pictured at the Harland & Wolff shipyard where it was built. The project was cancelled but its small-wheeled configuration with all-round tracks prefigured the A22 Churchill.

that battles were likely to be fast-moving and very different in character, it was cancelled.

The A20 specification called for a "shelled area tank." The Mechanisation Board was responsible for the initial design, which was deliberately drawn up to suit trench warfare. The tank had to be able to cross trenches and surmount a 5ft obstacle when moving forwards and a 4.5ft one when reversing, and the first design envisaged all-round tracks running on small wheels, and side sponsons for the armament, just like a First World War tank. There was to be a 2pdr gun in the front of the hull and the tank would have a crew of seven men.

The original concept was amended in September 1939 to replace the side sponsons by a turret (taken from a Matilda), although small sponsons remained in place for auxiliary machine guns. At the same time, 60mm armour was specified to withstand the German 37mm anti-tank gun. To save time, the War Office now wanted to use existing mechanical components, including the new 300bhp Meadows flat-12 engine that had been requested for the Covenanter tank.

A contract for 100 tanks was placed with the Harland & Wolff shipyard in Belfast, and that company was asked to complete the detail design before producing prototypes. Four pilot models in mild steel were ordered in February 1940 and the first one was trialled in June. It proved to have mechanical problems, and with a 15mph top speed was also considered underpowered.

However, by this stage the reality of armoured warfare had become clear from the experience of the BEF in France. So the A20 project was cancelled that same month and the pilot models (some say only two were built) were relegated to component testing work. In place of the A20, the War Office now drew up specification A22 – which would later enter production as the Churchill tank.

DIMENSIONS AND WEIGHT:
Length, Width 7ft 7in, and Height not available. Weight 43 tons

FURTHER READING:
Churchill Infantry Tank, David Fletcher.

A21 TANK

The A21 was a projected development of the A20 tank that did not progress beyond the drawing-board.

A22 TANK

See Churchill.

A23 TANK

The A23 was Vauxhall's proposal to meet the 1940 General Staff specification for a new heavy Cruiser tank. It was a shortened and lightened version of their A22 Churchill infantry tank design, sharing the same suspension and 21-litre Bedford Twin-Six engine. The A23 was intended to have 75 mm of frontal armour and a five-man crew, but its design was rejected in early 1941 in favour of the A24 Cavalier.

A24 TANK

See Cavalier.

A25 TANK

See Harry Hopkins.

A26 CRUISER TANK

The A26 was a projected lighter and faster cruiser version of the A22 Churchill. It was never built.

A27 TANK

See Cromwell.

A28 INFANTRY TANK

The A28 tank was the first of many attempts to adapt the A27 Cromwell cruiser tank for other roles, retaining as much as possible of the original design to simplify manufacture and ease battlefield logistics. The proposal came from Rolls-Royce, who suggested creating an infantry tank that would have thicker plate armour than the Cromwell, plus skirt plates to protect the suspension.

At this stage of the war, the General Staff was prepared to look at almost any new idea, and so allocated the project the A28 number. However, the project quite literally did not progress beyond the drawing-board, and was abandoned in December 1941. Only a single drawing of the proposal is known to have survived, together with a note that the anticipated weight was 28 tons.

FURTHER READING:
British Tanks: The Second World War, Pat Ware.

A29 CLAN

Specification A29 was yet another General Staff response to the needs identified in the African desert campaign. It was issued in late 1941 and called for a cruiser tank with the 17pdr gun. The job of designing it was handed to Rolls-Royce, who had already worked on a tank design (the Cromwell MkIII) at its Clan Foundry premises in Belper, Derbyshire. The tank's alternative name of Clan came from that.

The A29 design was based on the Cromwell, with an uprated 700bhp Meteor engine that was expected to give 30mph. It used thicker and inevitably heavier armour, but this in tandem with the new turret for the larger gun was too much for the Cromwell's suspension. Rolls-Royce dealt with this by proposing a new twin-track suspension, but problems arose and delayed the programme. Meanwhile, the A30 that was being developed by BRCW was closer to being ready for production and was also going to weigh some 10 tons less than A29, and so A29 was cancelled.

DIMENSIONS AND WEIGHT:
Length 24ft 5in, width 10ft 5in, height 9ft 7in. Weight 50.6 tons.

FURTHER READING:
The Rolls-Royce Meteor: Cromwell and other applications, Evans, McWilliams, Whitworth & Birch.

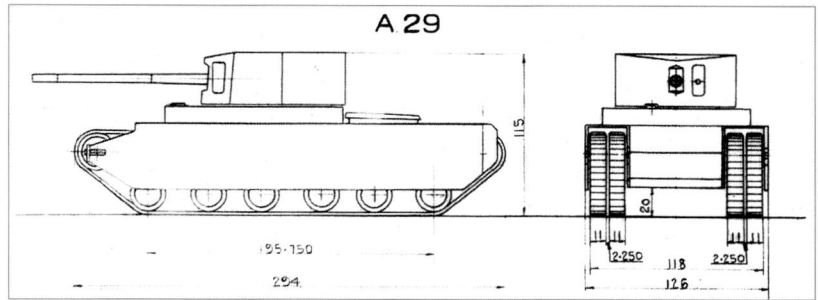

A30 TANK
See Challenger.

A31 TANK

The A31 designation was given to yet another enthusiastic proposal by Rolls-Royce for developing a new tank based on the A27 Cromwell. The poor performance of the A22 Churchill at the Dieppe Raid in August 1942 led to calls for its replacement, and this triggered the proposal to up-armour the Cromwell as an infantry tank. The proposal was not followed up.

A32 TANK

The General Staff allocated designation A32 to Rolls-Royce's proposal for yet another development of the A27 Cromwell. This time it was to be a more thorough redesign, with stronger suspension to support an extra 4.5 tons of weight created by armour equivalent to that of the Churchill. This was another proposal that came to nothing.

A33 TANK
See Excelsior.

A34 TANK
See Comet.

A35 TANK

The A35 was another Rolls-Royce idea for an up-armoured version of the Cromwell, and its design was carried out jointly with the LMS railway. With a projected weight of 36 tons, the A35 was going to need stronger suspension, but the project was not pursued.

A36 TANK

The A36 project was one more set of ideas that did not progress beyond the drawing-board. It was to be an up-armoured A30 Challenger, with stronger suspension to carry its additional weight, and a 17pdr gun.

Casting around for new tank designs after the retreat from Dunkirk, the General Staff called for a Cruiser with the then-new 17pdr gun. It became the A29 Clan and was developed by Rolls-Royce, but there was no production. (Rolls-Royce)

A37 TANK

This tank would have been a heavier version of the A33 Excelsior, with a longer hull, an extra suspension bogie on each side, and a 17pdr gun. It did not progress beyond the project stage.

A38 TANK

See Valiant.

A39 TANK

See Tortoise.

A41 TANK

See Centurion.

A42 TANK

The Mk VII A22 Churchill was redesignated A42 in 1945.

A43 TANK

See Black Prince.

A44 TANK

A44 was a project to make the A34 Comet capable of taking the 17pdr gun by adding a larger turret ring. The availability of the new "77mm" gun, which would fit the existing hull, led to the cancellation of the A44 project.

A45 UNIVERSAL TANK

See FV201 and Conqueror.

A46 LIGHT TANK

The A46 light tank was the last project numbered in the A series of specifications issued by the General Staff. Vickers picked up the contract to produce it in late 1943 and the War Office called for 80 production tanks in 1944 before even seeing the plans. Production was at one stage expected to begin in 1946 but in practice it never did, and the A46 project petered out in 1947.

Vickers chose to base the design of the A46 on the A17 Tetrarch and A25 Harry Hopkins light tanks, and the new tank resembled them with the same four large wheels per side and front-wheel steering. The plan was to fit gun tank versions with the new "77mm" compact development of the 17pdr gun, with a 7.62 co-axial machine gun. Several different engine options were considered, ranging from a 1000bhp Meteor through its 350bhp Meteorite V8 derivative and a 207bhp GMC diesel down to a 160bhp Rolls-Royce B80.

As the project progressed, it took on an almost modular aspect. Although the tank variants were to be rear-engined, there were to be related self-propelled guns and armoured load carriers with front-mounted engines. By 1947, work was under way on a related armoured personnel carrier known as CT-26, but the project had clearly lost its way by then.

DIMENSIONS AND WEIGHT:
Length 16ft (21ft 5in with gun forward), width 9ft 6in, height 6ft 6in. Weight 16 tons.

FURTHER READING:
Forgotten Tanks and Guns of the 1920s, 1930s and 1940s, David Lister.

ALECTO

The Alecto was a self-propelled gun derived from the unsuccessful Harry Hopkins tank (Vickers Light Tank Mk VIII). (Alecto was one of the Furies of Ancient Greek mythology).

Only small numbers were actually built. They were intended for close-support work by airborne forces, and had a 3.7in howitzer mounted low down in the hull. These were turretless vehicles and their armour was reduced as compared to the parent gun tank in order to save weight.

In a fit of enthusiasm, the War Office ordered 2200 of them, but only a few were built before their limitations became clear, and none ever saw active service. Some were later converted to bulldozers and used by Royal Engineers units.

AL JAHRA

The Al Jahra was a variant of the Vickers MBT Mk 1 that was supplied to Kuwait. The order for 70 tanks was met in 1970.

This strange-looking machine was the Alecto, a close-support derivative of the Harry Hopkins tank that mounted a 3.7in howitzer in its hull. Strictly speaking, it was a self-propelled gun rather than a tank.

The Al Jahra was the Kuwaiti version of the Vickers MBT Mk 1. (Tank Museum, Bovington)

Once again strictly a self-propelled gun, the Archer was a derivative of the Valentine tank that was introduced in 1943. Unusually, the gun faced the rear of the vehicle, which had a large open superstructure. (Morio, CC-by-SA 4.0)

ARCHER

The Archer was a derivative of the Valentine tank, but as a self-propelled gun it was operated by the Royal Artillery rather than the Royal Armoured Corps.

Once the 17pdr gun had been identified as an effective anti-tank weapon in late 1941, there was a rush to get it out to the front lines. Alongside various specifications for a 17pdr-equipped tank, the General Staff called for a self-propelled gun that could be put into production more quickly. Vickers took on the design and production of this, basing it on the Valentine tank chassis that was still in production but was now obsolete as a tank. The Archer entered production in mid-1943 with an order for 800 examples, although this was later reduced and only 665 had been built by the time production ended in May 1945.

The Archer was powered by an uprated (192bhp) version of the GMC 6-71 diesel engine. Its gun was mounted in a low-profile, open-topped superstructure and had a limited traverse. Unusually, it was installed facing backwards, which both reduced the length of the vehicle and enabled it to retreat rapidly after firing. The crew of four benefited from a well-arranged fighting compartment.

Archers did not enter service until October 1944, more than a year after production had begun. They served in Italy and North-West Europe during the war, and some were still in service with BAOR units into the 1950s. 200 examples were sent to Egypt after the 1948 Arab-Israeli War, and a further 36 to Jordan in 1952.

There are survivors at the Tank Museum in Bovington and at the National War and Resistance Museum at Overloon in the Netherlands. Others can be found at museums in Australia, India and Israel.

DIMENSIONS AND WEIGHT:
Length 21ft 11in, width 9ft, height 7ft 4in.
Weight 15 tons.

FURTHER READING:
Universal Tank: British Armour in the Second World War - Part 2, David Fletcher; *British Anti-Tank Artillery 1939–1945*, Chris Henry.

AVENGER

This was a planned self-propelled anti-tank gun variant of the A30 Challenger tank that did not enter production.

BARON

See Matilda II.

BIRCH GUN

See Vickers Medium Mark II.

BISHOP

The Bishop was a self-propelled gun derived from the Valentine tank. The rapid manoeuvres of the North African campaign lay behind the June 1941 request from the Ministry of Supply to BRCW to develop a self-propelled artillery vehicle based on the Valentine and mounting a 25pdr gun. The first order for 100 vehicles was placed in November 1941 and 50 more were ordered in July 1942, but production was halted before they had all been built.

Bishops were based on the Valentine Mk II with its 131bhp AEC A190 diesel engine. The enormous fixed turret needed for the 25pdr gun dwarfed the hull, giving the vehicle an unbalanced look and a very distinctive profile. The Bishop was used in North Africa and first saw action during the Battle of El Alamein. It was also used in the early days of the Italian Campaign but its slow speed and the limited gun traverse did not endear it to its four-man crews. By late 1942 the more effective US-built M3

This ungainly-looking machine is the Bishop, a self-propelled gun derived from the Valentine tank. The huge turret mounted a 25pdr gun. (Imperial War Museum, E-17430)

The A43 Black Prince was very obviously related to the Churchill, but mounted a larger turret with the 17pdr gun. (Public Domain)

Priest was becoming available, and the Bishops were moved into training roles.

DIMENSIONS AND WEIGHT:
Length 18ft 6in, width 9ft 1in, height 10ft. Weight 17.5 tons.

FURTHER READING:
Valentine Infantry Tank 1938-1945, Bruce Oliver Newsome PhD.

BLACK NIGHT

Black Night was the name given to a Challenger 2 Technology Demonstrator that aimed to upgrade the Challenger 2 with new night combat capabilities and an Active Protection System. The tank was shown by BAE Defence Systems at the September 2018 Defence Vehicle Dynamics exhibition and elements of it were incorporated into the Challenger 3 programme a year later.

BLACK PRINCE (A43)

In 1943, the General Staff issued specification A43 for an interim Infantry tank that would have a more effective main armament than the A22 Churchill. Sometimes known as the Super Churchill or Heavy Churchill for obvious reasons, this tank was formally known as the Black Prince, and was named after the son of King Edward III who distinguished himself as a military commander during the Hundred Years' War in the 14th century.

For speed, the A43 design was based on that of the Churchill itself, but the larger gun – planned from the start as the QF 17pdr or 76mm type – needed a larger turret with a wider turret ring, and as a result the hull also had to be widened. It was also welded instead of riveted like the contemporary Churchill hull.

The increase in size led to a major increase in weight, and the suspension had to be strength-ened and the tracks widened by 10 inches to cope. The 350bhp Bedford Twin Six engine of the Churchill was retained, but the tank proved badly underpowered with a road speed of just 10.5mph and a cross-country maximum of 7.5mph. A suggestion that the Rolls-Royce Meteor engine would improve the performance was not adopted, not least because production of the Meteor was already at full stretch.

By the time the Black Prince prototypes were ready in May 1945, the new Centurion tank was ready to enter production and the A43 had effectively become redundant. There would therefore be no production. The design had called for a pair of 7.92mm Besa machine guns to supplement the main gun, and probably all the prototypes had this configuration. Of the six that were built, one (number 4) survives in the Tank Museum at Bovington, while a hull recovered from Salisbury Plain in the 1980s is in private ownership.

DIMENSIONS AND WEIGHT:
Length 28ft 11in, width 11ft 3.5in, height 9ft. Weight 51 tons.

FURTHER READING:
British and American Tanks of World War Two, Peter Chamberlain & Chris Ellis.

CAERNARVON (FV221)

The Caernarvon tank was built to overcome delays in the Conqueror programme that were introduced when the decision was made in 1949 to use the American L1 120mm gun. The hull was almost ready, but the gun and turret were not, and the British Army anticipated an unac-ceptable delay.

The decision taken was to proceed as quickly as possible to troop trials of the hull by fitting it with the turret and gun from the A41 Centurion,

The Caernarvon was a stop-gap design in the early 1950s. This example was pictured at a press demonstration with a Centurion in the background.

and the resulting vehicle was given the FV221 designation and the name of Caernarvon. A first prototype was completed in 1952 to Mk I specification with a Centurion Mk II turret and 17pdr gun, but all subsequent Caernarvons had the Mk II specification with the Mk III Centurion turret and larger 20pdr gun.

The resulting tank was heavier and less agile than the Centurions already in service, but the 21 examples of the Caernarvon Mk II did allow troop trials of the hull intended for Conqueror and so allowed the entry into service of that tank to be brought forward by about three years. Pictures suggest that some of the trials vehicles had an extended gun barrel, which may have been intended to simulate the longer barrel of the 120mm gun intended for Conqueror.

Official documents do not agree on armour specifications but the maximum armour thickness (on the Centurion-derived turret) was probably 152mm. The Caernarvon was powered by a Rolls-Royce Meteor engine driving through a Merritt-Brown five-speed gearbox, and it rode on Horstmann suspension with a large gap between the centre bogies on each side. There was a four-man crew, consisting of a driver in the hull and the commander, gunner and loader in the turret, although the hull contained an unused position that had been designed for a fifth crew member in Conqueror. Maximum road speed has been quoted as 22mph.

Conqueror entered production in 1955, making the Caernarvon redundant. Some

Caernarvon Mk II hulls were re-used to create Conquerors, which may always have been part of the FV221 plan. The only one that survived was the Mk I prototype, which lost its turret and was then used for a time to test an experimental gas turbine engine. It survived until the late 1990s as the static commentary box at the Tank Museum in Bovington, but was then scrapped.

DIMENSIONS AND WEIGHT:
Length 25ft 4in, width 13ft 1in, height not known. Weight 55 tons.

FURTHER READING:
Conqueror Heavy Gun Tank, Michael Norman;
Britain's Lost Armour, 1945-1970, David Lister.

CARDEN-LOYD TANKETTE MKS I-V

The Carden-Loyd Tankette was the most successful of the one-man and two-man designs produced in the 1920s as cost-effective solutions to modernising armies around the world. The vehicle was important in the history of tank design mainly because it helped to clarify what a tank was and what it was not. In practice, the Tankette would evolve along a different path that would lead to the Universal Carrier and similar vehicles.

The first iterations of the design were built in 1925 by Carden-Loyd Tractors, Ltd of Kensington in London, and were intended for one-man operation. They were powered by a 40bhp Ford Model T four-cylinder petrol engine in the front of the hull and had a simple open-topped design with a mounting for a machine gun. The War Office evaluated the prototype, and the Mk I production model that followed was offered with either road wheels or tracks. Armament was a .303 Vickers machine gun. Mk II and Mk III tracked models followed quickly afterwards, with progressive evolutions of a suspension redesigned around four bogies on each side.

From 1926, the focus was on a two-man model. The first of these was the Mk IV, with a further modified suspension and a .50 cal Vickers heavy machine gun. After Mk IVA and Mk IVB evolutions, Carden-Loyd tried a wheel-and-track arrangement on their Mk V design. This unsuccessful prototype would however be followed by the very successful Mk VI.

The Mk VI appeared in 1927, still with its 40bhp Ford Model T engine and essentially an open tracked vehicle with armament limited to

Looking almost like a toy, this was the Carden-Lloyd two-man Tankette of 1926. (IWM, KID235)

Mk VII carried its machine gun in a squat fully rotating turret, and its Mk VIII successor was better known as the Light Tank Mk I that was adopted by the British armed forces.

Surviving examples include one at the Tank Museum in Bovington and a 1933 Mk VI trials vehicle in the Parola tank museum in Finland.

DIMENSIONS AND WEIGHT:
Length 8ft 9in, width 5ft 9in, height 4ft.
Weight 1.5 tons.

FURTHER READING:
Armour in Profile No 16, Carden Loyd Mark VI, R J Icks.

a Vickers .303 machine gun. Its main advance, however, was redesigned tracks that lasted much longer than earlier designs. The gunner was now positioned alongside the driver. Vickers did well with the Mk VI on export markets, and even sold the bulk of the 450 made to the British Army (although the total of 325 British examples is disputed). Vickers sold manufacturing licences overseas, too, and elements of the Mk VI design influenced indigenous tank designs in Czechoslovakia, Poland, the Soviet Union and even Germany – where the Panzer I light tank owed some of its suspension layout to this British design.

After the Mk VI, Vickers pursued two related lines of development. One eventually led to the Universal Carrier that proved so useful during the Second World War, and the other led to light tanks. On the light tank side, the two-man

CAVALIER (A24)

The Cavalier was an early stage in Britain's urgent response to the shortage of tanks after Dunkirk. It was planned as the Mk VII Cruiser Tank, was allocated the A24 designation and was originally to be named Cromwell. After the Meteor engine became available, it was renamed Cavalier to avoid confusion with other variants of the design.

The Tank Directorate decided in mid-1940 that future tanks should use the latest 6pdr gun, and in January 1941 the Tank Board decreed that the new cruiser should be in production by spring 1942. As a result, it would have to be based on an existing design to avoid the time delays associated with prototyping a new one. The job was allocated to Nuffield Mechanisation

The A24 Cavalier of 1942 was not particularly successful. It featured the 6pdr gun and a Liberty engine and was derived from the Crusader. This example was pictured by Nuffield Mechanisations, who developed it. The photograph was taken on 1st October 1942. (British Motor Industry Heritage Trust)

& Aero Ltd, who were to base the new model on their Crusader, and the War Office ordered six pilot models, under the name of Cromwell.

Delays in development of the turret were probably the reason why gunnery trials did not begin until December 1941, and the pilot-production Cavalier began trials at Farnborough in March 1942. A decision had been made that production should be shared between Nuffield and Ruston & Hornsby. In the mean time, the first A24 variants with Meteor engines appeared and immediately demonstrated their superiority over the Cavalier. Lord Nuffield refused to compromise by redesigning his tank to take the Meteor engine, and the War Office limited their order for Cavaliers to just 500 examples.

The Cavalier suffered from the same engine problems as the Crusader, and in February 1943 it was sidelined by the AFV Liaison Committee, who decided against developing it further with the new 75mm gun or 95mm howitzer. So those delivered were all relegated to training or auxiliary armour roles. Some were converted to ARV specification, their turrets being removed and a jib and other recovery equipment being added, but these were soon dropped. Beginning in 1943, 340 Cavaliers were completed as OP tanks with a dummy gun barrel, and proved useful as forward observation posts for the Royal Artillery. A dozen or so Cavaliers were handed over to the French in 1945.

Visually, the Cavalier was very similar to other cruiser tanks from the same family, although it had Crusader-type exhausts in the rear hull plate and shorter suspension arms (to cope with greater weight) than the Centaur and Cromwell. There would be Type A and Type B hulls, with minor differences. The turret was a boxy six-sided structure with an internal mantlet and the armoured outer skin attached to the inner walls by large and very visible bolts. Armour thickness varied between 20mm and 76mm. Internally, the hull was divided into four compartments by partial bulkheads which also had a strengthening function. There was a front compartment for the driver and the hull gunner, a fighting compartment behind it, an engine compartment behind that, and then a transmission and final drive compartment at the rear.

Mechanically, the Cavalier was very much the same as the Crusader, with a five-speed gearbox and pneumatic operation of the gears, brakes and the Wilson steering. The Nuffield Liberty engine was in 410bhp Mk IV form.

Cavalier gun tanks had a crew of five, consisting of commander, gunner, loader, driver, and co-driver. The 6pdr main gun was accompanied by a co-axial 7.92mm Besa machine gun, and a second Besa was mounted in the front of the hull. The tank had a maximum road speed of 24mph and a maximum off-road speed of just 14mph. It carried enough fuel for an operational range of 165 miles.

Just two Cavalier tanks are known to survive, and both are in poor condition. One belongs to the Tank Museum at Bovington and the other is at the Isle of Wight military museum.

DIMENSIONS AND WEIGHT:
Length 20ft 10in, width 9ft 6in, height 8ft. Weight 27 long tons.

FURTHER READING:
Cromwell Cruiser Tank 1942-50, David Fletcher & Richard C Harley.

CENTAUR (A27L)

Even though the A27 Cromwell promised to be the solution to Britain's need for a fast cruiser tank in 1942, there were not initially enough Meteor engines to meet this sudden new demand. As a result, the General Staff called for another interim tank that would essentially be a Cromwell with the older and much less powerful Liberty V12 engine. It was to be designed so that conversion to Cromwell standard would be straightforward when the supply of new Meteor engines had built up.

This interim tank was given the A27L designation (the L standing for Liberty) and was named the Centaur. The design was commissioned from English Electric in November 1941 and shared the Cruiser Tank Mk VIII classification with the Meteor-engined Cromwell or A27M. The pilot tank was completed in June 1942 and production began before the end of the year. The Liberty engine was coupled to the Merritt-Brown gearbox used with the Meteor (it had typically been used with a Wilson gearbox) and there were various other minor changes to make an eventual engine swap simpler. Centaurs nevertheless had different track tensioning arrangements from the Cromwell, and they had an angled rear plate with Crusader-style exhaust louvres.

About 950 were built in all. The Mk I had a 410bhp Liberty engine, which gave 27mph on the road and about 16mph across country. The

Mk II was only experimental and had wider tracks and no hull machine gun. A 75mm gun and uprated Liberty engine built by Leyland were the key features of the Mk III, of which 233 were built, and this improved engine was also used in the 80 Mk IV models, which were Close Support variants with a 95mm howitzer instead of the standard 6pdr gun.

During 1943, most Centaur Mk I models were up-gunned with the 75mm weapon. Others were converted as planned to Cromwell standard with Meteor engines (becoming Cromwell Mk X types, later redesignated Mk III), and a few were retained for training. Some Mk III Centaurs were converted for special-purpose roles, becoming AA tanks with Polsten cannon (AA Mk I for the Mk III or AA Mk II for the Mk IV); OP vehicles with extra communications equipment and a dummy gun for artillery observation duties; or ARVs, with a winch and a demountable A-frame jib instead of a turret). There were Dozer versions for the combat engineers, too, with a winch and jib for the dozer blade and no turret, and a very few lost their turrets to become Armoured Personnel Carriers.

Most of the unconverted Centaurs never saw action, being retained instead for training duties. The Close-Support variants nevertheless did see action during the D-Day landings and in their aftermath. In early 1946, 52 Centaur Mk I tanks were given to the Greek Army in the early period of the Greek Civil War. They saw limited service in the war because much of the fighting was in mountainous areas, but were retained until 1962.

Several Centaurs still survive. They include examples at the Imperial War Museum in Duxford and in France at the Musée des Blindés in Saumur and the Pegasus Bridge Museum in Ranville. Four survive in Portugal, one in Poland, and one at the Greek Army Tank Museum. Dozer conversions survive at the Tank Museum in Bovington and in India and Myanmar, and of course there are some gun tanks in private collections.

DIMENSIONS AND WEIGHT:
Length 20ft 10in, width 9ft 6in, height 8ft 2in. Weight 28.4 tons

FURTHER READING:
Cromwell Cruiser Tank, 1942-50, David Fletcher & Richard C Harley.

The Centaur was an A27 derivative powered by the Liberty engine, a poor cousin to the Meteor-engined A27 Cromwell. This one is a Centaur IV. Pictured in June 1944, it belonged to H Troop, 2nd Battery, Royal Marine Armoured Support Group. (IWM, B5457, Public Domain)

CENTURION (A41)
The Centurion was probably one of the most outstanding tank designs ever, and it was certainly one of the longest-serving. Centurions first reached armoured units of the British Army in 1946 and by 1948 were firmly established in service. They saw battlefield use from 1950 onwards, and the British Army was still using them in AVRE form during the Gulf War in early 1991. They were sold to a large number of overseas forces, and were extensively modified and upgraded by both Israel and South Africa for use into the 21st century.

When more effective tanks became available in quantity, many Centaurs were converted to special-purpose tanks. This one is a Centaur Dozer and is preserved in the Tank Museum at Bovington. (Makizox/ WikiMedia Commons)

Appearing just too late to make any difference at the end of the Second World War, the Centurion proved to be an excellent and long-lasting tank design. "Lily" is a Mk III type, without the side skirts commonly seen on Centurions, and is preserved in the Tank Museum at Bovington.

With side skirts firmly in place, this is a Centurion ARV, a variant which first appeared during the Korean War.

The origin of the Centurion can be traced back to 1943, by which time the weaknesses of then-current British tanks had become all too apparent. None could be adapted to take the highly effective new 17pdr gun that had been designed as an anti-tank weapon, and so the General Staff called for a new tank to be designed around it. It was conceived as a cruiser type according to the doctrines of the time and its main characteristics were laid out in October 1943; many of them were based on the German Panther or Pzkpfw V that had entered service that year.

Disillusioned with the efforts of commercial companies to produce tanks using their own designs, the General Staff entrusted the design of the new A41 Cruiser Tank to the Department of Tank Design. Dimensions were established primarily by the size of the turret ring needed for

the 17pdr gun, although the width was limited by such things as rail transport requirements. The armour specification was drawn up to cope with the powerful German 88mm anti-tank gun, and the choice of engine fell on the Rolls-Royce Meteor, which had already proved itself in the Cromwell and Comet tanks. The gearbox and steering system would be the same Merritt-Brown Z51R five-speed with two reverse speeds also used in those tanks. For the suspension, modified Horstmann double-bogie units (three on each side) were chosen because of their good performance and their ease of maintenance and replacement in the field.

The prototype A41s, and later the Mk 1 to Mk 3 production variants of the tank, were designed under the leadership of AEC at Southall, although design leadership would be transferred to Vickers-Armstrong Ltd for the Mk 5 and later variants produced from 1955. A first model was ready for examination at AEC in 1944, and the Tank Board called for 20 prototypes to be constructed by the Royal Arsenal and by ROF Nottingham. High losses in the Normandy campaign then called for a focus on production of existing designs, and as a result the first A41 prototypes were not built until January 1945. By this time, the A41 had acquired the name of Centurion (which had earlier been allocated to the aborted A30). The first prototype was delivered for trials at Chertsey in April 1945.

The basic layout of the Centurion hull was conventional, with driving, fighting, engine and transmission compartments divided by bulkheads. The tank was crewed by four men – the driver, commander, gunner, and loader (who also operated the radios). The turret traverse was power-operated, and there was an auxiliary generator to provide power for this and for the radios (as well as the vital boiling vessel in the turret that brewed the crew's tea). To avoid the need to use the main engine, the auxiliary generator was driven by a Morris four-cylinder car engine in the forward left-hand corner of the engine compartment.

Ammunition for the main gun was stored below the turret ring to reduce the risk of fire, which was one disadvantage of using the Meteor petrol engine. On each side of the tank, three detachable skirting plates protected the suspension and hull against hand-held anti-tank weapons. The Centurion had a maximum road speed of about 20mph and could reach 15mph in cross-country conditions.

The 20 prototypes had a variety of detail specifications; to meet a need for a heavy-calibre quick-firing weapon to respond to anti-tank fire, some had a 20mm Polsten cannon in the turret alongside the main armament and others had co-axial machine guns. Early trials went well, and six prototypes were shipped to Belgium in May 1945 for further trials. Again, the Centurion performed well, but out of these trials came a clear preference for the co-axial machine gun over the Polsten cannon.

Centurion Mks 1-8

The first order for 800 tanks was placed soon afterwards, and production began in November at Leyland Motors, ROF Leeds, the Royal Arsenal and Vickers Elswick. The first deliveries were made in February 1946. There were to be 100 Mk 1 variants with the 17pdr main armament and a co-axial 7.92mm Besa machine gun in the original design of fabricated turret. The next 700 tanks were initially ordered as Mk 2 (or A41A) types with an up-armoured hull and a newly designed cast turret that incorporated a new cupola that allowed the commander an all-round view under armour, a sighting periscope for the gunner, and stabilisation for the main gun.

The new turret had been approved by October 1946 for use with the latest and more powerful 20pdr gun, and a new and more powerful Meteor Mk 4B engine with 650bhp at 2250rpm had also become available. So with that improved specification, the Centurion became a Mk 3. Production of this first standard variant began in early 1947 and by 1948 the tank was widespread among British Army units. The Mk 3 was so much of an improvement on the two earlier Marks that a programme was developed to upgrade these to Mk 3 standard; those Mk 1s and Mk 2s which were not so modified were withdrawn from frontline duties and were turned into the special-purpose tanks described below.

The Mk 3's effectiveness was further improved by the availability for the 20pdr gun of APDS ammunition, which gave the weapon double the armour penetration capability of a German 88mm. The fire control system with its gun stabilisation was superbly effective, and allowed the gunner to track a target while on the move. In addition, the main armament could fire medium-velocity HE shells against unarmoured targets and pillboxes, making the Centurion an extremely versatile tank. Many examples went to BAOR units and stayed there as part of the Cold War deterrent, but the Centurion really came into its own on the battlefront in Korea between 1950 and 1953, when its agility and superb gun accuracy earned it praise not only from its users but from the Americans as well.

Nevertheless, frontline service highlighted various weaknesses, and nearly 250 modifications were made before Mk3 production ended in 1956. One weakness not satisfactorily cured was the tank's poor range of a theoretical 65 miles; in practice, it could be as low as 50 miles even on made roads. BAOR units experimented with supplementary external fuel tanks like those used on wartime Russian tanks, but these proved impractical. Much later, around 1956, a 200-gallon mono-wheel fuel trailer was made available for towing behind the tank, but its users generally regarded it as a liability. Fortunately, the Centurion proved to be a reliable tank, because another major criticism was that maintenance was difficult: it could take as long as 18 hours to change an engine in the field.

The next major variant of the Centurion was the Mk 5, previewed in 1955 and in production from 1956. There never was a Mk 4, which was planned as a close-support variant with a 95mm CS howitzer but was never built. On this new generation of Centurions, the anti-infantry 2in bomb-thrower on the turret was removed (it was a hindrance to the loader), the turret roof was reshaped and the rear escape door was deleted. At the same time, 7.62mm Browning machine guns (which used NATO standard small-arms ammunition) were fitted to the commander's cupola and the coaxial mount. An extra stowage bin was added to the glacis plate and a guide roller was added to the track run. From about the same time, a fume extractor was added to the barrel of the 20pdr gun.

The first of several upgrade programmes had already begun by the time the last major variant of the Centurion arrived in 1959, which is why it took the Mk 7 designation: the Mk 6 was a modified and redesignated Mk 5. For the Mk 7 , Leyland Motors had carried out a comprehensive redesign of the hull in order to incorporate a third fuel tank. This increased the tank's range to a reliable 100 miles (101 miles were claimed) in the right conditions. It was swiftly followed by the availability of the new L7 105mm gun, which began user trials in July 1959 and was quickly adopted as the new standard armament for the Centurion.

The last Centurions were built in 1962, and the final gun tank version was the Mk 8, which gained a more resilient mantlet and a new commander's cupola. In total, 4423 Centurions had been built, including many for overseas military forces and a sizeable number of special-purpose variants. There are details of all these below.

Upgrade programmes

An upgrade programme was introduced in 1959, converting existing Centurions to use the new 105mm gun and adding thicker hull armour as well. The upgrades were carried out during base overhauls, and the modified tanks gained new designations: the upgraded Mk 5 became a Mk 6; the Mk7 became a Mk 9 (alias FV4015); and the Mk 8 became a Mk 10 (alias FV4017).

A further upgrade programme began in 1965, as the tank's night-fighting capability was enhanced by a 22in IR searchlight mounted above the mantlet and aligned with the main gun. This programme affected the three major types of Centurion then in service, and again brought a change in the designations. The IR-equipped Mk 6 became a Mk 6/1, the Mk 9 became a Mk 9/1, and the Mk 10 became a Mk 10/1.

The last important change was then introduced in 1966, with the addition of a modified Browning M2 0.5in calibre ranging gun. This was mounted in the turret and was coaxial with the main armament and the existing 7.62mm machine gun. Once again, designations were changed, and Mk 6 variants became Mk 6/2, Mk 9 variants Mk 9/2, and Mk 10 variants Mk 10/2. Later in this upgrade programme, and somewhat confusingly, tanks already upgraded with IR equipment and now given the ranging gun were again given new type codes: Mk 6/1 became Mk 11, Mk 9/1 became Mk 12, and Mk 10/1 became Mk 13. Eventually, the Mk 6/2, Mk 9/2 and Mk 10/2 variants were also redesignated as Mk 11, Mk 12 and Mk 13 types respectively.

At some point in this final upgrade programme, a thermal sleeve was added to the barrel of the 105mm gun to reduce barrel distortion and improve long-range accuracy.

Other codes associated with the Centurion were FV4007 (for the Mks 1, 2, 3, 4, 7, 8/1, and 8/2); FV4011 (for the Mk 5); and FV4012 (for the Mks 7/1 and 7/2).

Special-purpose Centurions

As these improvements and upgrades worked their way through, many older Centurions were converted to special-purpose uses. Interestingly, the General Staff had believed in the late 1940s that the Centurion would not lend itself to such modification, and had planned instead to base its future special-purpose tanks on the new A45 Universal Tank (later FV201) that was expected to replace the Centurion as well. This plan was scrapped when it became clear that the modifications to the A45 would compromise the basic design to an unacceptable degree. After a false start using redundant Churchill hulls, the General Staff then discovered that the Centurion could be modified, and authorised the first special-purpose variants.

The most pressing need was for an ARV (Armoured Recovery Vehicle) variant to support Centurion units in Korea, and in March 1952 the first of about 180 were delivered. These were conversions based on Mk 1 or Mk 2 hulls, with the turret replaced by a boxy superstructure that housed a Bedford QL truck engine to power the winch. There was a rear spade so that the ARV could anchor itself during winching operations. Most of these MK 1 ARVs, designated FV4013 types, were withdrawn in 1959, but they continued into the 1960s as training vehicles.

A more considered Mk 2 ARV, or FV4006, entered service in 1956. These were based on Mk 1, Mk 2 or Mk 3 Centurion hulls, again with an armoured superstructure, an auxiliary engine for the winch, and a spade anchor at the rear. The winch could pull up to 90 tons when using pulley blocks, or 30 tons in a straight line pull. The Mk 2 ARV had a four-man crew and a single .30 inch machine gun for self-defence, mounted on the commander's cupola.

Further variants were the FV4008 (an amphibious Duplex Drive tank), and the FV4010 (a planned variant with Malkara anti-tank guided missiles). In 1961 came the Mk 5 Dozer, which had a primary purpose of digging hull-down fire positions for Centurion squadrons. As the name suggests, it was a Mk 5 gun tank fitted with a bulldozer blade for the purpose.

The last special-purpose Centurions then began to enter service in 1963, the year after production of standard gun tanks had ended. The AVRE (or FV4003) had the same hydraulically-operated bulldozer blade as the Dozer variant, and its turret had a 6.5in (165mm) low-velocity demolition gun to destroy fortifications and strongpoints. It could also carry a fascine or a roll of trackway, and some were used to tow the Giant Viper mine-clearance trailer.

Two further Royal Engineers variants entered service the same year, both based on Mk 5 Centurion hulls. One was the FV4002 Bridgelayer, which carried a no 6 Tank Bridge that could span up to 45 feet. For larger gaps in the terrain, up to 75 feet wide, there was the FV4016 ARK (Armoured Ramp Carrier), which itself drove into the gap that had to be crossed and acted as the centre support for the steel bridge it carried.

Lastly, the BARV also entered service in 1963, intended for beach recovery work in support of amphibious landings. Just 12 of these were built, all by ROF Leeds, and the last one was not withdrawn (by the Royal Marines) until 2003, which made it the last Centurion variant in British service.

Centurions overseas
The second largest buyer of new Centurions after the British Army was actually the US Government, which bought the tanks in quantity under the Mutual Defense Assistance Program to equip units of NATO-aligned armies in Europe. A major beneficiary was the Dutch Army, which took delivery of 592 Centurions, beginning in 1953.

Other major purchasers were Australia, Canada, India, South Africa, Sweden and Switzerland. Smaller quantities went to Egypt, Iraq, Jordan, Kuwait and New Zealand. The South Africans resourcefully modernised and upgraded theirs at a time when they had to be inventive and resourceful because of arms embargoes, and the result was the Olifant series of tanks that remained in service at the time of writing and was still considered the most effective tank in service on the African continent.

However, perhaps the best-known user of Centurions outside Britain was Israel. The Israel Defence Force took its first Centurions in 1959, all formerly in British service, and over the years it bought or captured many more; some of the Dutch Centurions, which were returned to the USA when their service was over, may also have gone to Israel. In the early 1970s, the Israelis upgraded them all with the diesel engines and automatic gearboxes that they also fitted to their Patton tanks. The tanks were then (unofficially) known as the SHO'T (which means "whip" or "scourge"), and distinguished themselves in the 1967 Six Days War. Many were up-armoured with Chobham-type armour or fitted with explosive reactive armour. In later years, many

were further modified to become armoured personnel carriers, and remained in service into the 21st century.

DIMENSIONS AND WEIGHT:
Length 25ft (32ft over 20pdr gun), width 11ft 1in, height 9ft 10.5in. Weight 51 tons (Mk 1 47 tons, Mk 3 49 tons).

FURTHER READING:
Centurion Universal Tank, 1943-2003, Simon Dunstan.

CHALLENGER (A30)
The first British tank to carry the Challenger name was the A30 Cruiser of 1942, which was never a great success. Based on the A27 (Cromwell) family, its main purpose was to get a tank into production as quickly as possible with the new 17pdr gun.

Although the 17pdr gun promised to provide the British Army with a weapon that could knock out all known AFVs of the time, there was as yet no tank suitable to carry it. It required a wider turret than could be fitted to the A27 that promised to be the basis of future British tanks, and so A27 "parent" BRCW developed a widened A27 hull that was also lengthened to take the extra bogie wheel on each side needed to carry the extra weight. A new and noticeably tall turret for the 17pdr was designed by Stothert & Pitt, and was based closely on their design for the TOG2 tank. It incorporated a co-axial .30 calibre Browning machine gun.

The plan was to deviate as little as possible from the mechanical specification of the A27, and the A30 retained its 600bhp Meteor engine and five-speed Merritt-Brown gearbox. There would be a five-man crew (commander, driver, gunner and two loaders). To make room for

The tall turret of the 1944 A30 Challenger made it highly conspicuous and it did not have a long service life.

stowage of the large 17pdr shells, the hull machine-gunner's position was deleted. Work began on three pilot models by May 1942 and the first was delivered for trials just three months later in August.

The A30 proved capable of 32mph on the road and 15mph across country, and carried enough fuel for 120 miles. However, the trials also showed up several problems: the weight caused suspension troubles, and the turret was slow to traverse. Yet the Challenger promised the quickest way of getting a 17pdr tank into production, and so the turret traverse problem was quickly fixed by using a Metadyne electric traverse gear, and some weight was taken out by reducing the armour thickness. Though the tank was not entirely satisfactory, an order was placed for 200 examples.

Even then, there were delays, and the General Staff did not sign off the design until February 1943. When the Sherman Firefly appeared as a much cheaper way of fielding a tank equipped with the 17pdr gun, the A30's original purpose evaporated. In November, the decision was therefore taken to order no more Challengers. Production eventually began in March 1944, and the 197 production models delivered in 1944-1945 made the Challenger total up to the original order of 200.

As the Challenger had not been drawn up with a deep wading capability, it could not be used in the initial phases of the D-Day landings.

Nevertheless the tank was used for reconnaissance work in the later stages of the European campaign alongside the Sherman Firefly. Among its users was a Czechoslovakian armoured brigade, and after the war the Czech army purchased 22 Challengers. These were put into reserve in 1951 and scrapped in 1959.

The tall turret of the Challenger was considered a liability, and this was probably the reason why a self-propelled anti-tank gun variant was developed with a lower-profile turret. This was called the Avenger, but it did not progress beyond trials and its development was cancelled in 1950.

Two examples of the A30 Challenger survive, one at the Overloon War Museum in the Netherlands, and the other at the Bovington Tank Museum in Britain.

DIMENSIONS AND WEIGHT:
Length 26ft 8¾in, width 9ft 6½in, height 9ft 1¼in. Weight 32.5 tons

FURTHER READING:
Cromwell Cruiser Tank, 1942-50, David Fletcher & Richard C Harley.

CHALLENGER (MBT)

Challenger was the British Army's replacement for the Chieftain MBT, entering service in 1983 and best known for its pioneering use of Chobham armour. It remained in service

The Challenger MBT entered service in 1983, and featured both Chobham armour and a rifled 120mm gun.

until 2001, when it was directly replaced by the Challenger 2.

Challenger began life as an improved Chieftain intended for Iran, but the order was cancelled after the Iranian Revolution in early 1979. At about the same time, the MBT-80 project for a Chieftain replacement collapsed, and the decision was taken – somewhat reluctantly – that MVEE should develop a new MBT on the basis of the Iranian Shir design. The project was briefly named Cheviot before being renamed Challenger, re-using the name given to the A30 cruiser tank of the Second World War. Its military designation was FV4030/4, which indicated a fourth version of the FV4030 Chieftain design.

Challenger was nevertheless a very great advance over Chieftain. It was powered by a 1200bhp Rolls-Royce Condor CV12 TCA turbocharged diesel engine that drove through a David Brown TN37 transmission with four forward and three reverse speeds. The suspension was a hydropneumatic system that gave both long travel and excellent control of bump and rebound, so giving the tank an outstanding cross-country performance. The main gun was a fully stabilised Royal Ordnance L11A5 120mm rifled type, and the secondary armament consisted of 7.62mm L8A2 and L37A2 machine guns. Challenger was designed to be operated by a four-man crew, consisting of commander,

driver, gunner and loader, and had a 280-mile range on the road.

Nevertheless, it was the Chobham armour that attracted the most interest – and its exact specifications remain secret more than four decades after its introduction. The name Chobham came from the fact that the MVEE (Military Vehicles Experimental Establishment) that developed it is located at Chobham in Surrey. The armour originated in the late 1960s, and was initially tried on an experimental aluminium-hulled tank (FV4211) that used Chieftain powertrain components. This line of development had been officially abandoned by 1972, but research continued and Chobham armour became a reality in the early 1980s. It would later be adopted for other designs, including the American M1 Abrams.

A total of 420 Challenger tanks were taken into British Army service, all of them built at the Royal Ordnance Factories in Leeds. ROF Leeds was acquired by Vickers Defence Systems in 1986, and with it the Challenger production line that remained active until 1990. Withdrawals of Challenger tanks began in 1998 and the tank had been completely replaced by its Challenger 2 successor by 2001. A number of Challenger hulls were converted into ARRVs, upgraded with the powertrain from the Challenger 2. Some of these were used to tow High Mobility

Trailers that could carry a single tank power pack for replacement on the battlefield.

Challenger tanks were used in the 1991 Gulf War, where they were fitted with additional Explosive Reactive Armour and were generally adapted for desert use. The British tanks destroyed around 300 Iraqi tanks without suffering a single loss in combat, and a Challenger achieved the longest range confirmed "kill" of the war when it destroyed an Iraqi tank at a range of 5100 metres. The British Army also used its Challengers during the conflict in Bosnia-Herzegovina.

Overseas users

The Jordanians ordered 274 Challengers, and between 1999 and 2002 also took a further 288 surplus examples from Britain to replace their Centurions. A total of 392 Jordanian Challengers were locally upgraded, with an unmanned Falcon turret that permits the crew to be reduced to two men, and were renamed Al-Hussein. The Jordanians also created several special variants of their own.

DIMENSIONS AND WEIGHT:
Length 37ft 9in (gun forward), width 11ft 6in, height 9ft 8in. Weight 62 tonnes (up to 70 tonnes with additional armour modules).

FURTHER READING:
Challenger Main Battle Tank, 1984-1997,
Simon Dunstan.

CHALLENGER 2

Challenger 2 or FV4034 was an extensive redesign of the first Challenger that entered British service in 1998 and within three years had replaced the earlier tank of the same name. A quantity of Challenger 2 tanks was also sold to Oman.

To a degree, the first Challenger had been a compromise, brought about by multiple factors beyond the control of the British Army. Well aware of this, Vickers Defence Systems began work on a second-generation version as a private venture in 1986. There was considerable scepticism from some MoD officials, but in late 1988, a prototype was ordered for 1990 delivery. This was evaluated against the US M1 Abrams, the West German Leopard 2 and the French Leclerc. MoD placed a first order for 140 Challenger 2 tanks in 1991, and production began in 1993 at Leeds and Elswick.

A further order for 268 tanks was placed in 1994, the same year when Challenger 2 somewhat embarrassingly failed its acceptance trials. Nevertheless, a subsequent programme of improvements enabled it to exceed all reliability requirements, and the tank finally entered British service in 1998.

Despite the clear similarities between Challenger 2 and its predecessor, there was little interchangeability between the two tanks. Challenger 2 retained the original hull, but its turret was new and was based on the Vickers Mk 7 private venture design. Its 1200bhp engine was similar to that in Challenger 1 (although now manufactured by Perkins rather than Rolls-Royce) and drove through a six-speed David Brown TN54E epicyclic gearbox, while the suspension was once again a hydropneumatic type. A diesel Auxiliary Power Unit was also fitted to power the electrical systems when the main engine was not running. Challenger 2 had a maximum road speed of 37mph and a maximum off-road speed of 25mph, with a range of 340 miles on road or 160 miles off it.

Although an automatic loader was investigated during the early stages of the Challenger 2 project, the British Army rejected it and settled for a four-man crew as in the earlier Challenger. They were protected by second-generation Chobham armour (also known as Dorchester armour) on the hull and the turret, and by an NBC system in the turret bustle. Explosive Reactive Armour and additional bar armour could be fitted as required.

The main gun was the L30A1 120mm rifled type that succeeded the L11 120mm type of the Chieftain and Challenger 1 tanks, and the turret could be rotated electrically through 360 degrees in nine seconds. Challenger 2 had a digital fire control computer, a gyrostabilised sight with laser rangefinder for the commander, and a second-generation Thales TOGS (Thermal Observation and Gunnery Sight) system for night vision. This was carried in an armoured housing above the gun barrel, so providing a ready visual distinction from Challenger 1 where it was mounted on the right of the turret. Secondary armament consisted of an L94A1 7.62mm chain gun mounted co-axially with the main gun, and a 7.62mm L37A2 GPMG on a pintle on the loader's hatch ring. Alternative options were available.

Challenger 2 saw operational service on peacekeeping missions in Bosnia and Herzegovina,

and in Kosovo. It was deployed in anger in Iraq in March 2003, where it demonstrated remarkable survivability. The tank has also undergone various in-service upgrades, the biggest being a Life Extension Programme announced in March 2021 that would keep a quantity of tanks in service until at least 2035. This programme was known as Challenger 3 and is discussed separately below.

Vickers offered the Challenger 2 on export markets but the Challenger 2E with a transversely-mounted 1500bhp MTU diesel engine lost a contract with the Greek Army to the German Leopard 2, and in 2005 BAE withdrew its export marketing. Challenger 2 found only one overseas customer, which was Oman. A total of 38 tanks were ordered, 18 in 1993 and 20 in 1997, and deliveries were completed in 2001. The Omani tanks had a number of differences from the British Challenger 2, affecting the cooling system, the armour and the secondary armament.

The Challenger 2 chassis was also used for the Titan armoured bridge-layer and the Trojan AVRE that replaced their Chieftain-based counterparts. There were 33 Titans, the first entering service in 2006, and a further 33 Trojans, which entered service in 2007.

DIMENSIONS AND WEIGHT:
Length 27ft 3in (44ft 3in with gun forward), width 11ft 6in (13ft 9in with appliqué armour), height 8ft 2in. Weight 64 tonnes; up to 75 tonnes with appliqué armour.

FURTHER READING:
Challenger 2, The British Main Battle Tank, Robert Griffin & MP Robinson.

CHALLENGER 3

After a long period of indecision about the future of tanks, the British Army decided in approximately 2015 that a new MBT would be too expensive and that it would instead focus on a Life Extension Project for the existing Challenger 2. Several companies were awarded assessment phase contracts in August 2016, and these were then whittled down to two teams, led by BAE Systems and the German company Rheinmetall, which produced the favoured smooth-bore 120mm gun.

A BAE Systems prototype called Black Night previewed the thinking about the Challenger upgrade in 2018, and incorporated enhanced sensor systems, a panoramic sight with both thermal and optical channels, night vision, and an Active Protection System capable of detecting enemy fire. Rheinmetall was meanwhile developing a new turret on its own initiative. The issue was resolved in June 2019 with the formation of a joint company, Rheinmetall BAE Systems Land (RBSL), at Telford to carry out the upgrades.

The plan for Challenger 3 was announced in more detail in the March 2021 Defence Command Paper. An upgrade of 148 tanks would extend the Challenger's service life to 2035, but the remaining Challenger 2s were to be retired and not replaced. Challenger 3 was to have "added mobility, survivability and lethality" and would enter service in 2027, reaching full operational capability in 2030.

An uprated engine with 1500bhp and an improved suspension would improve its maximum road speed to 60mph. There was to be a new turret, which could also be offered to allied forces and for export, and a new 120mm smooth-bore main gun made by Rheinmetall could fire the latest ammunition as used by the USA and other NATO partners. A new modular armour, a new suite of sights, an automatic target detection and tracking system, and a powerful digital battlefield communications ability were further key features.

CHARIOTEER

The FV4010 Charioteer tank was created in the early years of the Cold War to provide British units stationed in Europe with an up-gunned replacement for their outclassed Cromwells. Charioteers were converted from existing Cromwells in 1951-1952, but Army re-organisations in the early 1950s resulted in few entering service except with Territorial Army units. Many were later sold for further service overseas, and some of these remained on active duty into the 1990s.

The main purpose of the Charioteer was to destroy enemy tanks, although it was designed as a battlefield tank and not a dedicated tank destroyer. It retained the hull and mechanical elements of the parent Cromwell, which was reworked where necessary to Cromwell Mk VII standard; all were given fishtail exhausts as used on the Comet Model B, plus a large armoured telephone box at the rear that allowed communication with infantry units.

The host tanks were a mixture of Mk VI, Mk VII, Mk VIIw and Mk VIII Cromwells, and despite the rework some differences remained. The Charioteers were therefore known as Mk 6, Mk 7, Mk 7w and Mk 8 types, with hull types D, E and F. To create more room for ammunition stowage, the hull machine gun and its operator's position were removed. Conversions were carried out by Robinson & Kershaw Ltd at Dukinfield in Cheshire.

To accommodate the 20pdr gun and a co-axial machine gun, a new turret was designed. The weight limitations of the Cromwell-type suspension and the size of the 20pdr gun badly compromised the design of this. It was long and narrow, and tall as well. To save weight, relatively thin armour was used, with sloping turret sides to increase its effective thickness. Inside the turret, space restrictions limited the crew to two, with the driver as third crewman in the hull. That the design had been rushed into production became clear when commanders complained of restricted visibility when firing, and as a result a fourth crew member was added, whose role was to dismount from the tank and position himself as an external observer. There was also very limited space for stowage of ammunition, which was intended to be primarily APDS but with some conventional HE shells.

The plan in 1951 was to order 630 Charioteers, but the order was cut back as Army plans changed and the probable total built was 442. Some that did enter service were later fitted with the later version of the 20pdr gun with its mid-barrel fume extractor, and these were redesignated Charioteer Mk VIIB types. By the

This publicity picture of Challenger 3 was issued at the time the RBSL upgrade contract was announced. (RBSL)

The Charioteer was an up-gunned Cromwell of the early 1950s. This preserved example was pictured in Finland; the Finns took 38 examples of the tank and kept them in service until 1979. (©Methem, CC-by-SA 3.0)

1960s, these tanks had been relegated to reserve stocks, and a number were sold off to overseas armies. Austria took 56, Finland took 38, the Royal Jordanian Army took 24, and 43 went to Lebanon. Several took part in various Middle Eastern conflicts in later years.

Six Charioteers have survived. In Britain, there is one at the Bovington Tank Museum and a second at the East of England Tank Museum – in this case an experimental vehicle that was upgraded in 1969 with an L7 105mm gun to make it a more attractive export proposition. Austria has one at its Museum of Military History in Vienna, and Finland has three, including one that can be seen at the Parola Tank Museum. Two more are in Israel, at the Israeli Defence Force History Museum in Tel Aviv and at the Yad la-Shiryon Museum in Latron.

DIMENSIONS AND WEIGHT:
Length 28ft 10½in, width 10ft 2in, height 8ft 6in. Weight 28.5 tons

FURTHER READING:
AFV Profile No. 25, Cromwell and Comet, James Bingham; *Armour of the Middle East Wars 1948-78,* Steven J Zaloga.

CHASER
See Medium Mark A.

CHEVIOT
The Cheviot name was briefly used in the early stages of the Challenger MBT programme.

CHIEFTAIN
The Chieftain or FV4201 entered service in the mid-1960s and replaced both the Centurion and the Conqueror tanks in British service. Its specially-developed engine initially proved troublesome, but reliability improved gradually; export variants, of which there were a sizeable number, mostly had alternative powerpacks. The Chieftain remained Britain's main battle tank until it was replaced by the Challenger in 1995.

The British Army took a total of 900 examples, but despite the NATO drive towards standardisation, no other NATO countries adopted the Chieftain; most of them preferred the West German Leopard. Nevertheless, the tank was a major success as an export to the Middle East, where close to 1400 found buyers; there would certainly have been more but for policy changes consequent upon the 1979 Iranian Revolution.

The threat from Soviet heavy tanks in the early years of the Cold War had led to the Centurion being supplemented by the Conqueror as an interim move during the 1950s, but what the General Staff really wanted was a single tank that combined the mobility of the Centurion with the firepower of the Conqueror. When they issued a specification, it called for a tank with long-range engagement capability from defensive positions and a bigger angle of gun depression than on Conqueror. It had to withstand medium artillery, to have better frontal armour than Conqueror, and to be capable of firing 10 rounds in the first minute and six rounds per minute for the following four minutes.

Leyland Motors was called on to develop such a tank, and its first step was the prototype FV4202 or 40-ton Centurion that was built in 1956. The key features of this were a reclining position for the driver that allowed both a lower profile and sloping front armour, and improved depression angles for the main gun, achieved by omitting the traditional mantlet.

By the time work on the FV4201 itself began in 1958, NATO had called for multi-fuel engines in all members' military vehicles, and Leyland's response was the L60 engine, an opposed-piston diesel. This drove through a Merritt-Brown TN12 triple-differential gearbox operated by tiller controls, and the suspension was a Horstmann coil-spring type. Large steel side plates were added to provide stand-off protection from hollow charge attacks and to protect the tracks.

Notable features of the Chieftain were its steeply sloped front armour and a matching steep slope for the face of the turret. Both features were deliberately concealed on early vehicles. The turret was equipped with two six-barrel smoke dischargers and with a large searchlight, and had a large bustle to counter the weight of the main gun's long barrel. This bustle was used for radios, ammunition, and the fire control equipment. An interesting idea pursued during the development

stage was to make the FV4201's turret interchangeable in the field with that of the US T95 tank, but the ideal of increased NATO standardisation lost out to the difficulty of training crews to use two different guns.

The main gun chosen for the Chieftain was the L11A5, the first 120mm type designed and built in Britain. This was a rifled gun that was supported by full stabilisation and by a computerised fire control system, and by a 0.5in Browning ranging gun and an IR-capable projector that was co-axial with the main gun. Projectiles and charges were loaded separately, and a water-glycol jacket around the charge storage was designed to prevent a catastrophic explosion if the fighting compartment was ruptured. The tank's secondary armament consisted of a co-axial 7.62mm L81 machine gun and a second 7.62mm L37A1 gun mounted on the commander's cupola. The NBC protection system for the four-man crew was improved over that in the Centurion.

Seven FV4201 prototypes were built, the first commencing troop trials in 1959 and the others following between 1961 and 1963. These had early versions of the new L60 engine that fell considerably short of their 600bhp design target with outputs of no more than 485bhp. The small-diameter road wheels used initially to reduce height also gave insufficient ground clearance and were later replaced by Centurion wheels, and these prototypes had a short hull with internal exhaust silencers.

The FV4201 was accepted for service in May 1963 as the Chieftain. An order for 770 production tanks was preceded by a pre-production series of 40 training vehicles that incorporated a number of improvements. The engine now developed 585bhp and its exhaust silencers were now mounted externally on the rear hull, while the gearbox had also been strengthened. The rear hull had been lengthened to deal with engine vibration and cooling problems, and the original 45-ton weight rose to nearly 50 tons, which called for some suspension reinforcement. Meanwhile, the larger road wheels were accompanied by relocation of the drive and idler wheels and by tracks with rubber pads to protect the roads in West Germany where the tanks were to be stationed. The shape of the sloping front was once again concealed, this time by a dummy stowage bin on the glacis plate and a canvas cover over the nose of the turret.

The early examples of the Chieftain did not cover themselves in glory, and the L60 engine proved prone to multiple failures; notable among them were coolant leaks that led to white smoke in the exhaust which revealed the tank's position. Typical speeds were 19-22mph, and although the maximum of 27mph made

this a faster tank than the Centurion in theory, in practice it was somewhat slower overall. Nevertheless, the tank was relentlessly developed and improved throughout its service life. Most Chieftains were allocated to BAOR where they spent their lives on exercises, but experience with export models in the Middle East fed back to the manufacturers and contributed to upgrades and modifications.

There were no fewer than 12 Marks of Chieftain over the years, and a number of upgrades to models in service. Engine power was gradually increased, from 585bhp to 650bhp (Chieftain Mk 2 in 1967), 720bhp (Mk 3 in 1971), and finally to 750bhp (Mk 5 in 1975). By 1978, the engine had finally achieved its 4000-hour design life. The Mk 3 models had a new commander's cupola, and a laser rangefinder in place of the original co-axial machine gun allowed longer-range engagements. All earlier Chieftains except the original Mk 1s were upgraded to Mk 5 standard between 1975 and 1979, which involved fitting an improved Marconi fire control system, replacement of the searchlight by a Thermal Observation Gunnery Sight, additional NBC protection equipment in the turret bustle, and modifications to allow the use of kinetic FSAPDS (Fin Stabilized Armour Piercing Discarding Sabot) ammunition. From 1984, a further series of upgrades added the Stillbrew crew protection package that was

The Chieftain was sold to Jordan in modified form as the Khalid. This is a former Jordanian tank in preservation. (©Adamicz/ WikiMedia Commons)

designed to counter the latest Soviet 125mm tank guns through additional armour on the turret front and turret ring. Further upgrades were proposed, but were cancelled in the early 1990s when the Challenger replacement tanks were introduced.

A small number of early Chieftains were later converted to ARVs (FV4204) and armoured bridgelayers (FV4205), and various small-volume conversions included a Chieftain Marksman self-propelled anti-aircraft gun, an AVRE, a minesweeper, and even a remotely-controlled range target. The Chieftain also figured in the early days of the Chobham armour development programme. In April 1982, the Royal Ordnance Factories built a pair of Chieftain 900 prototypes, which were Iranian-pattern Chieftains fitted with the 900bhp Rolls-Royce Condor 900E engine and a fully automatic TN12-1000 version of the existing Chieftain gearbox. These were mocked-up with sheet metal cladding to simulate Chobham armour and were displayed at the 1982 British Army Equipment Exhibition (BAEE), but any idea of retro-fitting Chieftains with Chobham armour appears to have been abandoned by 1986.

The export Chieftains, the Khalid and the Shir

The Chieftain became a major export success, especially in the Middle East, although it should be no surprise that most export variants had engines other than the Leyland L60. Various changes in the political sphere led to the export Chieftain having a highly complex history.

During the later design stages of the tank, there were expectations that the Israeli Defence Force would take a quantity of a variant called the Chieftain Mk 4 and perhaps build this in Israel as well, but these plans were cancelled in 1969 for political reasons. Just two Chieftain Mk 4s were built and neither was delivered, but experience from the Chieftain tank project undoubtedly fed into Israel's design of its own Merkava tank. The Netherlands also trialled an early Chieftain in 1968 but severe engine oil leaks and other quality problems persuaded the Dutch military to buy elsewhere.

The earliest Chieftain exports were for Iran, which took a total of 707 examples of two types between 1976 and 1978, plus a number of ARV and armoured bridgelayer variants. Many of these were upgraded in later years with a package known as Mobarez. A second phase of the Iranian contract was to produce a derivative

known as the FV4030/2 or Shir (the name means Lion) with the rear of the hull reconfigured to take a 1200bhp Rolls-Royce CV12 diesel engine, but the project did not go beyond the prototype stage. There was also to be a third phase, a Shir 2 or FV4030/3 with Chobham armour and an 800bhp Rolls-Royce CV8 engine. The prototype was completed in 1978, an order for 1200 had been placed, and build of the first 250 had begun when the Iranian Revolution changed the political landscape in February 1979 and the order was cancelled.

Nevertheless, a contract with Jordan for 274 tropicalised tanks followed in June 1979. These were known as the Khalid types, and had the 1200bhp Rolls-Royce diesel engine. The first 125 were re-worked from Shir 1 tanks that had been in build for Iran, and the rest were new production examples. Deliveries were completed in July 1981.

Meanwhile, a contract with Kuwait had called for a total of 267 Chieftains, and these were delivered between 1976 and 1995. Many were lost during the conflict with Iraq, and some sources believe that the Iraqis captured between 50 and 75 examples and later put them into service, upgrading them with air conditioning and reinforced armour. A smaller quantity of 27 tanks was sold to Oman and delivered between 1981 and 1985. These were essentially Chieftain Mk 5 types, and they were upgraded in service with an L20 sight and a Type 520 laser rangefinder.

DIMENSIONS AND WEIGHT (CHIEFTAIN):
Length 24ft 7.3in (over hull), 35ft 5.2in (with gun forward), width 11ft 5.8in, height 9ft 6.2in. Weight 55 tons.

FURTHER READING:
Chieftain Main Battle Tank 1965-2003, Simon Dunstan.

CHURCHILL (A22)

The Churchill remains one of the best-loved British tanks of the Second World War, despite its many shortcomings. More than 5700 examples were built by various heavy engineering companies under the parentage of Vauxhall, and the tank proved a versatile design that lent itself to a number of special-purpose derivatives.

The General Staff had anticipated a requirement for an Infantry tank to fight a trench warfare battle similar to those of the First World

War, but the losses sustained by the British Army in France in 1940 made clear that a different kind of tank was required. The Director of Tank Design, Dr Henry Merritt, therefore scaled down the A20 tank then being designed, to produce one more suited to the battle conditions seen in Poland and in France and capable of entering production more quickly.

There was considerable urgency to get the new A22 or Infantry Mk IV design into production. The Army had lost large numbers of tanks in France and tanks were needed to counter the treat of a German invasion of Britain. So in June 1940, the design was handed over to car maker Vauxhall, who were instructed to have it in production within a year. The first prototypes ran in December 1940 and the first production vehicles were made on time in June 1941, but of course there had been insufficient time for thorough development and user trials. The handbook for the new tank came with a sticker that famously read, "All those things which we know are not as they should be will be put right. In nearly every case the cure has already been found, and it will be introduced as soon as the new material or new parts become available..... Fighting vehicles are urgently required, and instructions have been received to proceed with the vehicle as it is rather than hold up production."

The new tank took the name of Churchill, fitting neatly into the series of names beginning with C that was already in use, and creating a deliberate link with Winston Churchill who was then Prime Minister. The A22 Churchill had a conventional hull layout with four compartments (for driving, fighting, engine, and for the gearbox, steering and generators), and a five-man crew. Its all-round tracks alongside the main hull echoed the earlier A20 design, as did its sponson escape hatches. The suspension had 11 independently sprung two-wheel bogies on each side, with small wheels that gave the Churchill an immediately recognisable appearance. Power came from the 350bhp Bedford Twin Six engine also originally intended for the A20, and there was a brand-new four-speed Merritt-Brown gearbox with triple differentials for steering which, unusually, was effected by means of a tiller bar.

Unsurprisingly, the first Churchills suffered from multiple teething troubles. The gearbox had been put into production straight off the drawing-board, and suffered among other things

from difficult gear selection. There were bogie seizures, failures of the track links, and cooling and fuel vaporisation problems. By the time the tank was first used operationally, in the August 1942 Dieppe Raid, it had been made reliable – but in March and April that year Vauxhall had suspended production in order to rebuild about 700 earlier tanks with an improved specification. There was even talk of abandoning the Churchill in favour of the forthcoming Cromwell, but the success of the latest Mk III versions at El Alamein in October 1942 earned the tank an indefinite reprieve.

Some problems still remained. The tank was, and always would be, disappointingly slow. In theory it could achieve up to 17mph on the road, but at that speed it was extremely noisy, and its cross-country maximum was only 8mph. It was also under-gunned, and early examples had the QF 2pdr as a main weapon even though that had been considered obsolete by 1940; the need to keep producing guns after the losses in France prevented British industry from pausing to re-tool for the latest Ordnance 6pdr. Its armour with a maximum thickness of 102mm was only adequate, as it was not sloped, and in later versions would be made thicker.

The Churchill was deployed in the Western Desert, Tunisia, North-West Europe and Italy and

The Churchill was slow, noisy and under-gunned, but for all that was a firm favourite of the men who operated it. This is an early example, built before the improved Mk III earned the tank lasting respect at El Alamein in 1942. (IWM, KID1265, Public Domain)

Britain's car makers were enlisted to help when there was an urgent need for new tanks early in the Second World War, and Vauxhall became the design parent for the Churchill. This rear view shows one of the 1940 prototypes. (Vauxhall Heritage)

The MkVII or A22F version of the Churchill mounted the latest 75mm gun in a redesigned turret and was also up-armoured. This one has been carefully restored and was pictured on display at Carrickfergus in Northern Ireland, after which it was named. The round escape door in the hull side is clearly visible here. (Alan Wilson, CC-by-SA 2.0)

was used by both British and Commonwealth forces. Around 250 also served on the Eastern Front in the hands of Soviet troops after a total of 344 Mk I and Mk II types were despatched to Russia in August 1942 under the Soviet assistance programme. Of these, 91 were lost en route to attacks on the Arctic convoys, and most of the survivors were up-gunned by their new owners with the Soviet 76.2mm gun.

Churchill Mks I-II

The Mk I Churchills, of which 303 were built in 1941, had the QF 2pdr main gun with a co-axial 7.92mm Besa machine gun in a cast turret, and a 3in howitzer in the hull. Although many of these tanks were converted into special variants or sent to Russia, some were still in service by the time of the Gothic Line battles in Italy during 1944.

As supplies of the 3in howitzer were limited, it was replaced on the Churchill Mk II by a second machine gun. A few Mk IIs were built with the howitzer and 2pdr transposed to make a close support tank. A total of 1127 Mk IIs were built in 1941-1942.

Churchill Mks III-V

As supplies of the Ordnance 6pdr gun improved, so the Churchill was upgunned with this as its main weapon in a distinctive welded turret from

late 1942. The secondary armament was now standardised as one co-axial 7.92mm Besa and a second one in the hull, and the result was the Churchill Mk III. Track catwalks provided a further recognition feature. The production total is generally accepted as 675.

A shortage of steel plate for the welded turrets caused a reversion to a cast type in 1943. This created the Churchill Mk IV, still with the 6pdr gun, and there were 1622 examples of this. A close support variant with a 95mm howitzer was also built in 1943 and became the Churchill Mk V, although numbers were limited to 241.

Churchill Mks VI-VIII

Improvements came in two stages during 1944. First of all, the QF 75mm gun from the Cromwell was introduced, and 200 Mk VI Churchills were built to this specification (otherwise largely unchanged from the Mk IV) early that year.

The Churchill Mk VII was a more comprehensive revision, with its armour uprated to 152mm as well as the 75mm gun. These tanks had a slightly wider hull with round escape hatches instead of the square sponson escape doors of earlier Marks. More obviously, there was a completely redesigned turret that combined a main casting with top and bottom plates welded into position, a low cupola for the commander, and shoulder castings to improve protection for the gun mantlet. Weight now went up and maximum road speed went down to 12.5mph as a result. The Mk VII first saw action in Normandy during 1944, and 1400 examples were built. It was redesignated as an A42 in 1945.

The Mk VIII was a close support version of the Mk VII, with a 95mm howitzer in place of the main gun. Just 200 were built in 1944.

Churchill Mks IX-XI

As the design of the Churchill was improved, so earlier models were re-worked to incorporate appropriate upgrades. There were three major refit programmes, and there were also minor variations of them that presumably suited individual circumstances.

The first programme saw Mk III and Mk IV types being given appliqué armour plating to Mk VII standard. These were then known as Mk IX types. The second programme created a Mk X by adding appliqué armour to a Mk VI hull and fitting it with a Mk VII turret. The third programme then up-armoured the Mk V close-support variant and fitted some tanks (but not all) with a Mk VII turret. This became the Churchill Mk XI.

Special variants

The Churchill proved to be an adaptable tank, and in addition to the variants listed below there were various special-purpose derivatives that were used by assault engineers, particularly in the post-war period.

A field conversion in 1943-1944 created the Churchill NA75, which was a Mk IV adapted to take the Sherman 75mm gun and mantlet. It was created by the REME workshops in Algeria, where the guns from damaged Sherman tanks were fitted into Mk IV Churchills as an upgrade. The American gun reversed the positions of loader and gunner, and was therefore turned through 180 degrees in its mounting and the gun controls were given cross-over linkages. About 200 were eventually converted before June 1944, and most were used in Italy.

The Churchill Ark (Armoured Ramp Carrier) was created by removing the turret and fitting folding ramps at each end of the hull. The vehicle would be driven into a ditch, and the ramps were deployed to make a bridge over which other vehicles could be driven. The additional width and weight of the later Conqueror tank required two stronger ramps, and a different system was

devised, with the tanks operating in pairs as the Twin Ark between 1954 and 1965.

There were two versions of the Churchill ARV (Armoured Recovery Vehicle). The first, based on a Mk I or Mk II gun tank, was simply a turretless tank with a recovery jib mounted on the hull. The second type was based on a turretless Mk III or Mk IV with a fixed superstructure that incorporated a dummy gun. The recovery jib was mounted at the rear and was a more considered construction with a two-speed winch; there was also a ground spade.

The Churchill AVRE (Armoured Vehicle, Royal Engineers) had various forms. One had a special turret with a 290mm spigot mortar that fired a 40 lb explosive device known as General Wade's Flying Dustbin. Some carried box-girder bridges with a hydraulically-operated "launching" mechanism, and others were turretless bridgelayer types. By the end of the war, most Churchill regiments were using these, and many remained in service for some years after the gun tanks were withdrawn.

The Churchill Crocodile was a flame-thrower variant, where a flame gun replaced the hull-mounted machine gun. Developed from trials carried out with Valentine tanks during 1942, these were based on a Churchill Mk VII. The flammable liquid was carried in a 400-gallon armoured two-wheel trailer that was towed behind the tank. These special variants were used from D-Day onwards, but they were not the first Churchill flame-throwers. They were preceded by a field conversion known as the Oke (after Major Oke who designed it) that was used by the Calgary Regiment at Dieppe in 1942. In this case, the flammable liquid was carried in a tank mounted on the rear of the hull, and the flame-thrower was mounted at the front left.

The Churchill Crocodile flame-thrower was a later development of the tank. One is seen here demonstrating its fearsome capabilities. (IWM, Public Domain)

In late 1941, a total of 50 early Churchills were turned into Gun Carriers, using up stocks of the obsolete QF 3in anti-aircraft gun. This fairly crude conversion was known as the A22D. It had a squarish superstructure of thick plate and the gun in a ball mount low down at the front, next to the driver, with a very limited traverse. These conversions were reclassified as Self-Propelled Guns, and many were subsequently converted to other uses.

Churchills served in British units until the end of the war in Europe, and it was in Korea in 1951 that a Churchill squadron last saw action. The Irish Army took on four Mk VI Churchills in 1949 and kept at least two of them in service until 1969. Many Churchills survive in museums and there is a Churchill Trust project that aims to restore survivors to their original condition and working order. The Tank Museum at Bovington has four examples: a Mk II (cosmetically modified to look like a Mk I), a Mk III, a Mk VI and a Mk VII. The latter is a Churchill Crocodile, and also the last Churchill ever built.

DIMENSIONS AND WEIGHT:
Length 24ft 5in, width 10ft 8in, height 8ft 2in.
Weight 39.1 tons (Mk I); 40.7 tons (Mk VII).

FURTHER READING:
Churchill Infantry Tank, David Fletcher; *The Churchill Tank*, Peter Chamberlain & Chris Ellis.

COMET (A34)

The Comet or A34 tank was the last of the cruiser tanks based on the successful wartime A27 series. Fast, reliable, and armed with the formidable "77mm" main gun, it nevertheless arrived too late in the war to make a major difference.

When Leyland took over from BRCW as the "parent" company for the A27 series, they started work straight away on improvements. One aim was to develop the tank to take the 17pdr gun but without the compromises that had affected the attempt to do so with the A30 Challenger. In this aim, they were greatly aided by the continued efforts at Vickers-Armstrongs to reduce the size of the gun, which led to the lighter and shorter type that became known as the 77mm (although its actual bore was the same 76.2mm as in the 17pdr).

Most importantly, the new 77mm gun could be accommodated within a turret that would fit onto the A27 hull, although a new welded turret had to be specially designed for the job. It had a lower profile than the Challenger type, a cast gun mantlet, and a prominent counter-weight at the rear; it also used an electric traverse similar to that in the Churchill. The main armament was supplemented by two 7.62mm machine guns, one co-axial with it and the other in the hull front.

The mild-steel prototype began trials in February 1944, and those trials identified areas for improvement. In particular, return rollers were added above the main wheels, and became an easy recognition feature of the tank. Although still visually similar to the A27 series and sharing their engine and transmission, the new model had thicker armour and other hull revisions in addition to its new turret. Maximum speed from the 600bhp Meteor engine was limited to a more than adequate 32mph in order to minimise engine wear and track problems. Production deliveries began in September 1944 and the first tanks entered service the following January. Production was shared by Leyland, English Electric, John Fowler & Co, and Metro-Cammell, and by the end of the war 1186 had been made.

The earliest versions of the Comet had the exhaust venting through the top of the engine deck, but after the war a Type B hull with fishtail exhausts was introduced. Comets remained in British Army service alongside the new Centurion until 1958, when many of those still operational were sold to overseas armed forces.

Approximately 25 went to Burma (and were still in service in 2021). Cuba took 15, but these were soon retired because spares and support were denied under the armaments blockade that followed Castro's 1959 revolution. The Finnish Army took 41, and used them until 1970; and the Irish Army took a total of eight in 1959 and 1960. A total of 26 went to South Africa, where several were later modified as recovery vehicles or, more extensively, as armoured maintenance vehicles. Somalia also took nine Comets.

In British service, one Comet was modified as a Crocodile flame-thrower, but little is known about it. Elements of the A34 were also used in the construction of the experimental FV4401 Contentious self-propelled anti-tank gun in the early 1960s, but this did not enter production.

Several Comets survive around the world. In Britain, there is one at the Imperial War Museum in Duxford, another at the Muckleburgh Collection in Norfolk, and the Tank Museum at Bovington has at least three. There are further

The 1944 Comet was a further development of the A27 family, now meeting design specification A34 and mounting the latest 77mm gun. This preserved example was pictured during a display at the Bovington Tank Museum. (Alan Wilson/WikiMedia Commons)

preserved examples in Finland, France, Germany, Hong Kong, Ireland and the USA.

DIMENSIONS AND WEIGHT:
Length 25ft 1½in, width 10ft 0in, height 8ft 9½in. Weight 35.2 tons

FURTHER READING:
A34 Comet Tank, A Technical History, PM Knight; *British Cruiser Tank A34*, Chris Hughes & Dick Taylor.

CLAN
See A29.

CONQUEROR (FV214)

The FV214 Conqueror was a Heavy Gun Tank developed as a direct response to the Soviet IS-3, which was more powerfully armed and better armoured than any Western tank in the period immediately after World War II. British tacticians recognised that the new A41 Centurion then under development would not be able to face up to the IS-3 and that a tank with a bigger gun was needed. So from 1948 work began on the Conqueror, which was always intended as something of a stop-gap. The tactical plan was to use Conquerors to provide long-range anti-tank support for the Centurions in BAOR; in effect, the Conqueror became a tank destroyer.

To speed development, the Conqueror project drew on the work done for the hull of the A45 Infantry Support Tank, a project which had been started in 1944 and was later renamed FV201 but subsequently abandoned. The gun chosen was a new long-range 120mm type then under development in the USA, which would later be fitted to the American M103 heavy tanks whose role was similar to that intended for Conqueror. The gun fired APDS and HESH shells, and the size and weight of its ammunition meant that the projectiles and cartridges had to be loaded separately. As a result, there was space only for 35 rounds to be carried.

The Conqueror ended up as a very heavy tank with a 65-ton weight, thanks to its 7-inch frontal armour and the special turret that was designed to take the 120mm gun. This reduced

The Conqueror heavy gun tank was developed in some haste as a response to the Soviet IS-3. It entered production in 1955 but was another stop-gap design. The cast turret is apparent on this Mk I preserved at the Bovington Tank Museum. (Hohum, CC-by-SA 3.0)

its mobility, and also made it too heavy for many bridges in the BAOR region where it served. Nevertheless, Conqueror was respected for its good cross-country performance.

The first production Conqueror was completed in 1955, and production continued – at ROF Dalmuir – until 1959. In all, 185 examples were built. Of these, 20 were Mk I types and the rest were Mk IIs, with improved frontal armour and exhaust, and a single driver's periscope instead of the Mk I's three. Some were actually conversions of Caernarvon tanks, which had used the Conqueror's hull with a Centurion turret. The Conqueror tanks were withdrawn in 1966, by which time the Centurion had been up-gunned with a 105mm weapon, leaving the Conqueror with no real tactical role.

Conquerors had a cast turret and an advanced fire control system with a contra-rotating cupola that allowed the tank commander to locate a second target while the gunner laid on the first. Power came from an 810bhp M120 Rover-built

Meteor engine, driving through a five-speed Merritt-Brown gearbox and steering system. There were four suspension units on each side, each with two road wheels and three concentric springs. Conquerors carried a crew of four.

The FV215 design study was based on the Conqueror. A number of Conquerors were also converted to FV222 ARVs which had a 45-ton winch and were the only recovery vehicles capable of dealing with the weight of a Conqueror tank. There were two types of these, the Mk 1 with a box-like structure in place of the turret and the Mk 2 with a purpose-built hull incorporating a sloping glacis plate that extended to the top of the winch housing. Both had a folding spade at the rear for use in winching operations.

Several Conquerors survive, notably at the Tank Museum in Bovington, at the IWM in Duxford, and at the Kubinka Tank Museum in Russia. The REME Museum of Technology has a Mk 2 Conqueror ARV, and there are a number of derelicts on ranges and training areas.

DIMENSIONS AND WEIGHT:
Length 25ft 9in (39ft over the gun), width 13ft 1in, height 10ft 4in. Weight 65 tons.

FURTHER READING:
Conqueror, Rob Griffin; *AFV Profile No 38 Conqueror Heavy Gun Tank*, Michael Norman.

CONTENTIOUS (FV4401)

The Duncan Sandys Defence Review of 1957 had a major effect on the British Army, reducing the cost of overseas garrisons by creating an Army Strategic Reserve whose Brigades could be deployed swiftly by air to trouble spots within what remained of the British Empire. This placed a new emphasis on air portability that had its own impact on tank design.

Project Prodigal was initiated to look at the future of AFVs in these new circumstances, and would eventually lead to the CVR(T) series of light tanks. In the mean time, a requirement was identified for an airportable tank destroyer that would field a suitably powerful gun.

A mild steel prototype was produced under the name of FV4401 Contentious, and for speed of construction was based on a shortened Comet tank hull with only four road wheels instead of five. Power came from a Rolls-Royce B series engine. The hull was left open to minimise the vehicle's profile and its weight, and pending a

The Conqueror ARV was needed because no other recovery vehicles were capable of dealing with the gun tank's weight. This is a Mk 2 version. (Public Domain)

Contentious by name and not a little contentious by nature… this was an early 1960s design intended to be airportable and its basic design was not unlike that of the earlier Alecto. However, gun elevation was adjusted by means of a height-control system on the suspension, similar to that of the Swedish S-Tank with which it was contemporary. Only one mild steel prototype was built before the project was cancelled, and this is it. (Simon/WikiMedia Commons)

more satisfactory design the fuel tanks were mounted externally, above the track guards. There was room for only two crew members, so an autoloader was fitted for the fixed 105mm gun.

Gun elevation depended on a hydraulic system that gave independent height control of each wheel station, so that the whole hull could be tilted as necessary. The principle was similar to that used on the Swedish S-Tank (Stridsvagn 103) which reached prototype form in 1961. The Contentious prototype was built with a 20pdr gun as used in the contemporary Centurion tank, but was later reworked to mount a 105mm L7 gun. (Some sources argue that there was actually more than one prototype.)

Contentious was thoroughly tested but no production ensued. The prototype with 105mm gun survives at the Bovington Tank Museum in Britain.

DIMENSIONS AND WEIGHT:
Length 27ft 11in, width 10ft 2in, height (not known). Weight (not known).

CONWAY

In the early years of the Cold War, there were several different attempts to provide a tank or tank destroyer that could counter the perceived threat from the Soviet IS-3 heavy tank. The medium-term plan focused on the Conqueror tank but there were also attempts to create a tank destroyer with the new American 120mm L1 gun as a stop-gap response.

Two different but related vehicles were prototyped under the Conway name. The FV4004 was a self-propelled gun based on a Centurion Mk3 hull and mounted a 120mm gun in a large turret made from rolled plate. Just one prototype was built but the project was cancelled in 1951.

At about the same time, work re-focused on a tank destroyer that would use an even bigger gun, this time in the shape of the 183mm L4, a modified version of the BL 7.2in howitzer. This was numbered FV4005, but was apparently still thought of as part of the Conway project (although there is evidence that the name Centaur was also used). As a first stage, the

The first stage of the FV4005 Conway project was this self-propelled gun or tank destroyer, which combined a 183mm gun with a Centurion hull.

As a second stage of the Conway project, a massive turret was built for the 183mm gun. The turret survived at Bovington, and was later remounted on a spare Centurion hull; it now acts as a gate guardian for the Tank Museum.

gun was mounted to a Centurion hull using a low-profile limited traverse mounting, an automatic loader and a concentric recoil system. As a second stage, it was mounted in a massive turret with full 360-degree traverse and a hydraulic recoil system was employed.

The original prototype of this second-stage FV4005 was dismantled after the project was cancelled in August 1957 but its turret was retained at Bovington. In more recent years it has been re-mounted on a Centurion hull and is regularly on display outside the Tank Museum. The Bovington Tank Museum also has a scale model of the FV4004 Conway.

DIMENSIONS AND WEIGHT:
Length 25ft 7in (turreted FV4005), width 11ft 1in, height 11ft 8in. Weight 50 tons approximately.

FURTHER READING:
The Dark Age of Tanks: Britain's Lost Armour, 1945-1970, David Lister.

COVENANTER (A13)

The A13 Covenanter was an unsuccessful heavy cruiser tank built between 1940 and 1943. Although production quantities were high, and in all 1771 examples were built, the tank was never approved for overseas service, mainly because of persistent cooling system problems.

The origin of this tank lay in a 1938 War Office requirement for an improved heavy cruiser as an eventual replacement for the Nuffield-built Cruiser Mk IV that would enter service in 1940. When the first two designs proved too expensive, a new General Staff requirement was issued for a cheaper and lighter tank; this became the A13 Mk III, Cruiser Mk V.

Unlike the other members of the A13 family, the new one was really a heavy cruiser, although it did share with them its Christie suspension and its armament of a 2pdr main gun and a co-axial 7.92mm Besa machine gun. It was a quite radical departure from the design of the Mk III and Mk IV Cruisers. To achieve a low profile, the height of the hull was kept down by using cranked suspension arms; the four unevenly-spaced large road wheels on each side otherwise visually resembled the A13 Mk II design. The requirement also called for a welded hull rather than the traditional riveted type, an idea new to British tanks and which caused raised eyebrows in many quarters. Armour was to meet 30mm standards, and as sloped armour would meet this specification with thinner plate, it was used extensively as a way of reducing the tank's overall weight.

The plan was to use the Wilson transmission and epicyclic steering from the A16 tank, and Meadows were contracted to design and produce a new low-height engine with at least 300bhp to suit the low-profile hull. The one they eventually provided was a horizontally-opposed flat-12. The turret was to be a Nuffield design, and detailed design of the hull was to be done by the London Midland and Scottish Railway at Crewe, who had no previous experience of tank design. It is worth noting that Nuffield had been invited in February 1939 to play a larger part in the production of the new tank but had declined; they were allowed instead to draw up their own specification for a heavy cruiser tank, which subsequently became the A15 Cruiser Mk VI, or Crusader.

When the General Staff were shown the proposed design, they approved it with the proviso that the armour should be uprated to 40mm standard. This inevitably increased weight, but no redesign of the suspension was ever contemplated. The new tank was the first of the cruisers to be given a name, and the one chosen was Covenanter; it was suitably obscure, the Covenanters having been a Scottish religious faction at the time of the British Civil Wars in the 17th century.

This was a time when Britain was rapidly re-arming, and the first 100 Covenanter tanks were ordered off the drawing board in 1939 before any prototype had been built. The assumption was that any problems could be ironed out on a pair of pilot models and that full production could follow swiftly. The first of these was completed in May 1940 and performed well in trials; the second arrived in September and showed ominous warning of the cooling problems that would dog the tank.

These problems really resulted from the rushed design phase. The new Meadows engine was suitably low but it was also very wide, and left no space for radiators in the engine compartment. As a result, these had to be located at the front of the hull, with piping to the rear. Fears of supply problems with the planned Wilson gearbox and steering led to production models having the epicyclic steering units from the earlier A13 Mk II and a crash gearbox; a smaller transmission cooling fan had to be fitted, which did not help the overheating problems. The four-man crews (commander, driver, gunner and loader) would complain that the routing of the pipes to the radiator through the hull made their quarters uncomfortably hot as well.

Further orders followed, and by September 1939 both Leyland Motors and English Electric had been drawn in to build the Covenanter. Production actually began in late 1940, by which time the LMS Railway works had decided that they did not trust the strength of the planned welded construction and had switched to riveted construction, still using the original twin layers of steel plate. Weight increased, not helped by the need to use steel wheels instead of the planned aluminium types when aluminium was prioritised for the aircraft industry. Even so, the Covenanter still had a respectable top speed of 30mph and a range of 100 miles.

The first production models had several different designs of radiator louvre to deal with overheating, and an in due course an in-service solution was developed that added an oil cooler to one radiator. Tanks so modified became Mk II or Cruiser Mk V* types. The Covenanter Mk III (Cruiser Mk V**) was then a production type, with redesigned radiator louvres, an oil cooler mounted either side of the engine, a modified clutch linkage, air cleaners added inboard at the rear, and the exhaust silencers relocated at the ends of the track guards. The final Mk IV was another production model, built to Mk II standard but with the additional features of the Mk III.

There were also close-support versions of all four Marks, each armed with a 3in howitzer in place of the 2pdr main gun. Observation Post

variants of the Mk II and Mk IV models were created for artillery units, fitted with dummy guns and the necessary additional radios. There was also a Command version of the Mk II, again with a dummy gun and appropriate radios.

The tank's cooling problems were never fully resolved, and as a result Covenanters were considered unfit for overseas service. The majority were confined to training and home defence duties, although a small number were sent to North Africa for a rather fruitless evaluation by REME units. By late 1943 Covenanters were considered too poorly armed and too thinly armoured to face the latest German tanks and, as resolving these problems would have required major redesign, the type was declared obsolete by February 1944.

Just two special variants were created. A single ARV prototype was built in 1942, based on a turretless hull, and several Covenanters were converted to bridgelayers. These latter did see service in Europe after the Normandy invasion, and also in the Pacific theatre during 1945 in the hands of the Australian Army. Some gun tanks were fitted with the Anti–Mine Roller Attachment, which consisted of four rollers suspended on a frame attached to the front of the hull. Elements of the Covenanter were also used in the Medium Tank AT/1 amphibious prototype.

There are four survivors of the Covenanter in Britain. One is at the Bovington Tank Museum (which also has a turret from one of the pilot models), and another one was discovered in 2017. The other two are wrecks on a former gunnery range. There are two bridgelayer variants at the Australian Armoured Corps Tank Museum in Puckapunyal, and a third tank is at

The A13 Covenanter prompted the design of a new Meadows tank engine and pioneered welded construction in a British tank. Production began in 1940, but chronic cooling problems prevented the tank from becoming a success. (IWM, KID778, Public Domain)

the museum in the Parramatta barracks of the 1st/15th Royal New South Wales Lancers, near Sydney.

DIMENSIONS AND WEIGHT:
Length 19ft, width 8ft 7in, height 7ft 4in.
Weight 18 tons.

FURTHER READING:
Crusader and Covenanter Cruiser Tanks 1939–45, David Fletcher & Peter Sarson.

CROMWELL (A27)

The Cromwell name was initially allocated to the tank that became the A24 Cavalier, but the Cromwell as generally understood was a completely different design of cruiser tank that had the A27 designation. It was closely related to the Centaur, which was essentially the same design but with a different engine, and has a separate entry here. A total of 4016 Cromwells were built between 1942 and 1945.

The origin of the A27 Cromwell can be traced to Rolls-Royce's development of their Meteor tank engine from the Merlin aero engine in 1941. The General Staff wanted to use this hugely powerful new engine in a new version of the A24, but Nuffield would not agree to adapting their design to take it. The General Staff retreated hastily and decided to call for another new tank to take the new engine. It was

this that became the A27. With the new Meteor engine it became the A27M, and when a Liberty-engined derivative was drawn up as insurance, this became the A27L, that eventually took the Centaur name.

The first mild-steel A27M pilot model was delivered for trials in March 1942 and its performance proved exceptional. Major work put into the cooling system had reduced power losses, and also ensured that the engine did not over-heat, as it did on most other Cruiser tanks. With a 40mph top speed and a range of 170 miles on roads, the Cromwell was the fastest British tank of the Second World War and a huge improvement on earlier Cruiser types. (That high top speed was nevertheless a contributory factor to its reputation for throwing tracks.) Its new 6pdr gun brought increased firepower to the equation, and was backed up by a co-axial 7.92mm Besa machine gun and a second machine gun in the hull front. The tank had a crew of five: commander, driver, gunner, loader/radio operator and hull gunner.

Arrangements for production had been made with BRCW but that company could not meet the production quotas. Leyland Motors was therefore made the design parent for both the A27M and the A27L tanks; production would eventually be undertaken by Metro-Cammell, English Electric, and Fowlers of Lincoln. The War Office strategy was designed to ensure continuity of

Right at last: the A27 with Rolls-Royce Meteor engine, Christie suspension and 6pdr gun provided Britain with a really good tank from early 1943. This Mk IV model with the later 75mm gun was pictured in the Tank Museum at Bovington. (Morio, CC-by-SA 4.0)

production: A27L hulls were designed to take Meteor engines if necessary (and many did), while the A27L was built with its Liberty engine only until production of the Meteor had been reliably established. Both types were to use the new Merritt-Brown Z5 gearbox as designed for the Churchill which offered differential steering without clutching or braking. This was a major advance on previous designs and gave the tanks excellent manoeuvrability.

Production of the A27M began slowly in November 1942, at which point its name of Cromwell was confirmed and the Cavalier and Centaur names were allocated. In the beginning, supplies of the Meteor engine were slow to get under way and some tanks were built with modified Merlin aero engines taken from the repair programme, but by January 1943 Meteor production had been reliably established and full production of the Cromwell began.

In fact, production began before a final specification had been agreed, and the Cromwell was into its fourth (Mk IV) variant before one was. All Marks nevertheless had the same basic specification, with a hull divided by bulkheads into three compartments, a Christie suspension with five road wheels per side and angled springs to reduce the tank's height, and the 540bhp Meteor engine driving through the Merritt-Brown Z5 gearbox.

The final specification was not issued until February 1944, by which time well over 2000 Cromwells had been built and the Mk IV type was in production. In fact, only three of those Marks were actually made: the Mk II existed only as a pilot example. It was built by Vauxhall when they expected to join the Cromwell programme and used a cast turret similar to that on the Churchill; in practice, Vauxhall withdrew from the Cromwell programme when Churchill production was extended.

The Mk I and Mk III both had the original 6pdr main gun; there were 357 of the Mk I and about 200 of the Mk III, which used Centaur hulls at a time when production of Meteor engines had begun to exceed that of Cromwell hulls. The Cromwell IV was introduced in November 1943 and went on to become the most numerous variant, with a production total of at least 1935. These also had hulls originally intended for Centaurs but had a new 75mm gun. The last ones had the final production specification, with extra armour below the crew compartment, seam welding to add strength,

A Cromwell tank forms the memorial to the 7th Armoured Division (the Desert Rats) at Thetford Forest in Norfolk, beside the A1065 road. (Keith Evans/ WikiMedia Commons)

This rear view shows an ARV based on the Cromwell hull. (Public Domain)

and a commander's cupola that gave all-round vision.

The new 75mm gun was developed after experience with the American 75mm fitted to Lease-Lend Grants and Shermans. Developed by the ROF, it was essentially a 6pdr bored out to take American 75mm ammunition. It was a simple matter to fit the new 75mm in place of the 6pdr, and it brought an HE shell capability that the 6pdr did not have (although it had a lower armour-piercing capability).

There were four more subsequent Marks of Cromwell. The Mk V became the new basic type with a dedicated Cromwell-pattern hull incorporating thicker frontal armour, and with the 75mm main gun. The Mk VI was a Close Support tank with a 3.7in howitzer in the turret; 341 were built. Cromwells Mk VII and Mk VIII were then not production types but resulted from upgrade programmes that brought wider tracks and improved suspension. The Mk VII was the upgraded gun tank (of which about 1500 were created) and the Mk VIIII was the upgraded Close Support version.

Some Cromwells were converted to or built as Observation Post or Command tanks. The OP tanks retained their main gun and were fitted with additional radios; they were based on Mk IV, Mk VI and Mk VIII types. In the case of the Command tank, the main gun was removed to create more space in the turret, and a dummy gun barrel was fitted. There was also a Control variant used by regimental headquarters that was equipped with two radios and also retained its main gun.

The Cromwell first saw combat in Normandy in June 1944, and in the fighting that followed the D-Day landings its speed and mobility endeared it to crews and compensated for the heavier firepower of some German tanks. Those same qualities, together with its low profile, made it ideal for reconnaissance duties. Hugely respected afterwards, Cromwell tanks remained in British service until 1955, and several saw service in the Korean War. The Cromwell became the basis of several other British tank designs, and a number were also used by armed forces in Greece, Israel and Portugal.

More than 50 Cromwells still survive, some as wrecks and others in private collections. Among those normally available for public viewing are three Mk IV models in Britain: one at the Bovington Tank Museum, a Command version at the Imperial War Museum in Duxford, and one that forms a memorial to the 7th Armoured Division on the A1065 road near Thetford in Norfolk.

Australia has the only surviving Mk I Cromwell in the Royal Australian Armoured Corps Tank Museum at Puckapunyal. The others on public view are all Mk IVs: there are two in Belgium, two in Russia, one in the Netherlands, one in the Czech Republic, one in Israel and one in the USA.

> **DIMENSIONS AND WEIGHT:**
> Length 20ft 10in, width 9ft 6½in, height 8ft 2in.
> Weight 27.6 tons
>
> **FURTHER READING:**
> *Cromwell Cruiser Tank, 1942-50*, David Fletcher & Richard C Harley; *Cruiser Tank Warfare*, John Plant.

CROSSLEY-MARTEL TANKETTE
See Martel Tankettes.

CRUISER MARK I
See A9 Cruiser Tank.

CRUISER MARK II
See A10 Cruiser Tank.

CRUISER MK III
The Cruiser Mk III tank that served in the British Army between 1938 and 1941 was the first of the "Christie cruisers" – tanks that used the Christie suspension system to permit higher speeds and better cross-country performance than were available from the earlier bogie-type suspensions.

The first Cruiser tank to use a Christie suspension was the Mk III. It was built by Nuffield with their licence-manufactured Liberty engine and a 2pdr gun, but thin armour was a weakness and the tank lasted in service only until 1942. (Alan Wilson, CC-by-SA 2.0)

Walter J Christie was an American automotive engineer and inventor, and in 1928 he had developed a new "helicoil" suspension system for tanks, which gave each wheel its own spring-loaded mounting. The US military developed his design further, and the Russian military obtained its details by less orthodox means and developed their own tanks around it. It was a 1936 demonstration of Soviet tanks that enthused the new Assistant Director of Mechanisation at the War Office, General Giffard LeQuesne Martel. He arranged for the Nuffield Group to buy an example from the USA and to take out a licence to develop and build Christie tanks. Lord Nuffield seized his chance. He set up a new company, Nuffield Mechanisation & Aero Ltd, to manufacture the design; and he took out a licence to build the American Liberty aero engine that Christie favoured and that had also impressed Martel.

The General Staff then drew up a formal specification for a new cruiser tank, designated A13. The contract for development and manufacture of course went to Nuffield, who delivered the first prototype (A13E1) in 1937. A second prototype followed with a redesigned and larger hull that could take the turret of the A9 tank; the drive to the wheels was also replaced by a conventional sprocket on each side. Pending production of this promising new model, the War Office approved the A9 cruiser as an interim buy, and subsequently the A10 was ordered as an additional safety measure.

After satisfactory trials, an order for 50 tanks was placed in October 1937. The model now became the Tank, Cruiser, Mk III; the Vickers-designed A9 had become the Mk I, and the same company's A10 had become the Cruiser Mk II. Deliveries began in December 1938 and production ended in mid-1939 after 65 Cruiser Mk III tanks had been built; by that stage, work was already under way on an improved Cruiser Mk IV that was derived from it.

The Cruiser Mk III had armour of between 6mm and 14mm thickness, although the original General Staff specification had called for 30mm plate or its sloped equivalent. It shared its riveted turret design with the A9 and A10 tanks, although the commander's cupola was slightly different, with a larger hatch. There was a 2pdr gun as the main armament, with a single Vickers .303 machine gun, and the tank had a crew of four (commander, driver, gunner and loader). It was powered by a Nuffield Liberty V12 aero

engine of 340bhp, which could be started either by compressed air or electrically. There were four large and unevenly-spaced road wheels on each side, and the tank had a range of 90 miles with a top speed of 30mph.

As an early attempt at a cruiser tank, the Mk III was a step in the right direction. It had a good turn of speed and the best tank gun that Britain could supply at the time, but its armour was thin and it suffered from engine problems. Some were sent to France with the BEF in 1940, where their poor armour protection became apparent; many were lost in the fighting, and the rest were abandoned at Dunkirk. Others took part in the early North African campaign in the Libyan desert in 1940-1941, and some were transferred to Greece later in 1941 and were lost there. The Mk III's service life was over before the start of 1942.

There was just one special variant of this tank, which was a Close Support variant equipped with the 3.7in mortar, intended to fire smoke rounds for infantry support.

An example of the Mk III Cruiser survives at the Bovington Tank Museum. It was used to prove the planned turret armour upgrade for the Mk IV model, and survives with that modification.

DIMENSIONS AND WEIGHT:
Length 19ft 8in, width 8ft 4in, height 8ft 6in.
Weight 14 tons

FURTHER READING:
British Battle Tanks Vol 2, David Fletcher;
Cruiser Tank Warfare, John Plant.

CRUISER MK IV

The Cruiser Mk IV, or A13 Mk II, was the first mass-produced British Cruiser tank and was an up-armoured development of the Cruiser Mk III (A13 Mk I). It was built between 1939 and 1941, but exact quantities are in dispute. The figure of 600 seems about right.

Nuffield had built around 30 Cruiser Mk III tanks when the War Office realised that they needed thicker armour. So the original requirement for 30mm frontal armour (or its sloping equivalent) was resurrected and implemented by means of sloped armour added to the existing turret and at the rear. The upgrade was relatively straightforward and some of the later Mk IIIs were completed to Mk IV standard before they left the factory.

Everything else about the Mk IV was the same as the Mk III. It had the same Christie suspen-

sion with four road wheels on each side, the same Liberty V12 engine, and the same armament of a 2-pdr main gun with a Vickers .303 machine gun as the secondary weapon. It was configured in the same way for a four-man crew.

As the War Office called for more tanks, Nuffield was unable to meet the full demand and so three other manufacturers were called in to build Mk IVs. These were Leyland Motors, English Electric and the LMS Railway. In line with the new military policy that favoured the Besa 7.92mm machine gun over the Vickers .303, the Mk IV was modified with the new gun (and a new mantlet) early in 1940 to become a Cruiser Mk IVA, or A13 Mk IIA. There would eventually be more Mk IVA models than of the original Mk IV production version. This was the only production change of importance; there were also no special variants, although a Close Support variant was considered in 1939 and rejected.

About 40 of these tanks went to France with the BEF in 1940. Many were put out of action and many more abandoned at Dunkirk, but nine were captured and became command vehicles with the German forces during Operation Barbarossa, the invasion of Russia. The Mk IV was one of the main tank types used in the North African desert campaign, where it was well liked despite its vulnerability to anti-tank guns. These tanks were replaced by more modern Cruiser types after 1941.

The modified Cruiser Mk III at the Bovington Tank Museum is representative of the Mk IV specification.

DIMENSIONS AND WEIGHT:
Length 19ft 9in, width 8ft 4in, height 8ft 6in. Weight 14.75 tons

FURTHER READING:
British Battle Tanks Vol 2, David Fletcher; *Cruiser Tank Warfare*, John Plant.

CRUISER MARK V
See A13 Mk III Cruiser Tank (Covenanter).

CRUISER MARK VI
See A15 (Crusader).

CRUISER MARK VII
See A24 (Cavalier).

CRUISER MARK VIII
See A27L (Centaur), A27M (Cromwell), and A30 (Challenger).

CRUSADER (A15)
When the Nuffield proposal for the A16 heavy cruiser tank was deemed too expensive in April 1939, the General Staff turned to a cheaper specification called A13. Its design was allocated to the London, Midland and Scottish Railway,

The Crusader or Cruiser Mk VI was another Nuffield design that had a short life. Despite progressive upgrades, it proved unreliable. This early example, with hull-mounted auxiliary turret, nevertheless managed a convincing performance for the camera! (MoD)

Crusaders were better appreciated in the desert in North Africa, and this shows what was called the Sunshade – a camouflage rigged up around the tank to make it look like a lorry from the air during Operation Bertram just before El Alamein in October 1942. (Public Domain)

but Nuffield was not prepared to be sidelined, and chose to develop its own version of the A13 specification.

While the A13 became the Covenanter, the Nuffield version was developed in parallel and earned the General Staff designation of A15. Like the Covenanter, it was ordered straight off the drawing-board in 1939 without waiting for a prototype, and the A15 became the Tank, Cruiser, Mk VI, with the name of Crusader. Determined to demonstrate their abilities, Nuffield managed to deliver the pilot model of the Crusader some six weeks before the first Covenanter was ready.

Not surprisingly, the A15 was drawn up around the 340bhp Nuffield Liberty engine. This was reworked to suit the low height required for the engine compartment, which unfortunately compromised the design of the cooling fans and the water pump. This would become a major problem when early Crusaders were called on to serve in the deserts of the North African Campaign in 1941-1942. The transmission was another Nuffield product – the four-speed constant-mesh gearbox – and there was a Wilson epicyclic steering system.

The design worked out to be rather heavier than earlier cruiser tanks, and as a result its Christie suspension needed five road wheels on each side rather than four. The Crusader was designed for a crew of five men – a commander, gunner, driver, loader and hull gunner. The hull gunner manned a Besa machine gun mounted in a small hand-traversed auxiliary turret mounted at the left-hand front of the hull. However, this was not liked by the troops and in service many units left the position unmanned or even removed the turret, reducing the crew to four.

When the A13 Covenanter project had been allocated to the LMS, Nuffield had been invited to contribute, and did become involved with the design of the turret. They then used that same turret for their own A15 Crusader. It had a polygonal design to give maximum internal space for the size of the turret ring, and was designed to accommodate the 2pdr gun that was then standard on the British cruiser designs. There was no cupola for the commander, who simply had a flat hatch with a periscope running through it. The earliest versions of this turret had a semi-in-

This Crusader Mk III is preserved at the Bovington Tank Museum. These later Crusaders dispensed with the auxiliary turret, had the 6pdr gun, and benefited from improved engine cooling arrangements. (Alan Wilson/ WikiMedia Commons)

Anti-aircraft versions of the Crusader were prepared for D-Day and its aftermath. The twin Oerlikon 20mm guns are clear in this picture of a preserved example at the Musée des Blindés in France. (CC0/Public Domain)

ternal cast mantlet, but this soon gave way to a larger mantlet that offered better protection and was cast with slots for the main gun, a coaxial Besa machine gun, and a sighting telescope.

Crusaders entered service in May 1941, early examples going to North Africa where they became the primary tank of the British cruiser armoured regiments. The rapid build-up of production inevitably led to quality problems, and shortages of spares in North Africa led to part-worn items being cannibalised from dead tanks, which led to reliability issues. Worse, the compromised cooling system of the Liberty engine gave serious reliability problems in desert conditions, and it was some considerable time before modifications were developed as a cure. Then, when the Germans began to use face-hardened armour on their tanks, it quickly became clear that the Crusader was under-gunned with its 2pdr that could only fire AP rounds; no HE rounds were available at the time.

Nevertheless, the Crusader proved a rather better tank than that list of its failings might suggest. It used its mobility, its speed, and its ability to fire on the move to good effect. Its operational range of 200 miles on roads and 146 miles across country was also valuable in the desert.

Mk II (Cruiser Mk VIA) models had the benefit of 49mm of frontal armour as against the Mk I's 40mm, and when there were delays in the introduction of the planned heavy cruiser tanks, a Mk III model was produced that mounted the new 6pdr gun and was further up-armoured to 51mm. As the bigger gun took up more space in the turret, the crew of the Mk III was reduced to three men, the commander having to double as loader. The first Mk III Crusaders were built in May 1942, and these variants also benefited from the more reliable Mk IV Liberty engine with its improved cooling fan arrangements.

But by late 1942, the Crusader's useful life was largely over. Its unreliability problems had earned it a bad reputation with the troops who used it, and as American-built M3 Grants joined the British forces in North Africa, the Crusader tanks were relegated to secondary duties, although their speed of 26mph on the road and 15mph cross-country kept them useful when formed into light squadrons tasked with flank attacks on the enemy. The last new Crusaders were Mk IIIs built in 1943; a total of 5300 examples of all types had been built.

After the North African Campaign was over, many Crusaders were converted for other uses. There had already been some variants, such as close-support Mk I and Mk II types with a 3in howitzer in place of the main gun, and Command Tank Mk IIs with a dummy gun and multiple radios. The Royal Artillery also used some as mobile observation posts, again with a dummy gun and also a fixed turret. A prototype ARV was also built in 1942 but the variant was not pursued.

The special variants after that were created for use in the D-Day landings and in the ensuing campaign in north-west Europe. These were anti-aircraft tanks (which saw little usage thanks to Allied air superiority over Europe) and gun tractors. Crusaders were also used for experiments with anti-mine rollers, with flotation kits and, after the war, to create a self-propelled gun with a 5.5in medium gun mounted in the hull.

All the anti-aircraft tanks were based on Crusader Mk III types, the early Mk I having a Bofors 40mm AA gun in an open-topped turret and a crew of four: gun commander, gun layer, loader, and driver. However, those actually used in Europe probably all had a simpler arrangement with the Bofors gun mounted directly to the top of the hull and protected only by its standard shield. The Mk II mounted twin Oerlikon 20mm anti-aircraft guns and a single .303 Vickers in a small but heavily armoured polygonal turret; and the Mk III variant was the same but with the radio moved to the hull to give more room in the turret.

The gun tractor was developed to tow the 17pdr anti-tank gun, and also carried some of its ammunition. Its turret was replaced by a simple boxy superstructure that afforded some protection to the driver and the six-man gun crew.

The last Crusaders were withdrawn from

An alternative anti-aircraft version of the Crusader had a single 40mm Bofors gun. This one was pictured in March 1943 at Lulworth, the gunnery range on the Dorset coast. (IWM/Public Domain)

British service in 1948, but several were sold on for further service in Argentina, Egypt and South Africa. In Argentina, they were converted to self-propelled guns with a tall boxy superstructure and a French 75mm or 105mm gun.

Several Crusaders still survive in museums, most notably at the Tank Museum in Bovington (which has a running Mk III), at Overloon in the Netherlands (a gun tractor) and at the Musée de Blindés in France (an anti-aircraft variant).

Yet another use for an unwanted Crusader! This one was turned into a gun tractor and was pictured many years later at the Overloon museum in Holland. (Public Domain)

DIMENSIONS AND WEIGHT:
Length 20ft 8.5in, width 9ft 1in, height 7ft 4in. Weight approx 20 tons.

FURTHER READING:
Crusader, Milsom, Sanders & Scarborough; *Crusader and Covenanter Cruiser Tank 1939–1945*, Fletcher & Sarson; *A15 Cruiser Mk VI Crusader Tank: A Technical History*, Knight.

CVR(T) FAMILY

The CVR(T) family of light tracked vehicles included two reconnaissance tanks, the FV101 Scorpion and the FV107 Scimitar, which are discussed in more detail here under their own

The second prototype of the A33 Excelsior still survives, and looks every inch the Heavy Assault Tank that it was intended to be. (XRobb/WikiMedia, CC-by-SA 3.0)

entries. CVR(T) stands for Combat Vehicle Reconnaissance (Tracked), and these were small, highly mobile, airportable armoured vehicles that were designed to share common automotive components and suspension. Besides the two light tanks, the family also included the FV102 Striker anti-tank guided missile vehicle, FV103 Spartan APC, FV104 Samaritan armoured ambulance, FV105 Sultan command control vehicle, and FV106 Samson ARV.

The development contract was awarded to Alvis of Coventry in 1967. Size and weight were limited by the airportability requirement and by the Army's insistence on low ground pressure to improve the vehicle's mobility. These called for some new design solutions, and Alvis chose to fabricate both the hull and the turret from a welded aluminium-zinc-magnesium alloy. As a result, the Scorpion core variant of the CVR(T) family became the first tank ever to have a light-weight aluminium hull. The alloy armour did bring with it some compromise in protection, however, and a further weight-saving compromise was the absence of a powered traverse on turreted variants.

The limited development time-scale left no time to develop an all-new engine, and the physical size of the engine was limited by the space available for it at the right front of the hull next to the driver. The British Army would have preferred a diesel, but the best solution turned out to be the 4.2-litre petrol Jaguar six-cylinder car engine, which was detuned to 190bhp for military use and drove through a Merritt-Wilson semi-automatic gearbox.

The contract called for 30 prototypes, of which the first 17 would be Scorpions. The trials were successful and the British Army accepted the CVR(T) for service in May 70; production began in 1972 and the first vehicles entered service in 1973. By 1996, over 3500 had been built for both British use and for export.

EXCELSIOR (A33)

The poor performance of the Churchill tanks in the August 1942 Dieppe Raid prompted concerns about their future, and the inevitable result was a rash of proposals for replacements. At the time, there was some discussion of using the new A27 Cromwell as the basis of a whole family of tanks, both infantry and cruiser types, and Rolls-Royce drew up two proposals that gained the codes A31 and A32. Neither was followed up, but a third proposal from English Electric (who were building Cromwells at the time) did progress to the prototype stage.

This proposal was to create a Heavy Assault Tank by adding extra armour to the A27 hull and turret and mounting this heavier structure on the T1 suspension and tracks from the 50-ton US M6 tank that was under development for both British and American use. The General Staff gave this idea the designation of A33, and at a later stage it acquired the name of Excelsior.

The first prototype was completed in 1943 and mounted a 6pdr gun, although the original specification had envisaged a Royal Ordnance QF 75mm weapon. There were two 7.92mm Besa machine guns as secondary armament and the tank had a five-man crew of commander, gunner, loader, driver and co-driver. Maximum armour thickness was 114mm and the tracks were protected by an armoured skirt that left the top run exposed.

In the mean time, questions had arisen over the future of the American M6 heavy tank, and this may be why the second prototype of the A33 replaced the American-designed suspension with a heavy-duty type designed by the LMS works and known as the "R/L Heavy" type. This was largely concealed by deep side skirts that also concealed the top run of the tracks, and this second prototype had the anticipated 75mm gun. However, in the mean time the Churchill had redeemed itself in the Tunisian and Italian campaigns and there was no longer a threat to its future. As a result, the A33 requirement lapsed and the project came to an end in May 1944.

The second prototype A33 survives and can be seen at the Tank Museum in Bovington.

DIMENSIONS AND WEIGHT:
Length 22ft 8in, width 11ft 1½in, height 7ft 11in. Weight 45 tons.

FURTHER READING:
The Universal Tank, David Fletcher.

FLYING ELEPHANT

Once production of the first Mk I tanks was under way in 1916, Albert Stern (the Chairman of the Tank Supply Committee) began to look at the next stage. After sifting through various proposals that had been submitted, he settled on one from William Tritton at Fosters for a shell-proof tank, designed to carry armour thick enough to resist field-gun fire.

The Tank Supply Committee approved production of a prototype in June, but a final design was not settled until August. The new tank was known at various times as the Heavy Tank and the Foster's Battle Tank, and the plan to use 3in frontal armour and 2in side armour made it extraordinarily heavy even though it was shorter and narrower than the existing Mk I tanks. To cope with the estimated weight of 100 tons, Daimler were asked to produce a design for two of their 105bhp engines linked together, each one driving its own four-speed gearbox.

The design was really a big box on tracks, with the primary tracks under each side, tractor-fashion, and an auxiliary pair of tracks under the belly of the vehicle to assist progress in soft going. The roof was to be semi-cylindrical and the plan for a main armament in the domed nose gave an appearance that was probably responsible for the nickname of "Flying Elephant ". The gun was likely to be a 6pdr, as used in the male Mk I tanks, although there was also a proposal for a 12pdr. There would have been two Hotchkiss machine guns mounted in each side, plus a further pair at the rear. The crew would have numbered between eight and ten.

No prototype was ever completed. The project was aborted in late 1916 because, according to Stern, the War Office placed a higher priority on mobility than on protection. There is a model of the Design B version of the tank at the Tank Museum in Bovington.

> **DIMENSIONS AND WEIGHT (PROJECTED):**
> Length 27ft 5in, width 9ft 10in, height 9ft 10in.
> Weight 100 tons approximately.

FV201

The FV201 project grew out of work that had started in 1944 to meet General Staff specification A45 for a Universal Tank. Believing that the design could not be adapted to cover all the intended specialist roles, the General Staff called for a tank that could, and the FV201 project

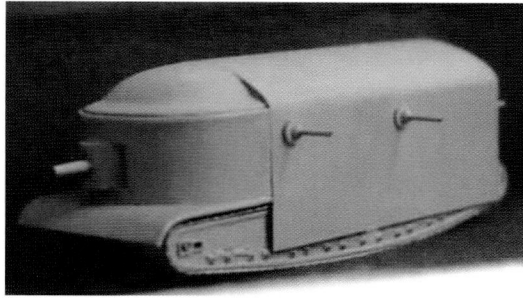

Only a model of the Flying Elephant heavy tank survives today. It is not hard to see where its nickname came from. (Public Domain)

was the result.

A first prototype with a Centurion turret and 17pdr gun was completed in October 1947 but it soon became clear that major hull modifications would be needed to cater for all the desirable variants. That led first to the cancellation of the gun tank variant in October 1948, and although work on the special-purpose variants continued into 1949, the project ran into the sand. Nevertheless, it was an FV201 hull that was modified to carry the 120mm gun as part of the Conqueror heavy tank development programme.

FV215

The FV215 was another concept for a heavy tank designed to support frontline Centurions and provide a counter to the Soviet IS-III. It was intended as an eventual replacement for Conqueror, with greater firepower. A first concept was outlined in 1951 and a prototype was ordered in 1954 but this was never completed. During 1956 it became clear that the War Office was no longer keen on the FV215 and the project was cancelled in 1957.

A full-size mock-up was constructed between 1955 and 1957, and the report on this is the main source of information about FV215. The tank was based on a modified FV200-series chassis with four Horstmann suspension bogies on each side and its hull was slightly narrower than that of Conqueror.

FV215 was to have the 183mm L4 gun, which

This picture of the FV215 wooden mock-up comes from the report on the proposed tank. The turret was mounted at the rear, probably because of the length of the 183mm gun barrel.

The FV4202 or "40-ton Centurion" prototypes incorporated several new ideas but were only ever intended as development models. This one still survives at Bovington. (Geni/WikiMedia, CC-by-SA 4.0)

would have had a very long barrel. This was probably the main reason that the welded turret was set at the rear of the tank, and this in turn prompted a rearrangement of the traditional hull configuration. The engine was moved to the middle, with its exhausts emerging through the hull roof just ahead of the turret; it also completely separated the driver's compartment from the fighting compartment. The intention was to use a Rover-built Meteor M120 No 2 Mk 1 with 810bhp, which would drive through a Merritt-Brown Z5R gearbox. Maximum speed was expected to be just under 20mph. As in the Conqueror and the Centurion, there would be a small four-cylinder auxiliary engine to power the generator when the main engine was not running.

The big gun required huge ordnance, which is why the five-man crew included two loaders; the other members were a driver, a gunner and the commander. The gunner, unusually, sat on the left of the gun and his ammunition stowage was limited to 20 rounds. Although a full 360-degree gun traverse was possible, a lockout mechanism prevented the weapon from being fired except in a 90-degree arc to the front of the vehicle and directly to the rear. This was arranged to

preserve stability.

Secondary armament was to consist of a machine gun on the turret roof and a Browning .30 calibre (7.62mm) machine gun that was mounted coaxially with the main weapon but was not integral to its main mounting. Maximum armour thickness was 4.9in on the glacis, which was sloped at 59 degrees.

Note that some versions of the *World of Tanks* video game incorporated a tank called an FV215b, which was an invention based on some elements of the real FV215.

DIMENSIONS AND WEIGHT:
Length 25ft, width 12ft, height 10ft 7in.
Weight 61 tons unladen, 65 tons in battle order.

FURTHER READING:
See www.tanks-encyclopedia.com

FV4202

The development vehicles that Leyland built to test early ideas for the Chieftain tank were known as FV4202 types, but are more familiarly known as the "40-ton Centurion". They used many parts from the Centurion but were some 10 tons lighter, with smaller road wheels and narrower tracks than the Centurion. Their lower weight also allowed the use of a more compact and lighter 520bhp Meteorite V8 engine, which drove through a five-speed Merritt-Brown gearbox.

The three prototypes featured a reclined driver's position, a crew of four and a 20pdr gun. One still exists in the Bovington Tank Museum, and one was used for a time as a recovery training aid at SEME in Bordon.

DIMENSIONS AND WEIGHT:
Length, width and height not available.
Weight 40.8 long tons.

FURTHER READING:
Chieftain Main Battle Tank 1965–2003, Simon Dunstan.

GRANT

When the British Tank Commission went shopping for tanks in the USA in June 1940, they quickly learned that the Americans were not prepared to build British tanks but would only sell Britain tanks of their own design. Britain badly needed a Medium tank and the only option at the time was the M3 Medium, a tank that was then still under development. The Americans nevertheless got it into volume production with unparalleled speed, placing some contracts in the traditional way with heavy engineering firms (American Locomotive and Baldwin Locomotive), but arranging for the majority to be built in the new purpose-built Detroit Tank Arsenal that opened in 1941. The M3 design was complete by March that year, and full production commenced in August. It was America's first mass-produced tank.

Britain ordered 200 examples as early as October 1940, and the Tank Commission was able to provide the American design team with advice based on recent combat experience in Europe. It was also able to negotiate construction of a special variant to suit British requirements, with the radio equipment relocated to the rear of the turret from its standard position within the hull. This variant had a distinctive cast turret with a long rear overhang, and was also 11 inches lower than the original American type.

These early British versions of the M3 Medium were known to the British Army as Grant tanks (after Ulysses S Grant, an American Civil War General who later became President). As a consequence of the Lease-Lend Act that was signed on 11 March 1941, later deliveries to the British Army were standard versions of the M3 Medium, and these were given the distinguishing name of Lee.

The Grant retained the basic configuration of the original American design, with a 37mm gun in the turret that was offset to the left of the tank, and a 75mm M2 gun mounted in a sponson at the right front of the hull, where it had a limited traverse of 15 degrees right or left. Both weapons had gyro stabilisers that allowed accurate firing while the tank was on the move. The turret and sponson were cast, but the hull was of riveted construction. The engine was a 340bhp Continental R-975 radial type and all variants of the M3 had vertical volute suspension. Grant tanks carried a crew of six – a commander, a driver, two loaders and two gunners. They had a maximum speed of 26mph and were capable of around 16mph across country, while the range was a useful 120 miles. Maximum armour thickness was 56mm.

All 200 examples of the Grant with its special turret were shipped to the British Army in the Western Desert from early 1942, where they made a major difference to the British tank

capability against the Afrika Korps. A further quantity of M3 tanks were delivered during 1942 as Grant II types, and were M3A5 diesel-powered variants with two General Motors 6-71 engines giving 375bhp. These had the standard American-pattern turret, and the longer M3 version of the 75mm gun. When the M4 Sherman became available in quantity, many of the remaining Grant tanks were shipped to Burma to strengthen British tank units that were dependent on older types; some went to the Australians; and a few were sent to Britain for training and for conversion to special-purpose tanks.

The first of these conversions appeared in 1943. The Grant ARV was based on either a Grant I or a Grant II, and carried a limited amount of recovery equipment. Some had a dummy turret, and some had no turret but carried twin anti-aircraft guns. From January 1943 there were Grant Scorpion III mine-clearing variants, with the 75mm gun removed to make room for the rotor frame, and a counterweight at the rear, and a further-developed Grant Scorpion IV added a Bedford engine at the left-hand rear to drive the rotors. There were Grant CDL conversions, too, which retained the sponson-mounted 75mm gun but had an armoured searchlight housing in place of a turret, with a machine gun in its front face. Some later examples had a dummy 37mm gun in

The camouflage on this Grant tank does a good job of disguising its real shape even at this distance. These US-built tanks proved of great value in the North African campaign. (Jonathan Cardy, CC-by-SA 3.0)

Removing the commander's cupola of the original design lowered the Grant's profile, but the tank was still a tall design.

the front of the turret as well. A small number of Grant Command tanks were created for senior commanders and carried extra radio equipment; some of these had either a dummy or no 37mm turret gun to create more space inside the tank. In 1944, somewhat confusingly, the name Grant ARV I was applied to examples of the standard T2 (M31) American ARV based on the M3 tank.

DIMENSIONS AND WEIGHT:
Length 18ft 6in, width 8ft 11in, height 9ft 4in (Grant I) or 10ft 3in (Grant II). Weight 60,000 lb.

FURTHER READING:
M3 Medium Tank: The Lee and Grant Tanks in World War II, David Doyle

HARRY HOPKINS (A25)

The Harry Hopkins tank was the last of Britain's light tanks, designed by Vickers and built between 1942 and 1945. It proved totally unsuccessful.

The tank was designed as a successor to the

Light tanks were out of favour by the time production of the A25 Harry Hopkins began. The tank also had some serious faults which cut its production run short.(IWM MH-9324, Public Domain)

Tetrarch or Light Tank Mk VII, and to Vickers was a Light Tank, Mk VIII. The new tank carried over many of the features of its immediate predecessor, but a key design aim was to improve its armour protection. The specification settled on a maximum thickness of 38mm for the front of the hull and the turret, with 17mm for the sides. The tank also grew in size, becoming both longer and wider than the Tetrarch. Features retained from the Tetrarch were the three-man crew; the 2pdr main gun and 7.92mm Besa machine gun; the Meadows 8.8-litre flat-12 petrol engine; and the unusual steering system (in which shallow turns were guided by the wheels themselves), although this time with power assistance.

The War Office asked for three prototypes in April 1941, and in September that year approved the design with an order for 1000; in November, that order was increased to 2410 tanks. The specification was now given General Staff number A25 and was assigned the name of Harry Hopkins. This was intended as a tribute to President Roosevelt's chief foreign policy adviser, who had been instrumental in arranging the Lend-Lease programme.

The contract was given to Metropolitan-Cammell in Birmingham, a Vickers subsidiary. Production began in June 1942 but immediately ran into difficulties. Problems were encountered with the early test examples and although these were not specified, they were quite clearly serious and included the front suspension.

In the mean time, the British Army had decided that its armoured units were not to use light tanks in the future, so the Harry Hopkins was theoretically sidelined before its production had even begun. In the light of this and the serious production difficulties, it is a wonder that the tank was not cancelled. Nevertheless, the War Office continued to support its production. By July 1943, serious defects were still showing up in test examples and only six tanks had been built. In November that year, the War Office confirmed an order for 750 examples (apparently in lieu of the earlier order for 2410), but production difficulties continued and no more than 100 tanks had been built by the time assembly was halted in February 1945.

The War Office tried hard to find a use for the Harry Hopkins tank, and discussed several quite radical ideas. These included a winged version that would be towed into action like a glider, but that idea was abandoned when the prototype crashed. The additional size and armour had made the tank too heavy to be carried by the Hamilcar glider in the same way as its Tetrarch predecessor, and eventually the few that had been built were handed over to the RAF for airfield defence duties.

A few examples of a self-propelled gun variant were built and were given the name of Alecto.

DIMENSIONS AND WEIGHT:
Length 14ft 3in, width 8ft 10in, height 6ft 11in.
Weight 8.5 tons

FURTHER READING:
The Vickers Tanks: From Landships to Challenger 2, Christopher Foss & Peter McKenzie.

HEAVY VALIANT

The Heavy Valiant project was related to the A38 Vickers Valiant of 1943, but was a very different vehicle. Like the Valiant itself, it proved a failure.

Very little hard information is available, although it is clear that the tank was proposed by Vickers in 1942. Based on the hull of the A33 Excelsior, it used the driver's compartment and turret from the A38 Valiant. The suspension was derived from the American T1 tank, itself based on the Vickers Six-ton type.

The tank was very heavily armoured, with 9in on the hull front and 10in on the turret. The turret was modified to take the 95mm howitzer from the Centaur Mk IV, but this ate into turret space with the unsatisfactory result that the commander was obliged to double as loader. Overall weight was estimated at 42 tons, and as a result the engine choice fell on the new 400bhp Rolls-Royce Meteorite V8 driving through an improved version of the Excelsior's transmission.

No information has survived about the dimensions of this tank, and there are no known photographs of what was probably a single prototype. This was trialled at Lulworth Cove in January 1945 but the project was clearly abandoned before going any further.

The Heavy Valiant has not survived.

DIMENSIONS AND WEIGHT:
Length, width and height unknown.
Weight 42 tons.

FURTHER READING:
Universal Tank: British Armour in the Second World War - Part 2, David Fletcher.

HORNET
See Medium Mark C.

INDEPENDENT
See A1 Independent Tank.

INTERNATIONAL
See Mk VIII Tank.

KHALID
See Chieftain.

LEE

The Lee was the standard US-built version of the American M3 Medium tank that was supplied to the British Army under Lend-Lease arrangements during 1942. It was of course in most respects the same as the Grant, the special version of the M3 that had been sold to the British Army under a contract placed in 1940. The Lee name was chosen in honour of the American General Robert E Lee, who led the Confederate Army during the American Civil War.

Although the British forces used examples of all the main M3 Medium variants, there were multiple sub-variants and derivatives that were used only by the Americans. The earliest deliveries to the British were the Lee I types (the initial M3 model), which had riveted hulls and 340bhp Continental R-975 engines. Like the Grant, they carried a crew of six and mounted a 37mm turret gun with a 75mm limited-traverse gun in a sponson at the right front. These were followed by Lee II types, which differed by having a cast hull and were essentially M3A1 models.

In British service, the Lee was the original US design of its M3 tank, with the commander's cupola that added to its height. The cupola is very clear in this picture.

Although the name Lee III was allocated (to the M3A2 variant), none were actually delivered to the British Army. The next new type to enter British service was therefore the M3A3 or Lee IV, which had the all-welded hull developed for the M3A2 but came with the Continental engine. The Lee V was then an M3A3 of the standard US pattern with the twin General Motors 6-71 diesel engines that delivered 375bhp. Final deliveries were of the Lee VI, which the Americans knew as an M3A4. This was the same as a Lee I but had the 370bhp Chrysler A-57 multi-bank engine and a slightly longer hull to accommodate it.

The last Lee tanks were built in December 1942, and by that time the M4 Sherman had become the primary American medium tank and was also equipping British units.

DIMENSIONS AND WEIGHT:
Length 18ft 6in (Lee VI 19ft 8in), width 8ft 11in, height 10ft 3in. Weight 27.2 tons.

FURTHER READING:
M3 Medium Tank: The Lee and Grant Tanks in World War II, David Doyle

LIBERTY
See Mk VIII Tank.

LIGHT INFANTRY TANK
The Light Infantry Tank was an experimental derivative of the Medium D model and came out of Philip Johnson's Department of Tank Design and Experiment in 1921.

Its configuration was similar to that of the Medium D but both suspension and tracks were modified. The cable-type suspension had a cam tensioning device that prevented the cable from going slack at the rear of the tank. The track, meanwhile, dispensed with the cable design of the Medium D and consisted of ball-jointed segments with the track shoes welded to the strut between the ball joints.

This was an 8-ton tank with an amphibious capability and was capable of a 30mph top speed. It was powered by a 100bhp Hall-Scott engine. Just one example was built, but the project was taken no further because the Light Infantry Tank had inherited many of the Medium D's faults.

FURTHER READING:
The British Tanks 1915-1919, David Fletcher.

LIGHT MARK IA SPECIAL (L) INDIA
See Vickers Medium Mark II.

LIGHT TANK, MK I (A4)
The Light Tank Mk I was the first of the six Marks of Light Tank that Vickers built for the British Army in the inter-war years. These were intended primarily for policing duties in the colonies, and to that end were light in weight, rapid, and armed (initially) only with a single machine gun. Just ten Mk I models are believed to have been made, in 1929-1931.

This first version of the design, known by the General Staff designation of A4, was based on the Carden-Loyd Tankette and used a stronger version of that vehicle's leaf-spring suspension with two twin-wheel bogies on each side. Instead of the elderly Ford Model T engine in the Tankettes, it had a 59bhp four-cylinder Meadows engine that had started life as a marine design. Each track was tensioned by a rear idler at same height as the drive sprocket – a feature new to British tanks – but the tracks themselves were the same as on the Tankette. This combination gave the vehicle a top speed of 30mph on the road and 21mph across country. Steering was achieved by de-clutching one track and braking to increase the turn speed.

The hull was essentially an armoured box with straight sides and a cylindrical turret broadly similar to that of the Vickers Six-ton or Mark E export tank. The armour was intended only to protect the two-man crew from such things as rifle bullets, and was therefore very light, varying between 4mm and 14mm in thickness. There was a cylindrical turret, similar to that used on the Type A (twin-turret) version of the Mark E and equipped with Vickers' own water-cooled .303 machine gun. Either four or five examples of this first version were built, which were primarily used for testing and then became training vehicles.

There was then a further-developed Mk IA derivative, which was only ever an experimental model. This had a larger superstructure and a larger turret, and a Horstmann suspension with horizontal coil springs that gave a smoother ride but was prone to uncontrollable bounce in cross-country work. Four of the five built were sent to India for trials in 1931, and were modified to improve engine cooling and to keep the crew cool as well. These tanks had probably been withdrawn by the time of the Second World War.

DIMENSIONS AND WEIGHT:
Length 13ft 3in, width 6ft 1in, height 5ft 7in.
Weight 4.8 tons.

FURTHER READING:
Light Tanks Marks I-VI, NW Duncan; *British Light Tanks 1927-1945*, David Fletcher & Henry Morshead.

LIGHT TANK MK II (A4)

The Light Tank Mk II was a Vickers design that followed on from the Light Tank Mk I in 1931. A total of 66 were built between then and 1933, many of them being sent to India.

The hull was shorter and slightly wider than on the Mk I, and the larger turret was rectangular rather than cylindrical; its extra size allowed for a radio to be mounted at the rear. An improved type of armour gave better protection for the two-man crew, although it was no thicker than on the earlier model, varying between 4mm and 12mm. Once again, the armament was a single water-cooled Vickers .303 machine gun, now with a pistol grip instead of the spade grips of the infantry version.

The first 16 tanks were built by Vickers-Armstrongs, with the four-cylinder Meadows engine driving through a Wilson preselector gearbox. Both were mounted on the right-hand side of the hull. Like the Mk I models, these Mk II tanks were capable of 30mph on the road and 21mph across country; they had an operating range of 173 miles. Most of these were later modified with a 66bhp Rolls-Royce six-cylinder petrol engine.

The early Vickers Light Tanks used a single .303 machine gun of their own manufacture. This is the Mk II, which met General Staff specification A4. (IWM KID-226, Public Domain)

These original Mk II types were followed by 29 Mk IIA types built at ROF Woolwich. These had a more powerful Meadows EPT six-cylinder engine with 85bhp but the four-speed gearbox of the Mk I models. They also had an improved cooling system, twin fuel tanks, and louvres on the sides of the turret.

The final batch of 21 tanks was again built by Vickers themselves with the Rolls-Royce engine. The suspension was also modified with dual coil springs, and the tank was now designated Mk IIB. Several of these were sent out to India, and those that were had an extra squared cupola on the turret.

DIMENSIONS AND WEIGHT:
Length 11ft 9in, width 6ft 3¼in, height 6ft 7in.
Weight 4.5 tons.

FURTHER READING:
Light Tanks Marks I-VI, NW Duncan; *British Light Tanks 1927-1945*, David Fletcher & Henry Morshead.

LIGHT TANK MK III (A4)

The third in the series of light tanks that Vickers built for the British Army was very similar indeed to the Light Tank Mk II. The first examples were built in 1934; the Belgians took a modified version the same year; and three years later a batch was built for the Netherlands as well.

The Mk III had a revised suspension, a Horstmann type with coil springs on bogies that each used a pair of rubber-lined wheels. It had the same Rolls-Royce six-cylinder engine and Wilson preselector gearbox as the Mk IIB types, and it shared its chassis and running-gear with Vickers' Light Dragon Mk IIB artillery tractor.

There was an extended superstructure and, to improve stability, these tanks were equipped with a slightly narrower turret that was also lighter in weight. This incorporated air louvres like the "Indian pattern" Mk II Light Tanks and carried the usual Vickers .303 water-cooled machine gun. Notably, it was also equipped with an electric traverse mechanism.

Of the 42 built for the British Army, 36 were sent to Egypt. The Belgian version took the name of Vickers T-15, and the Dutch one became a Mk IIIB, of which 37 were built in 1937 for use in the Dutch East Indies. The Belgians also bought a single Light Dragon Mk IIB artillery tractor and modified it with a 47mm anti-tank gun to make their own T-13 tank destroyer.

The Mk III Light Tank had turret and suspension differences from the Mk II to which it was otherwise similar. (IWM KID-333, Public Domain)

They then built this under licence from Vickers at Familleureux in Hainaut.

DIMENSIONS AND WEIGHT:
Length 11ft 9in, width 6ft 3¼in, height 6ft 7in.
Weight 4.5 tons.

FURTHER READING:
Light Tanks Marks I-VI, NW Duncan; *British Light Tanks 1927-1945,* David Fletcher & Henry Morshead.

LIGHT TANK MK IV (A4)

The fourth generation of the Vickers Light Tank was built in small numbers between 1934 and 1935. It was initially intended for colonial use in India but its makers also had hopes of quantity production for export.

In the beginning, this design was known as the Light Tank Mk II Indian Pattern No 1, or L2E1, and the first prototype was numbered A4E19 in the A4 series initiated with the first of the Vickers Light Tanks. It was really a new design, with a stronger chassis than before and a taller hull to provide more internal space and a small armoured superstructure over the driver on the left. The turret was offset to the right and now had a hexagonal shape but still incorporated Vickers' own .303 machine gun. The engine

Still meeting specification A4, the Mk IV Light Tank had a taller hull than earlier Marks and looks rather insubstantial in this rear view. (IWM KID-329, Public Domain)

was also on the right side, and was a Meadows six-cylinder ETS type with 88bhp. To simplify production, Vickers had designed a new suspension system. It was again a Horstmann type but the bogie wheels were differently spaced, and the guide wheels and supporting rollers were omitted, which allowed a small reduction in the length of the tank.

This first prototype showed up well in testing, with a high road speed of 36mph, but its shortcomings included poor visibility for the driver. So Vickers produced a second prototype (A4E20) in 1933, again known as the Light Tank Mk II Indian Pattern No 1, but this time with the alternative name of L2E2. Enough of the shortcomings of the first prototype had been overcome for the Army to place an order for a small batch. It then became the Light Tank Mk IV.

The production models, of which there were just 34, had a larger four-sided turret to a standardised design, with 9mm armour and improved elevation for the gun. Maximum armour thickness was 12mm, on the glacis plate. Production tanks also had a different version of the Meadows engine, this time the ESTE, still rated at 88bhp. However, the design again proved less than satisfactory. The taller turret compromised stability, and the simplified track system reduced mobility. In service, return rollers were added to the tracks as an improvement, and the turret traverse system was improved.

No examples of the Light Tank Mk IV were sold for export, and the British examples were used for training at home. A few went to France with the BEF in 1940, probably again for training duties, and some were captured and used by the Germans.

Just one example of the Light Tank Mk IV survives today, and is at the Bovington Tank Museum.

DIMENSIONS AND WEIGHT:
Length 11ft 3in, width 6ft 7in, height 6ft 9in.
Weight 4.25 tons.

FURTHER READING:
Light Tanks Marks I-V, NW Duncan; *British Light Tanks 1927-1945,* David Fletcher & Henry Morshead.

LIGHT TANK MK V (A5)

It was inevitable that the Vickers Light Tanks should increase in size sooner or later as more was asked of them. The Light Tank Mk V, first tested as prototype L3E1 in 1934, grew in size because of the need for an extra crew member. It became the first in the series to have a three-man crew, and was sufficiently different from earlier Marks of the Vickers Light Tank to be given the new General Staff designation of A5.

Exercises had shown time and again that the commander in British tanks was overloaded with tasks. Vickers' Medium Mk I had shown ten years earlier the advantage of reducing his workload by adding another crew member, and so the Light Tank Mk V was designed for a driver, commander, and gunner who doubled as the radio operator.

The extra crew member was accommodated in the turret, which was made larger and rounder, with sloping sides and a "bishop's mitre" cupola for the commander. Yet the newly created space was quickly used up: there was little room left for a radio set, and the addition of a second machine gun ate up more space. This second machine gun was a .50 calibre type, mounted coaxially with the single Vickers .303 machine gun traditional to this family of light tanks. It was expected to give the Mk V a better chance against the newer European light tanks of the period.

The hull in turn was widened, its height increased, and it was made around 18 inches longer as well, to accommodate larger fuel tanks. As in the Mk IV model, the power unit was an 88bhp six-cylinder Meadows ESTE type, although the extra half ton weight of the Mk V reduced maximum speed to 32mph. The larger fuel tanks allowed the range to remain similar, at 125 miles. Vickers had learned from their mistakes with the simplified track run of the Mk IV, and the tracks of the Mk V each had a single return roller.

Twelve Mk V tanks were built in 1934 and were delivered for testing to the newly formed 1st (Light) Battalion RTC. With them went a team of Vickers liaison engineers, whose task was to resolve problems quickly and implement improvements. It was a promising démarche that was not followed up with other designs.

Several of these tanks seem to have been used for experimental purposes. Some were converted for anti-aircraft duties by the addition of either twin 15mm Besa or quad Boulton & Paul machine guns. Two were converted for anti-tank duties with a 2pdr gun, one with an open-top turret and the other in a larger closed turret. Some were modified with a turret bustle to make

The need for a third crewman made the Mk V Light Tank larger again, and it was now covered by specification A5. The track design is recognisably that of the earlier Light Tanks.

more room for the radio; some had the "bishop's mitre" cupola removed; some had track modifications, and one was fitted with a Perkins diesel engine.

Some of these tanks went to France with the BEF in 1940 as training tanks, and none returned to Britain. The few still on the British side of the Channel were allocated to home defence duties, but probably did not last in service beyond 1941.

There are no known survivors of the Light Tank Mk V.

DIMENSIONS AND WEIGHT:
Length 13ft 0in, width 6ft 10in, height 7ft 4in. Weight 4.8 tons.

FURTHER READING:
Light Tanks Marks I-VI, NW Duncan; *British Light Tanks 1927-1945*, David Fletcher & Henry Morshead.

LIGHT TANK MK VI (A5)

The Light Tank Mk VI that Vickers produced between 1936 and 1940 was intended like its predecessors primarily for colonial policing duties. As deliveries of the new Medium tanks were very slow, it was pressed into service in several theatres during the early years of the Second World War.

The tank was a simple evolution of the Mk V that preceded it, and had the same General Staff designation of A5. It was most easily recognised by a larger turret that made room for a radio at the rear. It had the same three-man crew of driver, gunner and commander (who doubled as radio operator), and the same 88bhp six-cylinder Meadows ESTE petrol engine, although this now drove through a five-speed Wilson preselector gearbox and top speed was improved to 35mph. The Horstmann suspension

The Light Tank Mk VI was not what Britain needed as re-armament commenced in the mid-1930s, but it was all that was available. This is a later Mk VIB model in the Bovington museum. (Geni, CC-by-SA 4.0)

different, hexagonal cupola and relocated track return rollers. Ten of these were purchased by the Australians in 1936.

The 1937 Mk VIB's modifications were mostly intended to simplify production, and they included a circular cupola and a one-piece armoured louvre over the radiator; maximum armour thickness also increased to 15mm. This became the most numerous version, and there was an "India pattern" sub-variant of it in 1939 for the British Indian Army, with a hatch and periscope for the commander instead of a cupola in the turret roof. Then the final Mk VIC of 1939 had a further uprated engine with triple carburettors, a pair of domed hatches instead of a cupola, and was more powerfully armed with coaxial Besa 15mm and 7.92mm machine guns.

Just one special variant was created, which was an anti-aircraft type with a manually-traversed turret containing either four 7.92 mm Besa machine guns or a pair of 15mm Besa heavy machine guns. An improved Mk II version of this had a larger power-operated turret and improved gunsights.

gave the familiar problems of bounce and pitch on the move, which made gunlaying very difficult. Armour varied between 4mm and 14mm in thickness.

A total of 1682 of these tanks was built, and was spread over four major variants. The original (or plain Mk VI) mounted the same .303 and .50 calibre co-axial machine guns as the Mk V, and had a two-piece armoured louvre over the radiator. The Mk VIA of 1936 had a

When British rearmament began in 1937, the Light Tank Mk VI was the only tank that the War Office had ready to manufacture. As a result, the vast majority of tanks available at the outbreak of war in September 1939 were Mk VI types; the new Mediums were only just coming on-stream. Many went to France with the BEF in 1940 and were lost there; from late 1942, the Germans rebuilt captured examples as self-propelled guns with a 105mm or 150mm field howitzer. The Light Tank Mk VI also made up the majority of the tank force in the early stages of the North African campaign in 1940, and provided a large proportion of those sent to Greece in 1941. These tanks were also deployed to a limited extent against the Japanese in Malaya. They were used by Australian, Canadian and New Zealand troops during the Second World War, and some were in service with the Egyptians by the time of the 1948 Arab-Israeli War.

One example of the Light Tank Mk VI still exists at the Imperial War Museum in Duxford, there is a Mk VIA at the Royal Australian Armour Corps museum in Puckapunyal, and Bovington has a Mk VIB.

One of ten Mk VIA Light Tanks purchased by the Australians in 1936, this one has been preserved at the Royal Australian Armoured Corps Tank Museum in Puckapunyal. (Buckvoed/WikiMedia Commons)

LIGHT TANK, MK VII
See Tetrarch.

LIGHT TANK, MK VIII
See Harry Hopkins.

LITTLE WILLIE

After the Landships Committee issued its requirement for an armoured combat vehicle capable of crossing an 8ft wide trench, there were multiple experiments that failed. The one that worked was a prototype designed in July 1915 by William Tritton, the Managing Director of Fosters of Lincoln who had received a contract to develop a machine using tracks supplied by the Bullock Creeping Grip Tractor Co of Chicago.

Fosters assembled the prototype in August-September that year. It was initially known as the No 1 Lincoln Machine, and was built from riveted boiler plate. Fosters used powertrain components they had to hand, including the 105bhp Daimler-Knight 13-litre petrol engine that they were already building under licence for the Foster-Daimler heavy artillery tractor, and its two-speed gearbox. The vehicle had a box-shaped body and a dummy battleship-style gun turret on top, although this was fixed in place. The plan was to arm the turret with a 2pdr Vickers gun and several machine guns. There would probably have been a crew of six, and the vehicle was expected to have a top speed of approximately 2mph.

Tritton added a wheeled tail to aid steering, which increased the overall length by 7ft 3in. Early tests showed a need to redesign the unsprung track run with a more curved profile at the bottom to reduce resistance to steering turns; it then became clear that the tracks sagged and jammed during trench crossing. Tritton and the Admiralty engineer Lt Walter Wilson assigned to the project tried various alternative track types but it was Tritton who devised a system that worked in September 1915.

This view of the other side of a Mk VIB Light Tank shows the smoke discharger mounted on the turret. Most of these tanks were lost at Dunkirk and the remainder were withdrawn in 1942.

The turret was deleted without ever being armed, and the length of the track run was increased to improve trench-crossing ability. The prototype successfully demonstrated the basic technology that was needed but from December 1915 development focussed on the more promising rhomboid tank that Wilson had proposed in September. No 1 Lincoln Machine later acquired the nickname of Little Willie, which was a derisory British name for the German Kaiser, Wilhelm II.

The single prototype of the world's first tank is preserved at the Bovington Tank Museum.

Little Willie was the father of them all. This view shows clearly where the turret was removed during development. The torn metal around the vision slits in the front panel was caused by some thoughtless handling when the tank was being towed. Morio, CC-by-SA 4.0)

This Mk I male tank was pictured on 25 September 1916 in action on the Somme. These first rhomboid tanks had a wheeled tail to aid steering, and this one has anti-grenade netting on the roof. (Ernest Brooks, IWM Q2486, Public Domain)

MK I TANK

The Army Council wasted no time after watching demonstrations of the *Mother* tank (*see below*), and in February 1916 placed an order for 100 production examples. This was more than Fosters could handle, and so three-quarters of the order was given to the Metropolitan Carriage, Wagon and Finance Co in Birmingham, whose primary business was railway rolling stock and tramcars.

An order for a further 50 tanks followed in April, so increasing the demand for 6pdr guns beyond the number that could be supplied. As a result, a decision was taken to build 75 tanks with the 6pdr guns as planned, and the remaining 75 with four Vickers water-cooled machine guns. The sponsons were redesigned so that these could have a 180-degree arc of fire, with the result that the exit doors had to be reduced to dangerously small dimensions. The two types of tank would be distinguished by the descriptions "male" (with 6pdr) and "female" (with machine guns). Male tanks had three .303 Hotchkiss machine guns as secondary armament; female tanks had just one. Armour plate varied in thickness between 0.23in and 0.47in.

Like the *Mother* prototype, these production tanks had a tail wheel assembly that was intended to aid steering. This proved relatively ineffective and was later abandoned. The fuel tanks were mounted high up in the front horns of the track frames to provide a gravity feed to the engine, and proved vulnerable to direct hits by artillery shells; many tanks were burned out as a result. Another problem with these early tanks (in male form) was that the long barrels of the sponson-mounted 6pdr guns could foul on obstacles or dig into the ground when the tank was crossing a trench. Yet despite these failings, a maximum speed of about 2mph, and the unreliability only to be expected of an unproven design, the tank demonstrated its value on the battlefield.

When the Mk II tanks were introduced in late 1916, these first tanks understandably became known as Mk I types. As newer tanks became available later in the war, a number of them were converted into supply tanks, and some female Mk Is were turned into mobile radio stations.

Only one Mk I tank survives today, and it belongs to the collection of the Tank Museum at Bovington. Its history is unknown but it is believed to have been used for driver training, and spent nearly 50 years as a monument in the grounds of Hatfield House, where early tank testing was carried out. It has been restored to represent Number 705, C19, *Clan Leslie*.

DIMENSIONS AND WEIGHT:
Length 32ft 6in, width 13ft 9in, height 8ft 2in. Weight 28 tons (male) or 27 tons (female).

FURTHER READING:
The British Tanks 1915-19, David Fletcher.

MK II TANK

Although the tank remained unproven in battle at the time, the War Office ordered a further 50 of a slightly improved design in July 1916. This improved design became known as the Mk II and, as before, half of the order was for male tanks and half for females. The 25 males were built by Fosters and the 25 females by Metropolitan.

By the time actual construction began in December 1916, the tail wheels of the Mk I tanks had been discredited, and the Mk IIs were built without them. The Mk IIs were intended to be primarily training tanks, and as a result were probably all built with unhardened steel bodies. They also trialled a number of improvements suggested by experience with the first tanks, such as wider tracks and modified front idler wheels with greater adjustment to cope with track stretching. They had a narrower cab to suit the wider tracks, and a wedge-shaped structure on the roof aided observation and replaced the original circular hatch.

The last of the 50 Mk IIs were built in January 1917. Five were retained for development work; they were given to various bodies who were invited to propose engine and transmission improvements. The results were trialled at Oldbury during March 1917, and the most valuable improvement to emerge was a new epicyclic gear system designed by Walter Wilson. This was adopted for later production models to replace the secondary gearboxes and their gearsmen.

Twenty Mk IIs went to France and 25 were retained for training – which did not prevent them from joining the others in France when the need arose and serving at the Battle of Arras in April 17.

Just one Mk II tank survives in more or less complete condition, and this is at the Bovington Tank Museum. It is number F53, *The Flying Scotsman*.

DIMENSIONS AND WEIGHT:
Length 32ft 6in, width 13ft 9in, height 8ft 2in. Weight 28 tons (male) or 27 tons (female).

FURTHER READING:
The British Tanks 1915-19, David Fletcher.

MK III TANK

When the War Office had ordered 50 Mk II training tanks in July 1916, it had actually requested a total of 100 tanks. The second batch

The sole surviving Mk II tank is this one at Bovington, the Flying Scotsman of F Troop. (Mick Knapton, CC-by-SA 2.0)

This close-up of a sponson on the Mk II shows the arrangement of the Vickers machine guns of a female tank.

of 50 were all built by Metropolitan and incorporated a number of modifications that earned them the Mk III designation. The original plan was that they should incorporate all the modifications planned for the eventual Mk IV types, but in practice it took time for these improvements to reach production.

Like the Mk II tanks, the Mk IIIs are believed to have been unarmoured. They nevertheless had thicker side plating (0.47in thick instead of 0.31in thick) and a small difference in the arrangement of their vision slits. A major difference was that American-designed Lewis guns replaced the Hotchkiss machine guns on all variants and the Vickers sponson-mounted machine

This Mk III tank is attempting to haul itself out of a ditch. The length of the gun barrels which proved a handicap to early male tanks can be clearly seen. (Public Domain)

guns in the female tanks. The Lewis gun was lighter than the Vickers types and required a smaller mounting, and this in turn allowed a redesign of the sponson. Not only was it made smaller but it also had a pair of large flaps at the bottom that could be kicked open to allow the crew to get out in an emergency, an arrangement far more effective than the tiny door in the earlier female sponsons.

There are no survivors of the Mk III tank.

DIMENSIONS AND WEIGHT:
Length 32ft 6in, width 13ft 9in, height 8ft 2in.
Weight 28 tons (male) or 27 tons (female).

FURTHER READING:
The British Tanks 1915-19, David Fletcher.

MK IV TANK

The Mk IV tank was intended to incorporate all the lessons learned from service with the Mk Is and from experiments with the Mk IIs and IIIs. The first examples were probably built in early 1917 and Mk IVs began to arrive in France in May, but they were not used in anger before the battle of Messines Ridge in June.

In order to meet a War Office order for 1000 more tanks, additional manufacturers were co-opted into the tank programme. The original contractors of Fosters and Metropolitan were joined by Armstrong-Whitworth in Newcastle-on-Tyne, the Coventry Ordnance Works and the two Glasgow firms of Beardmore and Mirless Watson & Co. In the end, 1220 Mk IV tanks were built. There were 1015 fighting tanks (420 males

The Mk IV tanks had multiple improvements over their predecessors. This preserved example at Bovington is carrying a fascine on its roof to aid in ditch crossing. (Alan Wilson)

and 595 females) and a further 205 supply tanks.

The Mk IV was in many ways the definitive version of the early British tank, and it incorporated many improvements over the original Mk I. Some had been pioneered on the Mk II and Mk III training and experimental models, but the Mk IV also had major improvements in crew safety, in range, and in transportability.

Crew safety and range were both improved by the same modification, which removed the fuel tanks from the front horns and replaced them by a much larger, 70-gallon, armoured tank mounted between the tracks at the rear. The gravity-feed fuel system gave way to a more positive Autovac suction-feed type, and of course the additional fuel capacity improved the tank's range – although at about 0.5mpg this was never going to be great.

Then redesigned sponsons simplified the business of moving the tanks by rail. On earlier Marks, it had been necessary to partially dismantle the sponsons to reduce width to meet the rail loading gauge, which was a time-consuming operation. On the Mk IV, each sponson was split vertically down the middle, and the two outer ends were hinged. This allowed each sponson to be folded into the body cavity for rail transport, and a new short-barrel version of the 6pdr gun further simplified this operation. To ease the folding operation further, the sponsons were slightly streamlined, and the loss of angled front corners had the further benefit of reducing the risk of grounding in action.

The tanks were still far from perfect, and the swampy ground defeated most of them at the Third Battle of Ypres in July and August 1917. Nevertheless, around 432 Mk IV tanks took part in the Battle of Cambrai in November 1917, proving of great benefit on the first day even if mechanical unreliability saw their effectiveness diminish later. Of interest is that the first tank-to-tank battle was fought at Villers-Bretonneaux in April 1918 between Mk IV British tanks and German A7V types.

Some Mk IV tanks were used for development work. Field workshops added rails on the roof that carried an unditching beam. This steel-reinforced baulk of timber could be chained to the tracks and carried round under the tank to aid it to regain traction if it became stuck. However, attaching the beam under fire was hazardous. Fosters' William Tritton developed a rear extension called the Tadpole Tail, which made the tank longer to counter the wider trenches that

German troops had begun to dig to hinder the tanks' progress. However, it proved weak and was probably never used in combat.

There are seven known survivors of the Mk IV tank. The Tank Museum at Bovington has a male, named *Excellent*, and there is an incomplete Mk IV female at the Museum of Lincolnshire Life in Lincoln. Others survive at the Brussels army museum, at the US Army Ordnance Museum in Aberdeen, Maryland, at the Australian War Memorial, and at Ashford in Kent. Under restoration is D51 *Deborah*, a female excavated in 1999 at Flesquières in France that had been knocked out by shellfire at the Battle of Cambrai.

DIMENSIONS AND WEIGHT:
Length 26ft 5in, width 12ft 9in, height 8ft 2in.
Weight 28 tons (male) or 27 tons (female).

FURTHER READING:
The British Tanks 1915-19, David Fletcher.

MK V TANK

As originally conceived, the Mk V tank would have been more different from earlier designs than it became. Drawings and a wooden mock-up were completed at Metropolitan in June 1917, previewing a longer rear end, a more prominent driver's cab, redesigned sponsons and provision for a rearward-firing machine gun. The tank was also to have the new Wilson-designed epicyclic gearbox and a new Ricardo engine. However, for fear of disrupting production, many of these ideas were abandoned and the Mk V that entered production in December 1917 was really an improved Mk IV.

The new powertrain was employed, though. The Ricardo engine delivered nearly 50% more power than the old Daimler-Knight type, and it increased the tank's maximum speed to 4.6mph. However, it proved less than wholly reliable, mainly because of inadequate maintenance. The Wilson gearbox greatly simplified the driver's job, and the crew was reduced to eight because the two rear gearbox men were no longer needed. The planned rear machine-gun mount remained in the specification, and a second raised cabin was added to the roof towards the rear, allowing the crew to attach the unditching beam that was standard on the Mk V without leaving the tank.

One negative aspect of the new powertrain was a redesigned cooling system, which worked well for the engine but no longer drew outside air through the crew compartment. The engine was still mounted amidships in the crew compartment and the ventilation fan provided was inadequate, with the result that prolonged exposure to exhaust fumes and gun smoke led to crews becoming ill or losing consciousness in action.

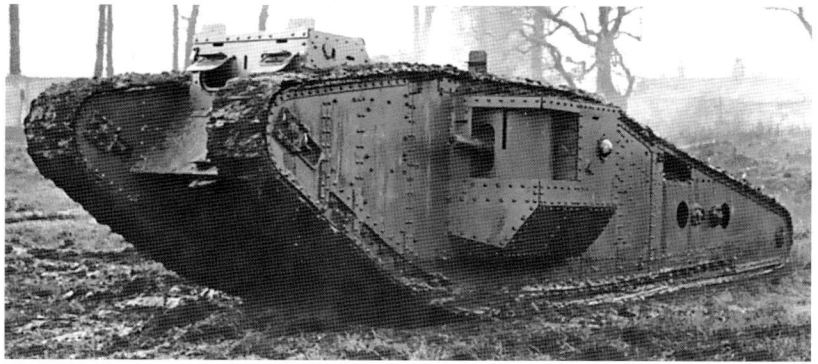

Metropolitan built 400 Mk V tanks, 200 as males and 200 as females. The first ones arrived in France in May 1918, and beginning in July most were converted to Hermaphrodite (or Composite) types by swapping sponsons to give each one a single 6pdr gun. The Mk Vs first saw action at the Battle of Hamel in July, and then in several more engagements during the closing months of the war.

Around 70 Mk V tanks were also shipped to Russia to support the White forces in that country's Civil War. Most were subsequently captured by the Red Army, and some were used in the defence of Tallinn against German forces in August 1941.

The Tadpole Tail extension added to the rear of Mk IV tanks proved weak and was not a success. (IWM, Public Domain)

This Mk V male tank carries a de-ditching beam on rails mounted to its roof.

Nine Mk V tanks still survive. There is a Mk V male at the Tank Museum in Bovington, and a second heavily restored example belongs to the Imperial War Museum in London. Seven more are in Russia or the Ukraine: a Mk V female is a memorial in Arkhangelsk, and the other six are Composites: one in the Kubinka Tank Museum, four at Luhnask in Ukraine and one at the MF Sumtsov Kharkiv Historical Museum in Ukraine.

DIMENSIONS AND WEIGHT:
Length 26ft 5in, width 12ft 9in, height 8ft 8in. Weight 29 tons.

FURTHER READING:
The British Tanks 1915-19, David Fletcher.

MK V TANK

The Tadpole Tail extension of the Mk IV tank had been an unsuccessful attempt to deal with the problem of wider trenches that hindered the tanks' progress. At Central Tank Workshops in France, a Mk IV was experimentally modified by adding 6ft to its centre section, and this design was adopted for the Mk V* (Mk V Star), together with a reshaped rear cupola that incorporated two machine-gun mounts, plus another machine gun position above a new door on each side.

A total of 700 tanks were ordered to this revised design, of which 500 were to be males and 200 females. Only 579 had been built by the time of the Armistice in November 1918, and it appears that 66 more were actually delivered, bringing the total to 645 by March 1919. Shortly before the Armistice, 90 of the new Mk V* tanks were supplied to the French forces, but they were not used in action. Several nevertheless remained in French service into the 1930s.

Adding length to the middle of the tank rather than at the tail did not compromise the structural integrity and resulted in the Mk V, but the extra length made steering more difficult. (Public Domain)*

In service the Mk V* proved disappointing. The extra weight restricted its performance and the extra length made it difficult to steer.

Only one Mk V* tank survives, in the National Armor and Cavalry Museum at Fort Benning in Georgia, USA. It saw service with a US Heavy Tank Battalion in the Great War.

DIMENSIONS AND WEIGHT:
Length 32ft 5in, width 12ft 9in, height 8ft 8in. Weight 33 tons.

FURTHER READING:
The British Tanks 1915-19, David Fletcher.

MK V** TANK

The steering difficulties of the Mk V* tank prompted development of a further version of the Mk V that became known as the Mk V**. The overall length remained the same but the contour of the track frames was changed so that ground contact was reduced in order to make steering easier; the engine was also moved rearwards to change the centre of gravity. Wider tracks ensured there was no loss of mobility.

Weight increased to 35 tons in male form, and this was countered by a more powerful Ricardo engine, bored out to give 225bhp. The relocated engine allowed a rearrangement of internal space, and the front and rear cabs were now combined. At the same time, the final drive chains and the fuel tanks were relocated.

Metropolitan received an order for 900 Mk V** tanks, of which 750 were to be males. However, the first one was not delivered until November 1918 and so the Mk V** came too late for war service. As a result, the order was drastically reduced, and only 25 examples were eventually built.

One Mk V** tank survives, at Bovington Tank Museum. It is a female called *Ol' Faithful*

*With reduced ground contact to aid steering, and a more powerful engine, the Mk V** unfortunately arrived too late to make any real difference. The extra length of the mid-section is clear in this picture. (Public Domain)*

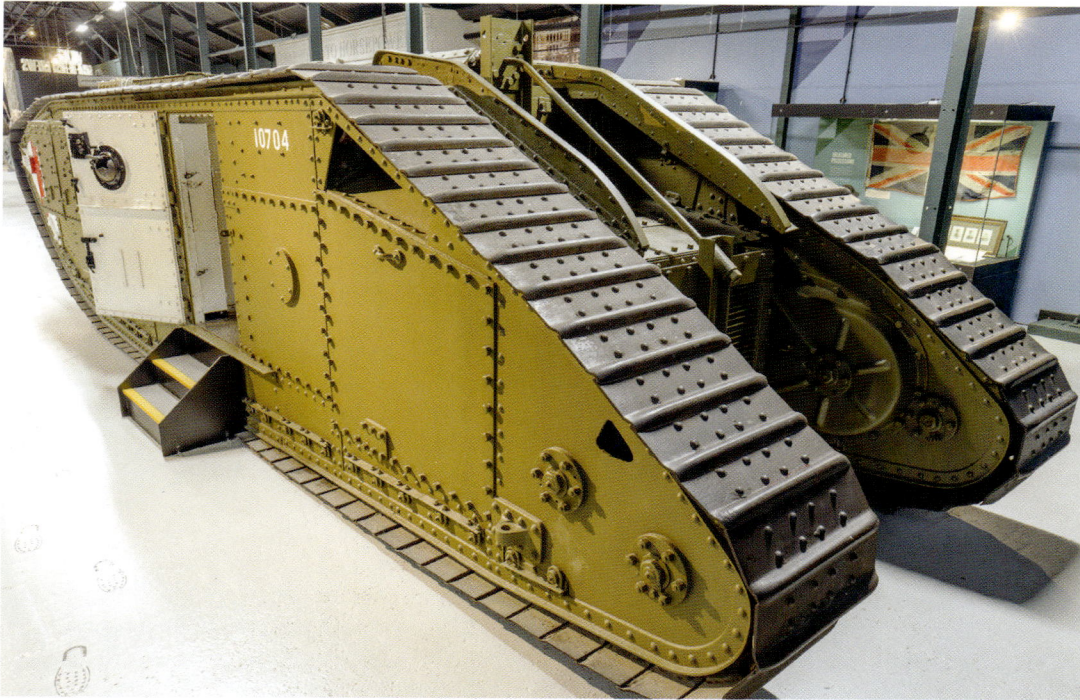

Ol' Faithful is a Mk V** tank preserved at Bovington after being used on engineering work for many years. A side access door in the mid-section allows museum visitors access to the interior.

that was modified for various engineering tasks in later years.

DIMENSIONS AND WEIGHT:
Length 32ft 5in, width 12ft 9in, height 9ft. Weight 35 tons.

FURTHER READING:
The British Tanks 1915-19, David Fletcher.

MK VI TANK

The Mk VI tank was never built, although Metropolitan did make a wooden mock-up at the same time as the original (and more radical) Mk V mock-up in June 1917. It clearly impressed somebody, because the US military placed an order for 600. However, this order was cancelled in December 1917 and interest switched to the US-British agreement signed in January 1918 to build the Mk VIII or International tank. The Mk VI project was terminated at the same time.

The Mk VI was another rhomboid design, but this time with a taller superstructure that combined the driver's hood, commander's observation post, and a rear section that mounted four machine guns. The main armament was a 6pdr gun with very limited traverse, set into the forward end of the hull. There were two further machine gun ports in miniature sponsons on door panels in the front sides of the track runs,

What might have been.... the Mk VI was to have a gun in its nose, auxiliary guns in small side sponsons, and much wider tracks than earlier tanks. It did not progress beyond this wooden mock-up. (Public Domain)

and the tracks themselves were much wider than any used up to that point.

DIMENSIONS AND WEIGHT:
No details available (mock-up only).

FURTHER READING:
The British Tanks 1915-19, David Fletcher.

MK VII TANK

A hydraulic drive system had been one of the proposals seen at the Oldbury Trial is March 1917, but it had overheated and had been ruled out of contention. That did not stop Brown Brothers in Edinburgh getting a contract to develop a tank with such a system in October 1917.

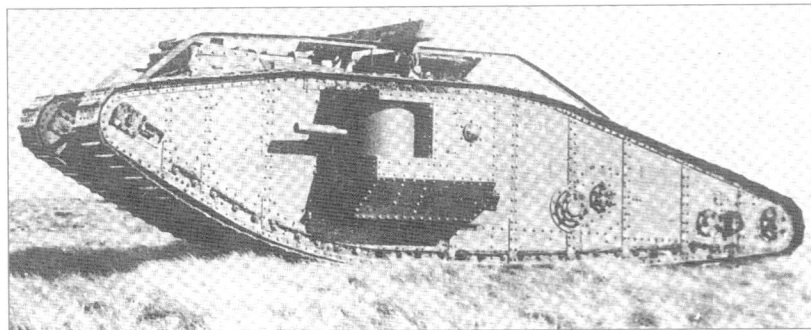

The Mk VII had a hydraulic drive system and was again lengthened, but only pilot models were built. (Public Domain)

The first one was ready in July 1918 and prompted an order for 74 more (to make a total of 75), which were all to be males and were to be built by Brown Brothers and by Kitsons in Leeds. In practice only three were built, all by Brown Brothers, and there is no record that they went through the usual military test procedures. Perhaps they could not be made to work properly and were not submitted for trials.

The hydraulic-powered tank gained the Mk VII designation. It was visually similar to a Mk V but had a longer tail, extra length being a preoccupation of tank designers at the time to cope with wider German trenches. It would have had an eight-man crew and was supposedly capable of 4.5mph. The Ricardo engine had an electric starter (a hand crank was standard in other tanks) and drove a pair of pumps that were coupled to a hydraulic motor on each side of the tank. From these, drive was transferred to the track sprockets via the usual intermediary of chains.

One thing the Mk VII did get right was hull ventilation, which was vastly improved over that of the Mk V with both extractor fans and armoured louvres in the hull roof.

There are no survivors of the Mk VII.

DIMENSIONS AND WEIGHT:
Length 29ft 11in, width 12ft 9in, height 8ft 7in. Weight 33 tons.

FURTHER READING:
The British Tanks 1915-19, David Fletcher.

MK VIII AND MK VIII* TANKS

The Mk VIII or International tank was born out of a grand idea for a standardised tank to be shared by the Allies, and the initial plan was to create a large fleet for a planned 1919 offensive. The USA had joined the war in April 1917 and had initially ordered 600 of the planned Mk

VI types. However, the order was superseded by the new project for a joint design. The Mk VIII came too late to see active service during the Great War and in practice only just over 130 were built.

Complex political manoeuvrings lay behind the Mk VIII plan, but the idea that came together in the final quarter of 1917 was for British design and US resources and ideas to be combined to build a tank on French soil – which would remove the logistics difficulties of shipping tanks into the Allied bases in France. Early design work was done by Lt John Rackham (later a pioneering designer of bus chassis) and by November 1917 the initial design envisaged a 38.8-ton tank with a 300bhp version of the 27-litre American Liberty aero engine and the ability to cross 14ft trenches. The plan was to build 1500 tanks but there was also ambitious talk of ramping up production later to as many as 1200 a month. Some components would be supplied by Britain and some by the USA.

There were many delays. The first prototype was built in Britain and was sent to the USA for completion and testing, which began in October. The Liberty engine was not ready until that same month. The new factory at Neuvy-Pailloux, 200 miles south of Paris, was not finished until November and never built a single tank.

Meanwhile, Britain had made contingency plans in case the co-operative venture stalled. On the one hand, a Mk X was drawn up as a design that could be rapidly put into production; and on the other, plans were made to build Mk VIIIs in British factories. Ricardo was commissioned to design a 300bhp V12 engine that could replace the US-made Liberty V12, and a Rolls-Royce V12 was used to make the mild-steel prototype mobile. A fleet of 1450 tanks was ordered from Beardmore in Glasgow, Metropolitan in Birmingham, and the North British Locomotive Company, also in Glasgow. In practice, North British was the only company to complete any Mk VIIIs before the war ended in November 1918, with a total of seven. After the war, a further 24 were built from parts, of which nine became training tanks at Bovington and the rest were scrapped.

The Americans chose to build 100 of their own in 1919-1920 at the Rock Island Arsenal, buying the armour plate from Britain. The US Army used five Browning machines guns as the secondary armament and operated the Mk VIII with a crew of ten. Despite the tanks' poor reliability, they were retained in service until 1932.

The Mk VIII tank was also known as the Liberty tank, after the aero engine that was to power it. Its shape was broadly similar to that of the existing rhomboid heavy tanks, with a sponson on each side mounting a short-barrelled 6pdr gun. From the aborted Mk VI design it took the enlarged superstructure and wider tracks, and from the Mk V* it borrowed the idea of side doors behind the sponsons with a machine gun mounting in each one. Like the Mk IV, its sponsons were retractable, but in this case as a whole assembly rather than in two sections. New features were a compartmentalised hull, which separated the engine from the 12-man crew compartment by a steel bulkhead. The crew included a gunner for each of the seven Hotchkiss .303 machine guns, plus a designated mechanic. In theory, there was to be room within the hull for 20 more infantry in full kit, but this was clearly pure fantasy in a hull whose width had been reduced by the wider tracks.

The Mk VIII had a maximum speed of 5.25mph and a range of 50 miles. Its 0.66in armour was slightly thicker than that of earlier rhomboid tanks. Like the Mk V* tank, its length-to-width ratio was far from ideal and it proved difficult to steer.

An even longer Mk VIII* tank was mooted during 1918, lengthened by four feet at the front and by six feet at the rear to make it capable of crossing an 18-foot ditch. As on the Mk V**, the contour of the tracks was altered to reduce resistance when turning. Total weight was estimated at 42.5 tons, but the Mk VIII* did not progress beyond the drawing-board.

Three Mk VIII tanks survive. One British-built example is at the Bovington Tank Museum, and there are US-built examples at Fort Meade in Maryland, USA and at the National Armor and Cavalry Museum at Fort Benning, Georgia, USA.

DIMENSIONS AND WEIGHT:
Length 34ft 2in, width 12ft 4in, height 10ft 3in. Weight 37 tons.

FURTHER READING:
The British Tanks 1915-19, David Fletcher.

MK IX TANK

The Mk IX Tank was really intended as an armoured personnel carrier, but as insurance against the failure of the contemporary Mk VIII fighting tank it was drawn up over the summer

The Mk VIII was a joint Anglo-American venture intended for a 1919 offensive that never took place. (IWM Q64476, Public Domain)

of 1917 to be fitted optionally with sponsons. It soon became clear that this complicated the design unacceptably and the Mk IX went ahead as a troop carrier that could double as a supply tank.

To save time the Mk IX was based on the existing Mk V with a lengthened hull. It had a redesigned front end with a turned-up lower track run that was the probable source of its "Pig" nickname. Internal space was maximised by moving the 150bhp Ricardo engine forward, putting the gearbox at the back, and removing most of the inner track frames, and in theory the Mk IX could carry 30 standing infantrymen or 10 tons of stores, plus more stores in an open tray on the roof. Each side contained two large oval access doors and eight rifle ports. The tank had a four-man crew, consisting of a driver, commander, mechanic and a machine-gunner who manned one Hotchkiss gun at the front and one at the rear. It had a maximum speed of 4.2mph.

Work began on two prototypes at Armstrong-Whitworth in Newcastle-on-Tyne during September 1917, and an order for 200 produc-

The Mk IX tank was primarily a "battle taxi" or armoured personnel carrier. It arrived just before the end of the war and was never built in quantity. This one was pictured at the Dollis Hill experimental ground in north-west London. (Public Domain)

Martel's first prototype of a light tank was built in 1925 and was clearly a very different beast from the huge rhomboid tanks of the previous decade. (Public Domain)

Morris built a pair of further-developed "tankette" prototypes, but lost interest in the project when they realised a planned agricultural tractor variant was not viable. (Public Domain)

Crossley now took an interest in Martel's ideas, but the project foundered in 1927 after just two prototypes of a one-man tankette had been built. (Public Domain)

tion models was placed with Marshalls, the traction engine makers in Gainsborough. Just 34 examples were built before production was halted by the Armistice; three of them had been delivered to Central Workshops in France. A 10-ton supply sledge was trialled that could be towed behind the tank in quantities of three at a time. One Mk IX was converted to an armoured ambulance in France, and a second was used for amphibious experiments after the war.

The only surviving Mk IX is at the Bovington Tank Museum.

DIMENSIONS AND WEIGHT:
Length 31ft 11in, width 8ft 1in, height 8ft 8in.
Weight 27 tons (unladen).

FURTHER READING:
The British Tanks 1915-19, David Fletcher.

MK X TANK
The Mk X tank, initially known as a Mk V***, was drawn up on paper as insurance against failure of the Mk VIII or International project. It was based on the Mk V that was already in production, with improvements to manoeuvrability and crew comfort. A provisional production run of 2000 was planned for 1919, but in the event no Mk Xs were built.

MARTEL TANKETTES
After the First World War, when Col JFC Fuller revived the idea of light armoured vehicles being used to assault enemy positions, Major Gifford LeQuesne Martel (then still a serving officer) set about designing one. His design went through several iterations in the mid-1920s but never progressed beyond the prototype stage.

Martel's first prototype was built at home in 1925 with a slab-sided and utilitarian wooden body, an American Maxwell engine, a set of tracks from the Roadless Traction Company (which had been established in 1919 by Philip Johnson of the Tank Design Department), and a steering "tail" like that used on early rhomboid tanks. Martel showed it to the War Office, and agreement was reached that two pilot models should be built by Morris Commercial Motors, using the Morris-Martel name. Unsurprisingly, Morris wanted to use their own engine – and also developed the chassis with one eye on the possibility of using it for an agricultural tractor as well.

In 1926, the War Office ordered eight more examples of a two-man version with a wider body, each equipped with a single Lewis gun. These were trialled by the Experimental Mechanisation Force on Salisbury Plain during 1927 against a rival two-man Tankette design by Carden-Loyd, which proved superior. Morris had meanwhile discovered that its planned agricultural tractor variant was not viable, and lost interest in the project.

Martel now took his ideas to Crossley Motors, who already had government contracts for armoured cars. Here, he worked on a one-man Tankette that shared elements of Crossley's three-axle BGV lorry chassis. Some of these chassis had the four driven wheels running on rubber tracks, made under licence from Citroen-Kégresse in France, and the Crossley-Martel Tankette was developed on this, with the chassis turned round so that the steered wheels were at the rear. The engine chosen was

The idea of swarms of small tanks supporting the infantry lay behind development of the A11 or Matilda I tank. This picture of a preserved early example belonging to the Bovington Tank Museum shows its spidery appearance. (Alan Wilson, CC-by-SA 2.0)

a Crossley 2.4-litre 14hp type. The vehicle was said to ride well but the tracks threw dust into the engine, which led to rapid wear. After two prototypes had been built in 1927, the project was abandoned.

MATILDA I (A11)

The original Matilda tank was a completely separate design from the larger and much better known Matilda II that took over the name in 1940. This earlier design had General Staff designation A11 and was yet another development by Sir John Carden at Vickers. The project name of Matilda probably came from Vickers (although there are alternative theories), but from June 1940 it was officially known as the Tank, Infantry, Mark I.

The original idea was to develop a small tank that could be used in large numbers to support the infantry. Development of the A11 began in 1935, to meet a General Staff specification for a cheap tank based on commercially available components. It was designed around a 70bhp Ford 3.6-litre V8 engine and a Fordson gearbox, using steering similar to that in the Vickers light tanks and a sprung bogie suspension derived from the Dragon artillery tractor, itself derived from the Vickers Mark E Six-ton tank. The hull was quite well armoured but was cramped for the two-man crew (driver and commander, the latter also being the gunner and radio operator),

The Matilda I's sprung bogie suspension was derived from the Dragon artillery tractor that Vickers were building.

and the tank had a spider-like appearance with the tracks mounted alongside the hull with no protection at all. The small cast turret contained only a single Vickers heavy machine gun and the tank had a maximum speed of 8mph with a range of 80 miles.

The A11 Matilda entered production at Vickers-Armstrongs in 1938, but by this time it was clear that war was inevitable, and the General Staff refocused its attention on plans for a heavier tank that could be equipped with a cannon. So the swarms of little tanks that had been envisaged a few years earlier never materialised, and only 139 production examples of the A11 Matilda were built, the final order for 19 being placed in January 1939. The last of these little tanks were built in August 1940, later examples having a .50 calibre gun in place of the original .303 weapon.

The A11 Matilda proved quite successful with the BEF in France during May 1940, where its armour was sufficient to resist German anti-tank guns of the time. However, with relatively little armament its uses were restricted. Just two were still running during the retreat to Dunkirk, and over the summer of 1940 all those remaining in the UK were withdrawn and used for training.

The Tank Museum at Bovington has all three known survivors of the A11 Matilda, of which two still run (one with a non-original power-train). The third is a badly damaged hull that was recovered from a gunnery range.

DIMENSIONS AND WEIGHT:
Length 18ft 5in, width 8ft 6in, height 8ft 3in. Weight 11 tons.

FURTHER READING:
Matilda Infantry Tank 1938–45, David Fletcher & Peter Sarson.

MATILDA II (A12)

The Matilda II was one of the best-known British tanks of the Second World War, and was the only one that served from the beginning in 1939 to the end in 1945. It must not be confused with the much smaller Matilda I or A11 tank of similar vintage, with which it shared only a name.

It was drawn up to meet the A12 specification issued by the General Staff in 1936 for a larger tank that could carry out the same infantry support duties as the A11. Designed by the Mechanisation Board, the tank was initially known as the Matilda II or Matilda Senior, becoming simply "the Matilda" after the smaller tank was withdrawn in 1940. Early handbooks and other documents simply called it the "I" tank (for Infantry).

The first build contract for this 27-ton tank was given to the Vulcan Foundry at Newton-le-Willows in Lancashire in November 1936. A mock-up was ready in April 1937 and the first mild-steel prototype was delivered in April 1938. Testing revealed the need for only minor changes, and the first order for 140 tanks was placed in June 1938. Just two had entered service by the outbreak of war.

Much of the design of the A12 was based on the earlier A7 Medium tank, with which the Matilda shared the concept of paired commercial vehicle engines – in this case two AEC water-cooled diesel six-cylinder bus engines that delivered 87bhp each and drove through a common shaft to a six-speed, air-operated Wilson epicyclic preselector gearbox. These engines were handed, an A183 type being

The Matilda II or A12 was intended for infantry support duties but was pressed into service in all the roles demanded of a tank as the war progressed. Though slow and under-armed, it was much liked by its users.

installed on the left of the hull and an A184 on the right, and in theory if one engine failed the other could keep the tank mobile.

The suspension was also carried over from the A7, and was essentially the one that Vickers had designed for their Medium Mark C prototype of 1927. There were five double-wheel bogies on each side, four of them in pairs on bell-cranks with a common horizontal coil spring. A fifth bogie at the rear was sprung against a bracket on the hull, and there was an additional sprung jockey wheel between the first bogie and the idler wheel. The whole track run was protected by steel plates that incorporated large mud chutes.

The layout of the hull was conventional, with the driver's compartment at the front, the fighting compartment in the centre, and the engines at the rear. The cast turret had a hydraulic traverse and a QF 2pdr main gun, and the auxiliary weapon was a 7.92mm Besa machine gun. The turret was well provided with a rotating cupola for the commander and a periscope for the gunner, and much of the ammunition was stowed in a basket on the outside of the turret, the loader having access through a hatch in the roof. Commander, gunner and loader were all stationed in the turret, the fourth crew member being the driver.

As an Infantry tank, the Matilda II was heavily armoured by the standards of the day, and even by the end of the war the tank was better armoured than many more modern designs. The glacis plate was 78mm (3.1in) thick, the side armour was 65-70mm, and the rear armour was 55mm; and the thick 75mm armour on the cast turret became legendary, earning the Matilda the admiring name of Queen of the Desert during the North African campaign of 1940-1941. The disadvantage of this thick armour was of course extra weight, and the Matilda was a slow tank with a top speed of 16mph on made roads and about 6mph across country. This was nevertheless considered adequate for its Infantry support rôle. A special block-pattern camouflage scheme was drawn up for the Matilda, based on the dazzle pattern used on ships in the First World War, and became closely associated with the tank.

After the first order from the Vulcan Foundry, more orders were placed with Fowler's of Leeds, Ruston & Hornsby, the LMS railway works at Horwich, and the North British Locomotive Co in Glasgow, and by the time the last one was delivered in August 1943, 2987 Matildas had been built.

Matildas first saw combat in France during 1940, but all battle survivors were abandoned at Dunkirk. The tank was also very effective against the Italians in the North African campaign, but its vulnerability became apparent when the Germans introduced the 88mm anti-tank gun in June 1941. Some Matildas were converted in the field to Scorpion types with a mine flail, and there were both Mk I and Mk II versions. Nevertheless, a serious weakness of the tank was always the lack of an HE round for its 2pdr gun; one had been designed but for reasons unknown it was never issued. One tank was fitted experimentally with the larger turret from an A27 with its 6pdr gun, but the War Office considered that up-gunning was not a practical proposition. Vickers therefore proposed the Valentine as an alternative, and when that began to arrive in autumn 1941 Matildas were gradually phased out.

Matildas were also supplied to Australia and the USSR. The Soviets were sent 1084 and received 918, many being lost on the Atlantic convoys. They modified some Matildas with their own weapons, but generally found the tank unreliable, slow and cumbersome. Few were used after 1942, although some remained in service as late as 1944.

Between 1942 and 1944, a total of 409 Matildas were supplied to the Australian Army, and in 1944 these were supplemented by a further 33 transferred from New Zealand. The Australians used them extensively, keeping

A special dazzle camouflage was developed for the Matilda II in desert use. There are examples at both Bovington and (pictured) the Musée des Blindés in Saumur. (Fat-yankey, CC-by-SA 2.5)

The Matilda II was also used for the CDL project, with a hugely powerful searchlight in a special turret and no main gun. This example survives at Bovington. (Makizox, CC-by-SA 4.0)

them in action until the last day of the war in the Pacific. For jungle warfare, they found the CS version effective with its 3in howitzer. They also created flame-thrower versions, the Matilda Frog seeing service in Borneo although the later Murray and Murray FT types arrived too late for war service. There were bulldozer tanks, too, and a Matilda Hedgehog mortar tank was developed successfully but was also too late to see war service. The final Matildas saw service with the Australian Citizen Military Forces until around 1955.

German troops paid the Matilda the ultimate compliment by using captured examples themselves, and after the war Matildas also saw service with the Egyptian armed forces, who used them in action during the 1948 Arab-Israeli War.

There were several variants of the Matilda. The first deliveries had a Vickers machine gun, but this was later changed to a Besa gun and the designation became Matilda IIA. The Matilda III (also known as the Infantry Tank Mark IIA*) had 95bhp 7.4-litre Leyland diesel engines in place of the AEC type, and many earlier examples were converted to this specification during major overhaul – much of it carried out by MG Cars at Abingdon. Further improved engines delivered the Matilda IV, which also lost its turret lamp. The Matilda IV CS was a close-support version, more used by the Australians than by the British. The last production version was then the Matilda V, with an improved gearbox and a Westinghouse servo.

Unsurprisingly, there were also several experimental versions of the tank. The experimental 6pdr conversion has already been noted. There were at least four versions of an experimental mine-flail version called the Baron, which did not see operational use. The second prototype (A12E2) was converted in 1941 to a radio-controlled tank with multiple planned uses, but an order for 60 more was cancelled because of the need to swap the standard Rackham clutch transmission to a Wilson type. This was called the Black Prince, a name later used for the A43 Infantry tank.

Perhaps the best known of these conversions was the CDL or Canal Defence Light – a name which concealed the tank's true purpose. It was fitted with a cylindrical turret containing a powerful searchlight that was projected through a vertical slit, and its aim was to temporarily blind and so disorientate the enemy at night. This conversion retained a Besa machine-gun for self-defence.

There are around 70 survivors of the Matilda II worldwide, some in private ownership. In Britain, the Tank Museum has a running Mk IIA and the only surviving CDL version, while the Imperial War Museum at Duxford has a Mk V model. Belgium has one at its Royal Museum of the Armed Forces and Military History in Brussels, and France has one at the Musée des Blindés in Saumur. There are examples at the American Heritage Museum in Stow, Massachusetts; at the Kubinka Tank Museum in Russia; at the Indian Cavalry Tank Museum at Ahmednagar; and at the Yad La-Shiryon museum in Latrun, Israel.

As many as 30 still exist in Australia, notably five at the Royal Australian Armoured Corps Memorial and Army Tank Museum at Puckapunyal; these include a Frog, a bulldozer, and a Hedgehog.

DIMENSIONS AND WEIGHT:
Length 18ft 5in, width 8ft 6in, height 8ft 3in.
Weight 25 tons.

FURTHER READING:
Matilda Infantry Tank 1938–45, David Fletcher & Peter Sarson.

MBT-80

The MBT-80 was designed during the 1970s and was intended to replace the Chieftain. In practice, it became collateral damage of the 1979 Iranian

Revolution. Production of the Shir tank designed for Iran was cancelled, which threatened jobs at ROF Leeds at a time when MBT-80 was still several years from production. Controversially, the MBT-80 programme was therefore cancelled in favour of Challenger, which could be put into production more quickly and would keep the Leeds factory in work.

Work on MBT-80 began in September 1978 after an evaluation of the US Abrams (then the XM1) had concluded that it would not meet future British requirements. It was allocated the code FV4601 and its design drew on work already done by MVEE, including on the experimental FV4211 tank (see Challenger) and on an unmanned turret. MBT-80 was drawn up with Chobham armour on a hull structure that made extensive use of aluminium to reduce weight, and with increased mobility from a new hydropneumatic suspension system. The 1500bhp Honeywell gas turbine engine from the Abrams was considered but rejected because its accompanying transmission would not fit the MBT-80's hull without a major redesign, and so the Rolls-Royce Condor turbocharged diesel with the same 1500bhp was chosen. This would drive the tracks through a David Brown TN-38 transmission.

The intention was to use the 120mm EXP-28M1 rifled gun, a development of the L11A5 type that incorporated a new barrel material designed to reduce wear. Secondary armament would include a 7.62mm L37A1 GPMG on the commander's cupola, with a remote-firing capability.

The MBT-80 had multiple other advanced features. These included an extensive electronic counter-measures capability, and a compartment for the four-man crew that incorporated heating, cooling and a full NBC defence system. Its fire control system was to incorporate a stabilised panoramic sight for the commander and, as on the Valiant MBT, the tank's thermal signature would be reduced by mixing cooling air with the exhaust gases. Concepts were also drawn up for several special-purpose variants of the tank.

Two test rigs were built, and both survive. One is in private hands, and the second, known as ATR2, survives at the Tank Museum in Bovington. Among other things, its hull was a composite construction with a conventional steel front welded to an aluminium rear in order to test structural strength.

DIMENSIONS AND WEIGHT:
Length, width, and height data not available. Weight 62 tonnes (with crew, fuel and ammunition).

MEDIUM TANKS

Note that there is potential for confusion between the Medium tanks developed by the British military authorities at the end of the Great War and the Vickers Medium tanks that were developed primarily to gain export sales in the 1920s and 1930s.

The "official" Medium tanks were the Medium Mark A or Whippet (1917), the Medium Mark B (1918), the Medium Mark C or Hornet (1918), and the Medium Mark D (1919). The Vickers Mediums are listed alphabetically under V.

MEDIUM, MARK A

It was Fosters' MD William Tritton who proposed a faster and cheaper tank to the Tank Supply Committee in October 1916, apparently after discussions with Albert Stern. The idea was for a smaller and more manoeuvrable model than the existing rhomboid types, capable of exploiting the gaps that they created, more or less cavalry-style.

The War Office approved this plan a month later, and build of a prototype began at Fosters in December. At this stage it was known as the Tritton Chaser, and it was demonstrated at the Oldbury trials in March 1917, possibly mounting the revolving turret from an Austin armoured car. General Haig placed an order with Fosters for 200 the next day, and this was confirmed formally in June.

The Medium A or Whippet showed that the tank's potential went far beyond that of the slow and heavy rhomboid types. This one is preserved at Bovington. (Alan Wilson/ WikiMedia Commons)

Tritton's design sat on unsprung tracks similar to those of Little Willie, with the side plates incorporating large mud chutes designed to prevent mud clogging the tracks. It was powered by two 45bhp Tylor four-cylinder engines, one driving each track – an arrangement that Tritton also used for the Flying Elephant super-heavy tank that he was working on at the time. This simplified the driver's task and made it possible for him to control the tank on his own, although it did call for a high degree of skill as he had two clutches to operate.

The new tank became known as the Medium Mark A type, and had a very distinctive appearance with an angular superstructure at the back. It also acquired the name of Whippet, probably from Tritton himself. Four Hotchkiss .303 machine guns were mounted in the superstructure, and in theory these would be manned by two machine gunners. In practice, space was tight and the Whippet usually ran with a three-man crew, consisting of driver, commander and a single machine gunner.

With a weight of 14 tons, the production versions were a couple of tons heavier than the Chaser prototype, but they were still much smaller and lighter than the heavy rhomboid tanks. They were much faster too, with a speed of 8.3mph. However, the difficulty of accurate steering tended to slow them down in the field.

The first two production Whippets arrived in France during December 1917 and the tanks first saw action in March 1918. They proved very successful as fast attack vehicles but attempts to co-ordinate then with horse cavalry units were not. Losses were also high. They distinguished themselves particularly during the Amiens Offensive in August 1918.

There were some experiments to improve the Whippet's trench-crossing ability, and at Central Workshops in France Major Philip Johnson fitted one example with leaf springs and sprung track rollers, plus a 360bhp Rolls-Royce Eagle V12 aero engine and Wilson epicyclic transmission. This tank achieved a remarkable top speed of 30mph.

Improved replacements for the Whippet were in preparation as the Medium Mark B and Medium Mark C even before the tanks had entered production. As the war ended in November 1918, the Whippets' active service was short, but some were sent to Ireland to deal with civil unrest there and others went to Russia to support the White forces in the Russian Civil War. About six were sold to Japan, where they remained in service until about 1930.

Five Whippets still survive. The one at the Bovington Tank Museum is the tank that Lt Cecil Sewell was commanding when he won a VC in August 1918. The others are in Brussels, at the Royal Museum of the Armed Forces and Military History; at Base Borden Museum in Ontario, Canada; at the Army College in Pretoria, South Africa; and at the United States Army Ordnance Museum at Fort Lee in Virginia.

DIMENSIONS AND WEIGHT:
Length 20ft, width 8ft 7in, height 9ft. Weight 14 tons.

FURTHER READING:
Medium Mark A Whippet, David Fletcher; *Medium Tanks Marks A-D*, Peter Chamberlain and Chris Ellis.

MEDIUM, MARK B

The Medium B tank was yet another design that arrived too late to be of use in the Great War. It was designed by Lt Walter Wilson as a replacement for the Medium Mark A or Whippet, and Wilson's first drawings were probably done in July 1917, just four months after the Whippet had made its bow as the Tritton Chaser prototype. Drawings certainly existed by August and approval was given for prototype build at Metropolitan in Birmingham, which began in September.

The Medium B was quite different from the Whippet, and was based on a scaled-down rhomboid style hull with a large fighting compartment on top. Its engine was a 100bhp four-cylinder derivative of the Ricardo six-cylinder in the larger tanks of the time, mounted at the rear and driving the tracks through a four-speed gearbox and Wilson's favoured epicyclic steering system. The fuel tanks were mounted at the rear and there were five machine gun positions in the superstructure, plus two more in the hull doors at the side, which were configured like small sponsons. For space reasons, crews typically worked with just four machine guns, moving them around as required.

The engine and gearbox were separated from the crew by a bulkhead, which improved conditions in the fighting compartment but did not allow access to the engine from inside the tank. The need to deal with engine problems from the outside while under fire understandably made the Medium Mark B unpopular with crews; worse, the lack of space in the engine compartment ensured that the engine was usually too hot to work on if it failed while the tank was operational. Armour still showed no improvement, with a 0.5in maximum thickness, and with a 6mph top speed, the Medium Mark B was actually slower than the Whippet it was intended to replace.

Such was the demand for tanks that the Army ordered 450 of the Medium Mark B before the first prototype had been completed. This order was soon increased to 700. Production began at the North British Locomotive Company in Glasgow, and Metropolitan in Birmingham, the Coventry Ordnance Works and the Patent Shaft and Axletree Co at Wednesbury near Birmingham were all lined up to join in. However, only 102 had been built before the war ended; 45 entered service with the British Army and the rest were almost certainly scrapped. The last known use of the Medium Mark B was in the 1919-1921 Irish War of Independence.

There are no known survivors of this tank.

DIMENSIONS AND WEIGHT:
Length 22ft 9in, width 8ft 10in, height 8ft 6in.
Weight 18 tons.

FURTHER READING:
Medium Mark A Whippet, David Fletcher; *Medium Tanks Marks A-D*, Peter Chamberlain and Chris Ellis.

MEDIUM, MARK C

The Medium Mark A or Whippet had not even entered service when its designer, Sir William Tritton of Fosters in Lincoln, learned that Major Walter Wilson had started the design of a new model intended to replace it. His reaction was to set his own chief designer, William Rigby, to work on a rival design.

Lagging slightly behind the Wilson design, the prototype Fosters tank was actually completed a few weeks before its rival but, as a later proposal, it took the military name of Medium Mark C. The fact that the Army approved both designs for production is symptomatic of the enthusiasm for tanks that was developing, and perhaps also points to a policy of what might be called multiple sourcing.

The first prototype was completed in August 1918 and was tested by Fosters with the name Hornet painted on its side, although this name

was never formally adopted. This tank was nearly as big as the Mk V heavy tanks, and had a scaled-down version of their rhomboid shape surmounted by a large armoured superstructure that incorporated the cab and a revolving observation turret for the commander. There were ball mounts for five machine guns, and once again none of the armour plate was thicker than 0.5 inches.

The Medium Mark C had the six-cylinder Ricardo engine with 150bhp, this time with the gearbox and epicyclic system mounted ahead of it. Maximum speed was just under 8mph and the rear-mounted fuel tank was big enough to give the tank a useful range of 140 miles. There were plans for a male version of the design, too, with a long-barrelled 6pdr gun mounted in the front of the superstructure.

The Medium B was a follow-up to the Medium A but reverted to the basic design of the larger rhomboid tanks. This one was pictured in 1918 without its machine guns. (Public Domain)

The Medium C was a deliberate rival for the Medium B and shared its rhomboid shape. Only 50 were built because the Armistice rendered them superfluous. (IWM Q70983, Public Domain)

An initial order for 200 tanks was later increased to 600, of which 200 were expected to be male types. In practice, no male types were ever built, and Fosters had only 36 partially-completed female types by the time of the Armistice. A further 14 were subsequently assembled from parts, making a total of 50. However, it was all too late for the tanks to see active service. Some were used for victory parades (where they looked more impressive than the battle-damaged tanks that had seen real fighting), and their most high-profile use was for riot control duties in Glasgow during 1919. After 1925, they were gradually replaced by the Vickers Mediums.

There are no survivors of the Medium Mark C tank.

DIMENSIONS AND WEIGHT:
Length 25ft 10in, width 8ft 4in, height 9ft 6in.
Weight 20 tons.

FURTHER READING:
Medium Mark A Whippet, David Fletcher;
Medium Tanks Marks A-D, Peter Chamberlain and Chris Ellis.

MEDIUM, MARK D

The Medium D tank could trace its origins to some work done in the experimental section of the Central Tank Corps Workshops in France during 1918. Lt Col Philip Johnson was then in charge, and he had a Whippet modified with leaf springs, sprung track rollers, a Wilson epicyclic transmission and what was probably a 360bhp Rolls-Royce Eagle aero engine. The result was a tank capable of travelling at 30mph – considerably faster than the 8mph of a standard Whippet.

Johnson also designed a new "snake track", based on a cable with track sections that were

fixed to it but were free to swing laterally. This reduced the risk of throwing a track at speed and, when tried on a Mk V tank, it allowed a maximum speed of 20mph.

The new track and suspension systems now became the basis of a new tank design by Johnson and his team. What became the Medium Mark D tank was long and narrow, with deep track frames and an oval fighting compartment mounted between them at the front end. It carried machine guns to cover the front and sides but the idea of creating a male version with a main gun in the nose had to be shelved for reasons explained later.

During 1918, Col JFC Fuller had begun to plan for a full mechanised offensive against the German army that was called Plan 1919. He saw the medium tanks as useful to exploit breakthroughs by the heavies, and encouraged the design. So a total of 11 mild-steel prototypes was ordered in August and September 1918 from Fowler's in Leeds and from Vickers in Newcastle-on-Tyne. Ruston & Hornsby were also lined up to participate in production.

The end of the war put an end to Plan 1919, but Fuller enlisted Churchill's help as Minister for Munitions to get an order for 500 of the new Medium Mark D tanks approved in December 1918. Johnson had returned to the UK to head the (civilian) Department of Tank Design and Experiment, and a wooden mock-up of the new tank existed by early 1919. There was then a reaction: by July 1919 the order had been reduced to 75 tanks, and subsequently went down to just 20.

The first prototype was completed in June 1919, powered by a 240bhp Siddeley Puma aero engine. With a top speed of 23mph on the level, it was fast and showed promise. Unfortunately, later models proved no more mechanically reliable than the prototype (whose teething troubles could perhaps be forgiven).

Meanwhile, Fuller had decided that the Medium D would be needed for future overseas wars where an amphibious capability might be needed, and this further complicated the project. It meant that no male version could be produced, because the gun would have to be mounted low down for stability, which was incompatible with half the tank being submerged. Admiralty experts also pronounced the existing hull design as likely to be unstable in the water. So two of the Vickers batch were completed as variants called the Medium D* and Medium D**.

Johnson's Medium D introduced a new shape to tank development, as well as its creator's "snake tracks". This is one of the two DM or modified pilot models built in 1921. (Public Domain)

The Medium D* was built in late 1919, with a wider hull and a different transmission. It was clearly not the answer and so it was followed in 1920 by the Medium D** with an even wider hull. This was also lengthened and gained more internal bulkheads. It had a Puma engine uprated to 300bhp, and later a 370bhp Rolls-Royce Eagle. It was also used for transmission experiments: a cam-operated clutch and brake system initially replaced the epicyclic steering gear, and in 1921 it was rebuilt with an experimental Williams-Janney hydraulic transmission.

Undeterred by the multiple setbacks that came with peacetime, Johnson pursued his design and created the Mark DM (D Modified), of which two were built by the Woolwich Arsenal in 1921. These had Rolls-Royce Eagle engines, plus an additional cupola for the commander, but their amphibious ability was poor and one demonstrated on the Thames had difficulty climbing out of the water into the bank.

Two Medium D tanks were sent to India in 1922 for tropical trials but, predictably, they broke down and the trials were abandoned. The military authorities were already losing interest and, when Johnson's Department of Tank Design and Experiment was closed down in 1923, the Medium D project died with it.

There are no surviving examples of the Medium D tank in any of its guises.

DIMENSIONS AND WEIGHT:
Length 25ft 10in, width 7ft 3in (8ft 5in for D*; 9ft for D**), height 9ft 6in. Weight 13.5 tons (14.5 tons for D*).

FURTHER READING:
Medium Mark A Whippet, David Fletcher; *Medium Tanks Marks A-D*, Peter Chamberlain and Chris Ellis.

MEDIUM TANK, AMPHIBIOUS (A/T 1)

One of the most ungainly tank creations ever made was the AT/1 or Medium Tank, Amphibious. An exceptionally deep hull kept the turret above water when the tank was wading, but gave it a curiously unbalanced look on dry land. Probably only one prototype was built, although this appears to have been modified progressively with improved suspension systems.

The AT/1 was built by Braithwaites in Newport, and used the turret and 285bhp Meadows flat-12 engine of the Covenanter with a Meadows gearbox and a Wilson steering

Perhaps barely credible in hindsight, the deep-hulled Amphibious Medium was created as a prototype in the early years of the Second World War.

system. The hull was of riveted construction with a maximum armour thickness of 40mm, and all joints were caulked for waterproofing. The tank had a crew of five (commander, gunner, loader, driver, plus one extra hand) and could achieve 10mph on land and 5mph in the water. The main armament was a QF 2pdr, supplemented by a co-axial 7.92mm Besa and a .303 Bren gun in an AA mount.

DIMENSIONS AND WEIGHT:
Length 24ft 2in, width 12ft 11in, height 11ft 3in. Weight 30.75 tons.

MORRIS-MARTEL TANKETTE
See Martel Tankettes.

MOTHER
Mother was the name given to the first prototype of the rhomboid-shaped tanks that inaugurated the genre. It was more formally known as His Majesty's Landship *Centipede* and was completed in December 1915. Successful demonstrations in early 1916 led to an Army Council Order for the first 100 tanks in February.

The rhomboid shape was an idea from Lt Walter Wilson, the Admiralty engineer assigned to the Landships Committee, and it was made feasible when William Tritton, MD of Fosters of Lincoln, proposed a track design made from pressed plate. This did not suffer from the problems encountered on the experimental Little Willie, and the new shape enabled the tank to meet its design target of crossing an 8ft wide trench.

Fosters made a wooden mock-up of the design in September while the new tracks were tested successfully on Little Willie. The tank was drawn up without a turret, which would have been detrimental to its stability; instead, the plan was to have a sponson on each side to contain the main weapons. By December 1915, the Admiralty had agreed to supply 50

The FV107 Scimitar reconnaissance vehicle was a member of the CVR(T) family. This one belonged to a Royal Marines recce unit and was pictured during a 1996 Combined Joint Task Force exercise held in the USA. (Lance Cpl RL Kugler Jr./ WikiMedia Commons)

pairs of its 6pdr (57mm) quick-firing guns for the job. There was some initial hesitation over secondary armament, although a machine-gun mounting was provided between the driver's and commander's visors in the cab superstructure at the front.

The basic construction of   depended on a steel skeleton that formed a box to which armour plates were riveted. The tracks ran in their own housing alongside, with projecting "horns" at front and rear that created the rhomboid shape. The engine was mounted roughly in the centre of the box, and was a 13.5-litre Daimler-Knight six-cylinder sleeve-valve type, as used in the Foster-Daimler tractor, developing 105bhp at 1000rpm. Its exhaust had no silencer, and exited through the roof of the box.

The cone clutch and two-speed and reverse gearbox also came from Foster-Daimler tractors, but there was then a quite complex drivetrain involving half-shafts, a secondary two-speed gearbox at the rear of the track on each side, and roller chains to the track driving sprockets. Steering could be effected by braking one track, but the tank also came with a wheeled tail (improved from the one developed for Little Willie) that could be steered by long cables that ran into the tank; it could also be raised and lowered hydraulically if necessary.

Mother was designed for a crew of eight men, whose discomfort must have been enormous thanks to the engine noise and heat and the lack of any suspension. They were a driver,

a commander (who shared some driving tasks), two men to operate the rear-mounted secondary gearboxes, two gunners and two loaders.

DIMENSIONS AND WEIGHT:
Length 31ft, width 13ft 8in (over sponsons), height 8ft. Weight approximately 27 tons.

FURTHER READING:
The British Tanks 1915-19, David Fletcher.

NO 1 LINCOLN MACHINE
See Little Willie.

SABRE
See Scorpion.

SCIMITAR (FV107)
The FV107 Scimitar was a tracked reconnaissance vehicle that is also sometimes described as a light tank. It was a member of the CVR(T) family (see separate entry) and was powered by the Jaguar J60 petrol engine which gave it a top speed of 50mph. The first examples entered service in 1971.

The Scimitar was one of two light tank versions of the CVR(T) range, the other being the FV101 Scorpion. The two types were very similar, the key distinguishing feature of the Scimitar being its high-velocity 30mm L21 RARDEN cannon. This was backed up by a co-axial 7.62mm L37A1 machine gun. More than 600 Scimitars were built, of which just under half went for export to Belgium and to Latvia.

Scimitars had a crew of three (commander, gunner and driver) and an operational range of 280 miles. Beginning in early 2011, the British vehicles were upgraded to Mk II standard by BAE Systems at Telford as part of a Life Extension Programme. They were given new hulls which provided more space and better crew protection against mines, new armour, mine-protected seating, and several detail changes designed to reduce maintenance costs. Their Jaguar engines were also replaced by 190bhp Cummins diesels and the gearbox was changed to a David Brown TN15E fully automatic type.

Scimitars saw action with British forces in the Falklands War, the First Gulf War, the 2003 Iraq invasion, and in Afghanistan.

DIMENSIONS AND WEIGHT:
Length 16ft 1in, width 7ft 3in, height 6ft 11in.
Weight 7.8 tonnes (with Jaguar engine);
11.8 tons (Mk II).

FURTHER READING:
Scorpion, the CVR(T) range, Simon Dunstan;
Scorpion and Scimitar, British Armoured Reconnaissance Vehicles 1970-2020, David Grummitt.

SCORPION (FV101)

The FV101 Scorpion was the lead vehicle of the CVR(T) family, whose origins are discussed under that heading. Over 3000 were built, of which 1500 served with the British Army and the Royal Air Force Regiment, while a similar number were exported.

These rapid, light reconnaissance vehicles, sometimes described as light tanks, differed from the similar FV107 Scimitar primarily in their use of the ROF L23A1 76mm low-velocity gun with a co-axial L43A1 7.62mm machine gun. Smoke and fumes from the main gun proved problematical, as they would fill the turret, especially when it was closed down. The Scorpion had a crew of three (commander, gunner and driver) and with its original Jaguar six-cylinder petrol engine had a maximum speed of 50mph. One example was recorded as achieving 51mph on test.

Examples were exported to Belgium, Botswana, Brunei, Chile, Honduras, Indonesia, Iran, Ireland, Jordan, Malaysia, New Zealand, Nigeria, Oman, the Philippines, Spain, Tanzania, Thailand, Togo, Venezuela and the United Arab Emirates. Some of these were Scorpion 90 types, with the special export specification of a long-barrel Cockerill Mk 3 M-A1 90mm gun instead of the 76mm type.

Scorpions saw action in the Iran-Iraq War, in the Falklands, and in the First Gulf War. After withdrawal in 1994, some Scorpion hulls were refurbished and fitted with turrets from FV721 Fox armoured cars to create a new reconnaissance variant called the Sabre; these remained in service until 2004. Some were also sent to BATUS, the British Army's training ground in Canada, where they were visually modified to represent the Russian T-80 tank with its 125mm gun. The Scorpions belonging to the

That the FV101 Scorpion had a larger main gun than the Scimitar is immediately obvious in this picture that was taken during BAOR exercises in Germany. (MoD/BAOR)

The CVR(T) design was deliberately adaptable, and this picture shows a Scorpion Command variant. (MoD/BAOR)

Irish Defence Force were given a new lease of life with 190bhp Steyr M16 six-cylinder diesel engines and remained in service until 2017.

DIMENSIONS AND WEIGHT:
Length 17ft 4.2in, width 7ft 0in, height 6ft 11in.
Weight 8 tonnes.

FURTHER READING:
Scorpion, the CVR(T) range, Simon Dunstan;
Scorpion and Scimitar, British Armoured Reconnaissance Vehicles 1970-2020,
David Grummitt.

SHERMAN

The American-built M4 Sherman was the most widely used Allied tank of the Second World War. It was supplied in large numbers to the British Army under Lend-Lease arrangements between 1942 and 1945, and was used in both unmodified and modified forms. The major modification developed by the British was to replace the original 75mm gun with the British-made 17pdr. This created the Sherman Firefly, which was the only British tank capable of taking on the German Panthers and Tigers in the aftermath of D-Day. The Sherman tank was a superb all-rounder which had an extensive history, and this entry deliberately focuses on the variants used by British forces.

To the Americans, the tank was an M4 Medium; the General Sherman name (usually abbreviated to Sherman) was applied by the British and was subsequently adopted almost universally. The tank was drawn up in 1941 with the basic chassis of the previous M3 Medium and a 75mm gun, and by the end of 1942 it was in production at no fewer than 11 plants across the USA. Engine production could not keep up with the volume of tanks being produced, and alternative engines (plus other modifications) led to new marks of the tank. A 375bhp GM 6046 twin diesel was used in the M4A2; the M4A3 had a Ford GAA petrol V8 with 450bhp; the M4A4 used the 370bhp Chrysler multi-bank engine, and the M4A6 had a 450bhp Caterpillar D-200A radial diesel.

The first British deliveries were predominantly of the M4A1 variant, which had a cast hull instead of the original welded design. They began to arrive in October 1942 and were shipped straight to the 8th Army in North Africa,

A Scorpion on patrol in Iraq in 1991. These compact vehicles were powered by a Jaguar petrol engine mounted alongside the driver. (PHC Holmes/ WikiMedia Commons)

Fitting the British 17pdr gun to the Sherman produced one of the best British tanks of the Second World War – the Sherman Firefly. This one is a Mk VC type on display at Bovington. The length of the main gun is immediately apparent, and was a distinguishing feature used by German tankers, who would try to take out these tanks before the less threatening ones. (Alan Wilson, CC-by-SA 2.0)

where their first major engagement was at the Battle of Alamein. A steady flow of Sherman deliveries followed until the end of the war, the major British types (in approximate descending order of quantity) being the M4A4, M4A2, M4, M4A1, and M4A3. The British naming system was to use mark numbers (I-VII) for the different hulls, and suffix letters for differences in main armament and suspension. A indicated the 76mm gun, B the 105mm howitzer, C the 17pdr, and Y the horizontal volute spring suspension (HVSS) with wider tracks for better weight distribution that was introduced on the M4A3 in August 1944. So the Sherman Firefly would be a IIC when based on the M4A1, a IVC when based on the M4A3, or a VC if based on the M4A4.

The Sherman normally had a crew of five – commander, gunner, loader, driver, and a co-driver who doubled as the hull gunner – but the Firefly dispensed with the hull gun and its associated crew member to make more room for ammunition.

Inevitably, there were multiple special conversions, and the British ones included Ark bridgelayers, ARVs, BARVs (developed for the D-Day landings), Duplex Drive amphibious tanks (with a canvas flotation screen and twin propellors, also developed for D-Day), flame-throwers, the Kangaroo APC, and mine-clearing flails.

There are many Shermans in preservation around the world, both in museum collections

The early Sherman with its 75mm gun is represented here by a Sherman II of the 44th RTR, pictured in North-West Europe. (Tank Museum, Bovington)

and in private hands. The Bovington Tank Museum has the first M4A1 delivered to Britain under Lend-Lease, as well as a 1944 Sherman Firefly and a Sherman Crab Mk II mine flail.

DIMENSIONS AND WEIGHT
(Depending on variant):
Length 19ft 4in-24ft 3in, width 8ft 7in-10ft 0.5in, height 9ft 0in- 9ft 9in. Weight 29.7-30.5 tons (M4A1-M4A3) or 31.25-32.5 tons (later types).

FURTHER READING:
M4 (76mm) Sherman Medium Tank 1943-65, Steven J Zaloga; *Sherman Tanks of the British Army and Royal Marines*, Dennis Oliver.

This Stuart M3A1 is preserved at the Aberdeen Proving Ground in the USA and wears the livery of the Desert Rats. (Pahcal 123 CC-by-SA 4.0)

SHIR

See Chieftain.

STUART

The Stuart was the first US-built tank to enter service with British forces under the Lend-Lease arrangements in the Second World War. Originally designed for recce work, the tank was known to its originators as a Light Tank M3, but the British Army named it the General Stuart after a Confederate army leader of the American Civil War. More commonly, it was just a Stuart, and its smooth ride also earned it the nickname of the Honey. The original M3 was further developed as the M5, and examples of these in British service were also known as Stuarts.

The M3 entered production in March 1941 and was an upgrade of the earlier M2 Light Tank that incorporated lessons learned from observation of the early stages of the war in Europe. The first examples were delivered to Britain in July 1941 and by November were in service in the Western Desert, where they were a valuable addition to the British forces. Early M3s had a riveted hull with a welded turret, but a welded hull was used from early 1942. The standard weapon was a 37mm M5 gun, supported by five Browning machine guns, of which two were in sponsons. The tank had a four-man crew of commander, gunner, driver and co-driver.

The limited 75-mile range of these tanks persuaded British troops to add external fuel tanks, and the sponsons were often removed to increase space. Yet these disadvantages were set against good mechanical reliability and the ability to fire HE shells, neither of which applied to the British-made tanks in North Africa.

The British Army received six marks of Stuart. The Mk I was an M3 with the standard 225bhp Continental 7-cyl R-670 radial engine, and the less numerous Mk II had the 250bhp Guiberson T-1020 9-cylinder diesel radial engine that had been introduced to counter a shortage of Continental engines. The Stuart Mk III was the improved M3A1, introduced in June 1942 with a new turret that had a basket but no cupola, with the sponsons removed and with a slightly longer vertically stabilised M6 main gun. With the Guiberson diesel engine, this became a Stuart Mk IV. The Stuart Mk V was the American M3A3 model from early 1943, with a redesigned and enlarged hull. The final Stuart Mk VI was what the Americans knew as an M5A1, which had twin Cadillac V8 engines with Hydra-Matic automatic gearboxes that had been introduced to counter a continuing shortage of engines for the M3. These entered production in 1943 as the M5 Light Tank and were visually distinguished by a taller rear deck.

Although the Stuart was outclassed by 1943,

"Hothead" is an M5A1 Stuart in the Bovington Tank Museum, and this rear view shows the taller rear deck that was needed to accommodate the twin Cadillac V8 engines. (Morio, CC-by-SA 4.0)

British units continued to use them in some theatres, including Burma and Italy, and they were still in service in north-west Europe after the D-Day landings. Many redundant British examples of M3 and M5 derivatives had their turrets removed to create one of three conversions. These were the Stuart Kangaroo, which was an APC with seats for infantry; the Stuart Recce, similar to the Kangaroo but with various additional machine-gun mountings; and the Stuart Command, with extra radio equipment (and often with grenade netting as well). Some were also used as artillery tractors and at least one was turned into an 18pdr self-propelled gun in the Middle East.

British Stuarts remained in service beyond the end of the war, and some were used in Indonesia before being passed on to the Dutch forces there.

DIMENSIONS AND WEIGHT:
Length 14ft 10.75in (Mk I to Mk V) or 14 ft 2.75in (Mk VI), width 7ft 4in (Mk I to Mk V) or 7ft 4.25in (Mk VI), height 8ft 3in (Mk I and Mk II) or 7ft 6.5in (Mk III to Mk VI). Weight 12.2 tons (Mk I and Mk II), 12.7 tons (Mk III to Mk V) or 15.1 tons (Mk VI).

FURTHER READING:
M3 & M5 Stuart Light Tank 1940-45, Steven J Zaloga.

TETRARCH (A17)

The Tetrarch started life as the next iteration of the Vickers Light Tank series, in which it became the Mk VII. It was designed both for export and in the hope of securing an order from the British Army, and the prototype was completed in 1937.

A key new feature was that the tank was designed to take a 2pdr main gun plus a 7.92mm Besa machine gun, and was no longer limited to the machine gun of earlier models in the Light Tank series. It was slightly wider and longer than its predecessors, with a two-man turret and a maximum armour thickness of 14mm. It also had a new track suspension system, with four large road wheels on each side and no separate driver or idler wheels. Each wheel was sprung independently by an oleopneumatic strut, and the front pair of wheels gave a limited degree of steering. However, for sharper turns the tank depended on the traditional track-braking method. The engine was also new in tank applications, and was an 8.8-litre Meadows flat-12-cylinder with 165bhp that gave a maximum road speed of 40mph.

The War Office did not need another Light Tank and the Mk VII did not fit the bill as one of the new Cruiser types, but this was a time of rapid rearmament in Britain and the Army was desperate for tanks. As a result, it was accepted for service with the General Staff designation A17,

The four large road wheels of the Tetrarch light tank gave it a very distinctive appearance. It was never very successful. (Public Domain)

The Tetrarch was found a role with the airborne divisions, and the Hamilcar glider was developed to carry it.

with a small number of changes that included an external fuel tank to increase the range to 140 miles. The first order was for 70 tanks; during 1938 the War Office dithered about how many it wanted and eventually settled on 220 when it learned that Metropolitan (to whom Vickers planned to sub-contract construction) had already ordered the armour plating for that quantity.

Production was delayed by War Office vacillation about the role of light tanks and in May 1941 by German bombing of the factories where these were to be built, but in the end at least 100 were made. Some authorities argue for a production total of 177. In the mean time, the War Office had allocated the name of Tetrarch to the new tank; a tetrarch was one of four ancient rulers, and perhaps the tank's distinctive four-wheel configuration had inspired the connection. The last of these tanks were delivered in late 1942.

Not long after the first A17s had been delivered in November 1940, the Army decided that light tanks were too vulnerable for use in its armoured divisions. It was also clear that the A17 was under-manned with its three-man crew of commander, gunner and driver, but

there was no space to accommodate a fourth man as loader. There were questions about the adequacy of its cooling system, and as a result none were sent to North Africa. So the future of the Tetrarch hung in the balance for a while, and during 1941 it was used to test Duplex Drive systems and was allocated to one of the RAC amphibious squadrons.

However, in mid-1941 the Army saw a role for the A17 with the new airborne divisions, and ensured that the new Hamilcar glider was developed to carry it. At this point, a number of the tanks had their 2pdr guns replaced with a 3in infantry support howitzer, and were redesignated as Tetrarch 1 CS (Close Support) types. Those that retained their 2pdr main weapons were fitted with Littlejohn squeeze-bore adaptors to increase muzzle velocity and armour penetration.

In early 1942, 20 Tetrarch tanks were sent to the Soviet Union under Lend-Lease arrangements. In May that year, the British Army used a few during the invasion of Madagascar, and in June a number were attached to the 1st Airborne Division for their new glider-borne role. A number took part in the 1943 invasion of Sicily as part of the 6th Airborne Armoured Reconnaissance Regiment, and about 20 were used in airborne landings in Normandy in June 1944. However, they were severely outgunned by German tanks and were withdrawn to infantry support roles.

By August 1944, Cromwell cruiser tanks had replaced most Tetrarchs in service, and the rest were replaced in the airborne role by the US-made M22 Locust in December 1944. By 1946, the tank was considered obsolete, and the last examples were withdrawn in 1950.

Two examples of the Tetrarch tank survive in museums today. One is at the Bovington Tank Museum and the other is in Russia at the Kubinka Tank Museum in Moscow.

DIMENSIONS AND WEIGHT:
Length 13ft 6in, width 7ft 7in, height 6ft 11in.
Weight 7.5 tons

FURTHER READING:
The Vickers Tanks: From Landships to Challenger, Christopher Foss and Peter McKenzie; *Airborne Armour: Tetrarch, Locust, Hamilcar and the 6th Airborne Armoured Reconnaissance Regiment 1938–1950*, Keith Flint.

There was just one example of the Three-man Light Tank, which was a mid-1920s design.

THREE-MAN LIGHT TANK (A3)

The idea that a light tank might prove useful was explored with a design that gained the General Staff specification number A3 in 1925. It was described as a Three-man Light Tank, or alternatively as Machine Gun Carrier No 1, and was probably the only tank designed and built by the Royal Ordnance Factories between the end of the Great War and the A7 tank in 1928.

Just one example seems to have been built, and was numbered as A3E1. It was a curious design, its otherwise unnecessary length of nearly 18ft presumably being intended to give it trench-crossing ability. At each end was a small turret, and in each turret was a crew member with a Vickers .303 machine gun. The third crew member was the driver, whose armoured box-like cab next to the front turret restricted its arc of fire. The crew were protected by armour half an inch thick.

The engine was mounted amidships, and drove the very simple steel tracks through a four-speed gearbox and reduction gearing. It was a four-cylinder type with 52bhp, was manufactured by AEC, and was supposedly chosen because it was readily available commercially. Exactly which AEC engine it was is not clear, the best bet probably being the 5.1-litre A118 type then used in both buses and lorries, although AEC never claimed more than 40bhp for that. One way or another, A3E1 was claimed to have a top speed of 16mph. Also unclear are the details of the suspension, which had nine twin road wheels on each side but was otherwise concealed by side-plates with integral mud chutes.

The A3 prototype was evaluated at MWEE in the spring of 1926, but the project went no further and the tank no longer survives.

DIMENSIONS AND WEIGHT:
Length 17ft 9in, width 9ft 0in, height 6ft 0in.
Weight 16.7 tons.

FURTHER READING:
Mechanised Force, David Fletcher.

TOG1

As war became inevitable in the first half of 1939, the government consulted the tank experts they had available, but their choice fell on men who had become experts in the 1914-1918 War rather than those who would fight in the next one. The Minister of Supply, who had responsibility for re-armament, had discussions with Sir Albert Stern, the former head of the Tank Supply Department, and two days after war was declared in September, he asked Stern to put together a committee to study requirements and designs for new tanks.

Stern of course turned to former colleagues, and among those he invited on to the committee were Sir Eustace Tennyson d'Eyncourt, Major-General Sir Ernest Swinton, Harry Ricardo, and Major Walter Wilson, all of whom had been prominent in tank development and production during the earlier conflict. Formally described as the Special Vehicle Development Committee of the Ministry of Supply, this group quickly became known as The Old Gang, and the initials of that name were later applied to their design proposals.

At this stage, the Army General Staff anticipated battle conditions similar to those of the Great War, and so the outline specification they issued was for a heavy tank that resembled the tanks used in that conflict. They expected all-round tracks, a top speed of just 5mph, and

When The Old Gang of Great War tank specialists got back together at the start of the Second World War, it was no surprise that their design proposals had much in common with those of 20 years earlier. Their first effort was known as TOG1. (Tank Museum)

armour thick enough to withstand current anti-tank guns and howitzers. There was to be a field gun on the front for demolishing fortifications, a sponson on each side would carry a 2pdr gun, and four Besa machine guns would cover all possible approaches by enemy infantry. The tank had to be transportable by rail and would have a crew of eight.

What the General Staff was calling for was a modern version of a Great War Tank, and that was what they got. In December 1939, the committee asked Fosters of Lincoln – again involved with the Great War tanks – to design the new heavy tank. Fosters proposed using a Paxman-Ricardo V12 diesel engine developed to give 600bhp, driving a pair of generators that would in turn power a motor for each track. They envisaged a complicated steering system that controlled the track motors through a potentiometer.

Construction of a prototype began in February 1940 and the tank was ready by October. Meanwhile, the design of the sponsons had been changed, and they were now to be smaller and carry only machine guns. In practice, no sponsons of any kind were ever fitted. TOG1, as it was known, had a 75mm howitzer mounted in its nose (borrowed from the French Char B), and a Matilda turret with that tank's 2pdr gun.

The electric transmission proved unsatisfactory on test, and the tank's great length – planned for trench crossing – made steering difficult. TOG1 was rebuilt with a hydraulic transmission as TOG1A and the modified prototype was ready by May 1943. By that time, it was of course clear that battlefield conditions

were not going to be the same as in the Great War, and a good deal of work had been done on a second design, called TOG2. TOG1 did not survive.

DIMENSIONS AND WEIGHT:
Length 33ft 3in, width 10ft 3in, height 10ft 0in.
Weight 63.5 tons

FURTHER READING:
The Great Tank Scandal: British Armour in the Second World War - Part 1, David Fletcher.

TOG2

TOG2 was the second proposal for a Heavy Tank from the Special Vehicle Development Committee of the Ministry of Supply. Like TOG1, it had a long hull for trench crossing, but that hull was now planned to be lower with the tracks running below it. Side sponsons were again in the design, and there would be a larger turret with a 6pdr gun. The single prototype was completed in March 1941 and, like TOG1, was never fitted with the intended sponsons. It was given a dummy turret that was taller than planned and carried a 77mm gun.

In early 1942, TOG2 became TOG2* when it was fitted with the new cast turret intended for the A30 Challenger, mounting a 17pdr gun. In this form, the tank required a crew of six, consisting of commander, driver, gunner, two loaders, and a co-driver.

A further development called TOG2R (R for revised) was also planned but was never actually built. It would have been about 6ft shorter than TOG2, with a different suspension featuring torsion bars, and no sponsons – but all the indications are that it was as badly out of touch with real-world requirements as the earlier TOG proposals.

DIMENSIONS AND WEIGHT:
Length 33ft 3in, width 10ft 3in, height 10ft 0in.
Weight 80 tons (TOG2*)

FURTHER READING:
The Great Tank Scandal: British Armour in the Second World War - Part 1, David Fletcher.

TORTOISE (A39)

The Tortoise or A39 was a heavy assault gun that is also described as a super-heavy tank. It was developed in anticipation of a requirement to assault heavily fortified targets such as the

TOG2 was a second design that was out of touch with battlefield requirements. The sole prototype survives at the Tank Museum in Bovington. (Makizox, CC-by-SA 4.0)

Siegfried Line (West Wall) during the eventual Allied invasion of Germany.

A general concept was issued to industry in March 1943, and the Nuffield Organisation came up with a series of design proposals (numbered AT1 to AT18) between May 1943 and February 1944, each one larger and heavier than the last. The final two were heavy flame-thrower designs, but design AT16 from February 1944 was approved by the Tank Board, and the War Office subsequently asked for 25 to be built straight from the mock-up, without the interme-

Super-heavy tank or heavy assault gun, the Tortoise was a mid-war design that did not appear until 1946, by which time it no longer met Army requirements. This example survives at Bovington. (Morio, CC-by-SA 4.0)

Johnson's Tropical Tank revealed problems on test in 1922 and the project was cancelled before a second example had been completed. The twin-turret design was characteristic of the inter-war period.

diary of a prototype. The A39 was required for operational service by September 1945, and was expected to enter service with the specialist 79th Armoured Division under Major-General Percy Hobart.

That target date was not met, and in any case the war in Europe ended in May 1945. The order for 25 tanks was reduced to just six, and all of these were built as mild-steel prototypes. Deliveries began in 1946. Two went to Germany for troop trials in 1948, when they demonstrated both reliability and their power and accuracy as gun platforms. On the negative side, their weight and size made both manoeuvring and transportation difficult. Now that the original intended use was no longer in prospect, the A39 project was allowed to wither and the prototypes fell into disuse after 1949.

The Tortoise was designed as a turretless vehicle, partly to avoid the weak spots of turreted designs and partly because its intended role did not require the full traverse available from a turret. The gun nevertheless had a limited traverse from its power-assisted mounting. Unusually, this incorporated a large armoured ball mount in the front of the hull. The weapon itself had not been used before in a tank, and was modified from the Ordnance 3.7-inch (94mm) heavy anti-aircraft gun; in tank form, it was described as a 32-pounder. The Tortoise also had a Besa machine gun in an armoured ball mount next to the main weapon and two more in a small turret on top of the hull.

The cast hull was made in three sections and was heavily armoured, with plate of between 7 and 9 inches' thickness (although the top armour was just 1.3in thick). This was the main reason for the tank's all-up weight of 78 tons. It carried a seven-man crew of commander, gunner, machine gunner, two loaders, driver and co-driver. The problem of ammunition storage had not been satisfactorily resolved, and of the 60 rounds for the main gun that were carried, only 12 were readily accessible; the rest had to be stored under the floor.

The Tortoise was powered by a 650bhp Meteor Mk V petrol engine, driving through a Merritt-Brown gearbox with six forward speeds that was also arranged to give all six speeds in reverse. There were four two-wheel track bogies on each side, each pair being linked to a transverse torsion bar, and the tracks and suspension were well protected by armoured side plates. The tank had a maximum road speed of 12mph

and a maximum off-road speed of just 4mph. It carried enough fuel for a road range of 87 miles.

One running example of the Tortoise is preserved at the Tank Museum in Bovington, and two others are known to survive as derelicts on gunnery ranges.

DIMENSIONS AND WEIGHT:
Length 33ft, width 13ft, height 9ft 10in.
Weight 78 long tons.

FURTHER READING:
Super-Heavy Tanks of World War II,
Kenneth W Estes.

TRITTON CHASER
See Medium Mark A.

TROPICAL TANK
Philip Johnson of the Department of Tank Design was sent to India in 1919 to determine whether tanks might be of value to the British Army stationed there. He reported back that they would, and proposed a whole family of tracked vehicles based on a single design. The 5-ton light tank derivative was known simply as the Tropical Tank, an unsuccessful design about which relatively little information survives.

Johnson specified his favoured spring cable suspension but chose conventional tracks rather than the snake type of his other designs. The tank was laid out with its 45bhp Tylor engine at the front and its transmission at the rear, like the Whippet. With a four-speed and reverse gearbox, it was capable of 15mph on the road and 7mph across country.

There was a boxy front superstructure over the engine and driving compartment, and behind that were two offset turrets. These were similar to those on Austin armoured cars and were most likely intended to be equipped with machine guns.

Beginning in October 1921, Vickers built a prototype at their Erith factory, but early testing showed several problems and by June 1922 it was still not satisfactory. Nevertheless, the tank was delivered to Farnborough in the summer or late autumn (sources differ on the date) for testing by the Army. There were still major problems with the tank, particularly its suspension, and tests were abandoned. Build of a second example had begun in July, but it was never completed.

DIMENSIONS AND WEIGHT:
No reliable dimensions are available.
Weight 5.15 tons.

FURTHER READING:
Mechanised Force, David Fletcher.

VALENTINE

The Valentine may not have been one of Britain's better tanks of the Second World War, but it was among the most numerous and was fondly remembered by those who used it. Valentine production began in 1940 and was supplemented from May 1941 by production in Canada. A total of 8316 Valentines of all variants was built, of which 1420 came from Canada, and Valentine production reached its peak in 1942. Of that total, 3665 tanks were sent to the Soviet Army.

However, the Valentine soon became outdated; its armour was thin and its main gun lacked the necessary punch. By the end of 1942 it had been declared obsolete, and by June 1943 it was no longer in front-line service with British forces, although it remained in service with Australian, Indian, New Zealand and Soviet forces and the British continued to use them for non-combat roles.

It was in February 1938 that the War Office asked Vickers to develop a Mk III infantry tank with some urgency, basing it on either the Matilda II or the company's own A10 Cruiser Mk II. A first mock-up the following month reflected Vickers' concerns about weight and was rejected because of insufficient armour, but Vickers insisted that they could deliver a new tank more cheaply than any derivative of the Matilda II.

Their design for the Valentine tank, ready by April 1939, weighed around 16 tons and, on War Office insistence, had a petrol engine. This drove through a five-speed Meadows gearbox and the tracks had a modified Horstmann suspension, with two units on each side, each consisting of

one large and two smaller wheels. There were 60mm of armour and a two-man turret, and the tracks were unprotected to save weight. Even so, the Valentine had fairly restricted performance, with a top speed of 15mph on roads and a range of 90 miles.

By spring 1939, war appeared inevitable, and the General Staff placed an order for 300 Valentines without calling for any pilot vehicles. To get production up to speed as quickly as possible, they arranged for Metropolitan-Cammell and BRCW to help. The first Valentines were delivered in May 1940 and, after successful trials, were put into service.

Most Valentines had a three-man crew, but the Mk III added a fourth to relieve the commander of loading duties. The main armament was initially the stalwart 2pdr, but the Valentine Mk VIII was upgraded with the 6pdr, when the crew went back to three because of space limitations in the turret. The final Mk XI Valentines built in February-May 1944 had the QF 75mm, but by this time better tanks had become available. Most variants had a 7.92mm Besa machine gun as secondary armament.

The first Valentines had a 135bhp AEC A189 petrol engine, but this proved unreliable and after 308 tanks had been built, the Mk II Valentine appeared with a 131bhp A190 diesel, which was retained for the improved Mk III variant. These early Valentines had a five-speed Meadows crash gearbox. However, the Directorate of Mechanisation wanted better, and the Mk IV and later Valentines had a GMC 6-71S diesel engine with 130bhp that drove through an American five-speed Spicer gearbox. The Mk IX, X and XI Valentines all had the improved A type of the GMC diesel with its bigger injectors and higher governed speed.

By the time this Valentine Mk X was built, the tank was powered by a GMC diesel engine and carried a 6pdr main gun.

"Hannibal" was the first Valentine to be converted to a bridgelayer in 1942, with a Number 1 Scissors Bridge. It is based on a Mk I tank, although most Valentine bridgelayers were based on Mk II and Mk III tanks. After use as a training aid, it was preserved at the Tank Museum in Bovington.

In its early days in service, the Valentine was viewed as a stop-gap cruiser tank, and in 1942 a number went to North Africa to replace Matildas. They earned themselves a solid reputation in the desert, where the diesel-engined versions came into their own. A large quantity was also sent to Egypt.

In later years, many Valentines were converted for use as command tanks or Observation Posts, as mine flails (Scorpion II) or with mine rollers for D-Day, as bridgelayers, and in connection with the Canal Defence Light experiments. From 1942, they were also used for Duplex Drive trials, and in the end a total of 625 Valentine DDs were converted by Metro-Cammell from Mk V, Mk IX and Mk XI models – but all were restricted to training duties because the Sherman tank was found to work better as a DD type. There was also a close-support derivative of the Mk III, armed with a 3in mortar.

The Valentine became the basis for two self-propelled guns, both of which have individual entries here. The earlier of the two was the Bishop, which appeared in 1942, and the second was the Archer, which entered production the following year.

Many Valentine tanks survive. The Bovington Tank Museum has a Mk IX in running condition, a Mk II and a bridgelayer. Others are displayed at the Imperial War Museum in Duxford, the Royal Military Museum in Brussels, the Musée des Blindés in Saumur, the South African National Museum of Military History and the Kubinka Tank Museum in Russia. There are also examples in museums in the USA and in India, and several survive in private collections.

DIMENSIONS AND WEIGHT:
Length 17ft 9in, width 8ft 7.5in, height 7ft 5.5in. Weight 16 long tons.

FURTHER READING:
Valentine Infantry Tank 1938-45, Bruce Oliver Newsome PhD & H Morshead.

VALIANT (A38)

The Valiant was an abortive attempt to develop an assault tank from the Valentine. Just one prototype was built, in late 1943 or early 1944, but had so many shortcomings that it was eventually used by the School of Tank Technology as an object lesson in poor tank design.

General Staff specification A38 called for a heavily armoured tank for use in the Far East, but placed tight weight restrictions on the design. Vickers proposed one based on the Valentine, and in August 1942 the Ministry of Supply called for three (later six) mild steel prototypes. Work was transferred to BRCW, and in October an order was placed for 500 tanks. It was cancelled soon afterwards.

By March 1943, the Ministry of Supply had designated Ruston & Hornsby as the design parent for the new tank, although in practice there would be considerable input from Rolls-Royce at Belper. The plan was for a 27-ton tank powered by the 165bhp GMC 6004 diesel engine, as used in the later Valentines, with six individually-sprung road wheels on each side and a 17pdr main gun. In practice, the sole prototype, made of mild steel and completed by Ruston & Hornsby at the end of 1943 or early the following year, had a different gun – possibly a 6pdr. The tank was designed for a crew of four, and its secondary armament was a pair of Besa 7.92mm machine guns.

Trials quickly demonstrated multiple faults. There was poor ground clearance, and an overhanging tail caused the tank to ground when climbing; the driver's controls had also been poorly thought out. The Valiant design was sidelined, although it was brought back briefly in April 1945 for suspension trials. These were aborted, mainly because of the risk of driver injury, and the tank was finally cancelled. It survives with a 75mm gun, which may not have been the original fitment.

There had been plans for a Heavy Valiant, also known as the Valiant Mk III and the Vanguard. This is discussed separately.

The sole Valiant prototype is now part of the collection at the Bovington Tank Museum.

DIMENSIONS AND WEIGHT:
Length 17ft 7in, width 9ft 3in, height 7ft.
Weight 27 tons.

FURTHER READING:
British and American Tanks of World War Two, Peter Chamberlain & Chris Ellis.

VANGUARD
See Heavy Valiant.

VICKERS COMMERCIAL TANKS
Between 1933 and 1940, Vickers built a series of light Commercial Tanks for export that were derived from the Carden-Loyd line of development. These were turreted designs that had some elements in common with the Light Tanks that the company developed for the British Army at the same time, but other aspects of their design lagged slightly behind the domestic variety, for some fairly obvious reasons.

These tanks are usually identified by their year of manufacture, and about 130 of them were built between 1933 and 1940. Known buyers were Argentina, Belgium, China, Finland, Latvia, the Soviet Union and Switzerland. Some changed ownership as a result of political or wartime developments.

The Vickers Commercial light tanks had a core design that could be configured to suit the customer. This one is a 1936-pattern tank that is preserved at the Bovington Tank Museum. (Simon Q/ CC by 2.0)

103

The 1933 model had a riveted hull and turret and was powered by an 88bhp Meadows ESTB six-cylinder engine. The design of the turret could be specified by the customer, who could also select the armament; the default option was a Vickers 7.7mm machine gun. The 1934 model had a revised suspension with helical springs, and the T-15 Light Tank (see separate entry) was a special derivative for the Belgian Army. There were further variations of the base specification for 1935, 1936 and 1937. There were individual models, too, and these included a 1932 Patrol Tank, a 1935 Tank Destroyer with a 2pdr gun, and a 1938 Light Command Tank. Experiments with amphibious derivatives also led to some export orders.

Typical performance of a Vickers Commercial Tank was 40mph with a range of about 90 miles.

DIMENSIONS AND WEIGHT (TYPICAL):
Length 11ft 9.5in, width 6ft 2.5in, height 6ft 2.5in. Weight 3.8 tons.

FURTHER READING:
The Vickers Tanks, from Landships to Challenger 2, Christopher Foss & Peter McKenzie.

VICKERS LIGHT TANKS
See Light Tank, Mks I to VI.

VICKERS MARK E (SIX-TON)
Though largely overlooked today, the Vickers Mark E was actually the most successful design of its time. From the outset, it was designed as a simple, reliable and versatile light tank for export; the British Army did evaluate it, but decided against buying any. (Nevertheless, some were taken on for training duties at the start of the Second World War, when there was an acute need for tanks of all kinds.) An overall build total of 153 examples is generally accepted.

The design team included John Carden and Vivian Lloyd, and the tank came together in 1928 as a scaled-up tankette with riveted steel hull plates and a revolving turret. Armour protection was good for the time, with 25.4mm (1in) for the front and the turret or turrets, and 19mm (0.75in) on the hull rear. The tank was marketed as the Vickers Six-ton type, but in practice most production models were considerably heavier than that.

Suspension was a simple design with two axles, each with a pair of twin-wheel bogies connected by a leaf spring, and high-strength steel tracks gave a longer life than most contemporary designs. Power was supplied by a derivative of the Armstrong-Siddeley RAF 1a engine (often wrongly cited as a Puma type), which developed between 80bhp and 95bhp, according to version, and gave a maximum road speed of 22mph.

From the start, the design team aimed for versatility, and to that end they prepared two versions of the Mark E. The Type A had twin turrets, reflecting the preoccupation with such designs at the time, and each of these carried a Vickers machine gun. The Type B had a single turret designed for two men, one operating a machine gun and the other the main weapon; Vickers called this the Duplex Mounting. The main gun was initially a low-velocity short-barrel Ordnance QF 3pdr, although many customers chose a high-velocity type instead. The two-man turret was nevertheless an innovation that was widely praised as allowing a much greater rate of fire, and it was later widely copied. All versions of the Six-ton tank had a crew of three.

Vickers' wide experience in export markets ensured that overseas sales of the Mark E would be a success, and it compared well with its main rival, the French Renault FT tank. The first buyer was the Soviet Union, which bought 15 Type A models in 1931 and then purchased a licence to build the Type B, which they adapted to become the T-26. More than 12,000 were built in various versions, including bridgelayers and flamethrowers. Poland also bought 38 examples in 1932, 16 Type As and 22 Type Bs.

The Vickers Six-ton tank was produced commercially and was a very successful export in the 1930s. This one, used by the Finnish Army, had a 37mm Bofors anti-tank gun adapted as its main weapon. It is preserved at the Parola Armoured Vehicle Museum. (Richard Allen/WikiMedia Commons, CC-by-SA 2.0)

They modified their tanks when engine cooling problems became apparent, and eventually adapted the Mark E design to become their own 7TP tank.

Other overseas buyers, though mostly of much smaller quantities, were Bolivia, Bulgaria, China, Finland, Greece, Portugal and Siam. Inevitably, some of these were captured during warfare and ended up serving with other countries as well. When the Belgians put in an order, they wanted to replace the engine with a Rolls-Royce six-cylinder car engine. This required a major hull redesign, with the engine on the left and the turret moved to the right and rearwards. The Belgians rejected the evaluation example of what Vickers now called the Mark F, but the redesigned hull was used with the original Armstrong-Siddeley engine for the tanks sold to Finland and Siam. One Type A went to Japan in 1930, where it served as a study model in the development of that country's Type 95 Ha-Go tank.

Vickers further developed the Mark E as a cargo vehicle in 1934, and sold a dozen to the British Army as artillery tractors. These were known as the Dragon, Medium Mark IV. Others were sold to China, India, Poland and Siam, although both of the latter modified theirs considerably.

DIMENSIONS AND WEIGHT:
Length 16ft 10in, width 7ft 11in, height 7ft 1in. Weight 7.2 tons.

FURTHER READING:
The Vickers Tanks: From Landship to Challenger, Christopher Foss & Peter McKenzie.

VICKERS MARK F
This was an unsuccessful variant of the Vickers Mark E (see above).

VICKERS MBT MK 1
The Vickers MBT (Main Battle Tank) was designed as a low-cost and simple tank for export, and the model that appeared in prototype form in 1963 was in fact the second attempt at a design. The original plan was for a 24-tonne tank armed with a 20pdr gun and eight Vickers Vigilant anti-tank missiles to make it as effective as a Centurion but at a substantially lower cost. However, when British, German and US tanks adopted the 105mm L7 gun, it was clear that such a tank would be outclassed. A complete redesign followed.

The redesigned MBT was built with welded homogeneous armour plates that had twice the effective thickness of the original design, and yet was still 12 tonnes lighter than a Centurion. Vickers also incorporated the new engine and transmission that were intended for the Chieftain tank that was then under development, and the result was an effective fighting machine with good mobility. The design was later adapted to take a Detroit Diesel 12V-71T engine.

This MBT Mk 1 found buyers in Kuwait and India. The version for Kuwait was called the Al Jahra, and a total of 70 were delivered between 1970 and 1972. Several of these were captured by Iraqi forces during the First Gulf War in 1990-1991 and saw limited use by their captors, but all were eventually destroyed. The Indian version was called the Vijayanta (*qv*), and the majority were built in India.

DIMENSIONS AND WEIGHT:
Length 31ft 11in (with gun forward), width 10ft 5in, height 8ft 0in. Weight 42 short tons.

FURTHER READING:
The Vickers Tanks: From Landship to Challenger, Christopher Foss & Peter McKenzie.

VICKERS MBT MK 2
Still pursuing export sales, in 1968 Vickers developed a specification for an improved MBT that they called the Mk 2. This was to have an uprated Detroit Diesel engine and improved tracks that together would give a 35mph top speed. There were to be improvements to the hull front and to the turret, which would have a new commander's cupola to accept the vision devices used in the Chieftain. Reduced total weight, modified tracks and repositioned wheel stations would also reduce ground pressure.

Pictured when new, this Six-ton tank was one of 20 sold to the Kuomintang (Nationalist Army) in China. The short-barrelled main gun was a 47mm type. (Noabrotato/ WikiMedia Commons, CC-by-SA 4.0)

The Mk 3 version of the Vickers MBT with its redesigned turret was ordered by Kenya, where this one was pictured in service. (Doge, CC-by-SA 4.0)

The Mk 7 version of the Vickers MBT combined a German-made hull with the turret from the company's own Valiant and a 120mm gun. It did not progress beyond the prototype stage. (Hugh Llewellyn/WikiMedia Commons, CC-by-SA 2.0)

AVLBs between 1983 and 1995) and Tanzania, which took four ARVs in 1989.

VICKERS MBT MK 4
See Vickers Valiant.

VICKERS MBT MK 7
The MBT Mk7 prototype used a chassis made by Krauss-Maffei in Germany that was essentially that of a Leopard 2 MBT. To this was mounted a third-generation Vickers Valiant turret, with a Marconi digital fire control system, thermal imaging equipment and a panoramic sight. The Mk 7 also had features designed to reduce its heat signature and the risk of detection by night sights.

VICKERS MEDIUM TANKS
The Vickers Medium Tanks are not to be confused with the Medium tanks descended from the Whippet and which are listed here under M for Medium. The Vickers tanks were built primarily for export, although some certainly did serve with the British armed forces.

The Vickers tanks were the Medium Mark I (1924), Medium Mark II (1925), Medium Mark III (1930), Medium Mark C (1927), Medium Mark D (1929), Mark E or Six-ton (1931), and Mark F (1929). They all have their own alphabetical entries here.

VICKERS MEDIUM MARK C
The Vickers Medium Mark C was one of the first commercial tank designs from Vickers-Armstrongs. It was only ever produced for the Imperial Japanese Army, who took delivery of one example in March 1927 to study in advance of producing their own designs. The Medium Mark C had an influence on the design of the Japanese Type 89 Medium Tank.

The Medium Mark C was essentially a heavily modified Medium Mark II, with the engine relocated at the rear and six pairs of coil-sprung double-wheel bogies. The powerplant was a water-cooled six-cylinder Sunbeam Amazon type with 160bhp at 2100rpm, which was nearly twice as powerful as the Armstrong-Siddeley V8 in the Medium Mk II. Despite that, this 11.5-ton tank had a disappointing maximum speed of just 11mph.

It was equipped with a short-barrel 6pdr main gun and four machine guns, and the five-man crew was protected by pitifully thin armour that was just 6.5mm (0.25in) thick.

There would also be two Swingfire wire-guided anti-tank missiles on either side of the turret.

Although a mock-up based on a Mk 1 MBT was displayed at Farnborough, no production followed, and the project was probably cancelled in late 1970.

VICKERS MBT MK 3
The Mk 3 MBT was introduced as an export model in 1975. The main differences from the Mk 1 lay in the design of the turret, which combined a cast front with a main structure fabricated from armour plate. The main gun could be depressed to a greater extent than on the Mk 1 and the Mk 3 carried more ammunition.

The Kenyan military took delivery of 76 examples, plus a further seven ARV derivatives between 1979 and 1982. Subsequent customers were Nigeria (136 MBTs, 12 ARVs and 26

DIMENSIONS AND WEIGHT:
Length 17ft 6in, width 8ft 4in, height 8ft.
Weight 11.5 tons.

FURTHER READING:
The Vickers Tanks, from Landships to Challenger 2, Christopher Foss & Peter McKenzie.

VICKERS MEDIUM MARK D

This was a one-off export design built specially for the Irish Free State in 1929. In all but minor details, it was the same as the Vickers Medium Mark C that was sold to Japan.

The tank was supposedly capable of 20mph, which was considerably more than the Medium Mark C could achieve even though the Mark D was a ton heavier; perhaps there was some massaging of the figures by the sales department. It carried a 6pdr main gun, two Vickers .303 machine guns on the flanks and two more in the turret bustle and upper glacis plate respectively. The five-man crew consisted of commander, driver, gunner, and loader, and probably a machine gunner.

Just the one tank was built, and was used for training. The Irish then bought a pair of more modern Swedish tanks in 1934-1935 and the Vickers Medium Mark D was taken out of service. After suffering major damage during a training exercise in 1940, it was scrapped, although its turret and 6pdr gun were retained for static defence at Curragh Camp in Kildare, and the gun remains in the camp museum today.

DIMENSIONS AND WEIGHT:
Length 17ft 6in, width 8ft 4in, height 8ft.
Weight 12.5 tons.

FURTHER READING:
Forgotten Tanks and Guns of the 1920s, 1930s and 1940s, David Lister.

VICKERS MEDIUM MARK I (A2)

The Vickers Medium Mark I tank was accepted into service with the Royal Tank Regiment in 1924, but never fired a shot in anger and was withdrawn in 1938. It replaced some of the Mark V heavy tanks in British service and for many years was the most modern design of tank anywhere in the world.

When the Army began to look for a new Light Infantry Tank in 1920, Vickers-Armstrongs decided to develop a design to compete with the one of that name from the Department

of Tank Design under Lt Col Philip Johnson. Their first attempt was an 8.5-ton tank with a Williams-Jenney hydraulic transmission that proved unreliable, and was abandoned in 1922. Nevertheless, Vickers persevered and carried over this first design's features of sprung suspension and a fully revolving turret to a second design.

The General Staff allocated the designation of A2 to the Vickers design, and the first prototypes went on trial at Bovington in 1923. Initially described as the Light Tank Mark I, it was renamed the Medium Tank Mark I in 1924. A single close-support variant (the second prototype, A2E2) was built in 1923 with a 15pdr mortar in place of the main weapon.

Thirty tanks were built to the original 11.7-ton design, which had a low track run that incorporated five double-wheel bogies mounted on unequal-length helical springs. The engine was an Armstrong-Siddeley 8.8-litre V8 with 90bhp.

The hull layout was unconventional, with the engine next to the driver at the front, the

The Vickers Medium Mk I entered service in 1924 and was withdrawn shortly before the Second World War. This picture shows three examples on manoeuvres in Britain. (Public Domain)

The sole surviving Vickers Medium Mk I is at the Special Service Battalion Museum in South Africa. (GC Hurley/WikiMedia Commons, CC-by-SA 4.0)

four-speed gearbox in the middle, and the final drive with an epicyclic gear for each track at the rear. There was no compartmentalisation to ease conditions for the crew, which in terms of design was a step backwards. On top of the hull was a bevelled cylindrical turret with a QF 3pdr main gun and four ball mountings for Hotchkiss machine guns; in practice, a single gun was moved from mounting to mounting because of space restrictions. There was also a single Vickers machine gun on each side of the hull. Armour was very poor, with a maximum thickness of just 0.25in (6.25mm).

The Vickers Medium Mark I had a five-man crew, made up of a commander, driver, gunner, loader (who also operated the turret machine gun) and hull machine gunner (who doubled as a mechanic). The turret was arranged to accommodate three crew members, which brought the advantage that the commander had only a single role and was able to concentrate fully on it. The tank had a range of 120 miles and a maximum speed of 15mph, but the double-wheel bogie suspension proved troublesome and was changed for the next iteration of the design in 1931.

There were 50 of that next iteration, which was called the Medium Mark IA and came with a stronger design of box bogie suspension. The armour was increased to 0.3in (8mm) on vertical surfaces, and there were other minor changes. An upgrade in service then created the Mark IA*, its turret rebuilt with an independently traversable "bishop's mitre" cupola for the commander. The Hotchkiss machine gun mountings were also removed and a co-axial Vickers machine gun was installed, counterbalanced by a lead weight at the rear of the turret.

One Mark I was rebuilt experimentally in 1926 with four large rubber-tyred wheels that could be lowered to improve its mobility on the road, but the experiment was abandoned because the tank was unstable when running on wheels. The original Mk I close-support tank was one of two CS types that were shipped to South Africa in August 1934; it was used for several experiments before being returned to standard in Britain and used for training at Bovington. A dozen Mark IA tanks were rebuilt as close support vehicles in the early 1930s with the 15-pound mortar and were redesignated Mark IA CS types.

Of the 140 Vickers Medium Mark I tanks built, just one has survived. This is preserved at the South African Special Service Battalion Museum in Bloemfontein.

DIMENSIONS AND WEIGHT:
Length 17ft 6in, width 9ft 1.5in, height 9ft 3in. Weight 11.7 tons.

FURTHER READING:
Mediums Marks I-II, NW Duncan; *The Vickers Tanks, from Landships to Challenger 2*, Christopher Foss & Peter McKenzie.

VICKERS MEDIUM MARK II

The Medium Mark II was a further development of the Vickers Medium Mark I that was introduced in 1925. The first 100 were modified in two groups in 1930-1931, and a further 20 were built in 1930 to Mk IIA standard for use in Egypt. Vickers also sold small numbers of the tank to Australia and South Africa. The British Army Medium Mark II tanks were gradually withdrawn from 1939 and replaced by the Cruiser Mark I, but a few were reactivated briefly in the summer of 1940 as preparation for the threat of a German invasion.

These tanks used the same chassis, engine, transmission and suspension as the Medium Mark I but now with Rackham clutches that provided an early form of mechanical servo control. They had a taller superstructure at the front with the driver's visor relocated at the top. They had a stronger box-bogie type suspension, this time protected by armoured skirts, and their extra weight made them slightly slower than the Mark Is, with a maximum speed down from 15mph to 13mph.

The main armament was again a 3pdr gun, this time the Mk I L32 with a longer barrel than on the Medium Mark I and with a Hotchkiss machine gun in a separate ball mount to its right. The turret contained three further machine guns, and its rear face was sloped so that the rear-facing gun could be used against aircraft. As on the Mark I, there was also a Vickers machine gun in each side of the hull to the rear.

The Medium tanks first saw combat in 1935 on the Northwest Frontier of British India (now Pakistan) against the Mohmands. Some went to Egypt in November 1939 where they were supposedly used for experiments by Major-General Sir Percy Hobart and his Mobile Division. At least one still survived as a pillbox in Egypt in early 1941, and there is some evidence that Mk IIs fought against Italian troops in the Western Desert.

Vickers sold 21 or 22 examples of the Medium Mark II to overseas armed forces. Two female

Mark IIs were built in 1927 for the Indian Government, with four Vickers machine guns in the turret instead of the main gun. These had the cumbersome official designation of Tank Light Mark IA Special (L) India. The Australians took four in 1929, with their favoured Vickers machine guns rather than the standard Hotchkiss type. These were the country's first tanks and were initially used purely for training purposes. The other 15 (possibly 16) sold overseas went to the Soviet Union in 1931, where Maxim guns replaced the Hotchkiss machine guns. Only one was supplied with a 3pdr gun, and the others were presumably fitted with Soviet-made main guns on arrival. These had no cupola, less pronounced bevelling of the turret, and cowled ventilation fans on the side of the hull. Some were sent to the Karelian peninsula, where they were dug in as bunkers.

Of the first 100 delivered to the British Army in 1924-1927, 56 were modified in 1930 to Mark II* standard. Their Hotchkiss machine guns were removed, a Vickers co-axial machine gun was added, the commander's post was moved rearwards and a lead weight was added to counterbalance the turret. The remaining 44 tanks of the original delivery were brought up to Mark II* standard in 1932; in this case, an armoured box for a radio was fitted to the back of the turret, and the turret roof was modified, losing its "bishop's mitre" commander's cupola. The weight of the Mark II** rose to 13.5 tons.

There was then a further order for 20 tanks intended for use in Egypt, and these were built in 1930 to Mark IIA specification. They were broadly similar to the Mark II* types but did not have the "bishop's mitre" cupola and had an armoured ventilator fan on the left of the turret. Probably all were later upgraded to Mark IIA* when they were retro-fitted with the cupola.

Five tanks were shipped to Egypt in 1928, where they were insulated against the heat with items that included spaced asbestos plates on the upper surfaces. A few Mark IIAs were rebuilt to CS standard when, like the similarly modified Mark Is, they lost their main guns to a 15pdr (3.7in) howitzer. The main intention was to provide smoke cover, although the tanks also carried some HE shells. Weight in these cases increased to 14 tons. There was also a project to convert Mark IIs into bridge carriers, but it did not go beyond prototype form because the bridge had to be laid manually, which exposed the crew to enemy fire.

Two Mark IIs were also converted to Command Tanks in the later 1920s, with a large rectangular superstructure in place of the turret and a single machine gun at the front of it for self-defence. Four more were supposedly ordered, but not built. A Mark II* was also converted in 1931 by fixing the turret in place, fitting a dummy gun in place of the main armament, and mounting an additional radio in the space freed up.

In the late 1920s seven prototype self-propelled guns were built from Medium Mark II chassis. These were known as Birch Guns (after Sir Noel Birch, Master-General of Ordnance) and had an open fighting compartment with an 18pdr field gun that enjoyed a 36-degree traverse. The design was progressively improved

The Birch Gun was an attempt to create a self-propelled gun on the chassis of a Vickers Medium Mk II. The project did not go beyond the prototype stage. (Public Domain)

The front of the hull on a Vickers Medium Mk II has some very obvious differences from its Mk I predecessor, and the armoured skirts are clearly visible here.

from one to the next, and some sources claim that one version had a lengthened chassis and a 75mm gun. A picture suggests that one was given a substantial casemate in place of the open fighting compartment. However, the Birch Gun project was dropped when the Royal Artillery decided to focus on towed field guns.

There are three survivors of the claimed 167 Medium Mark II tanks built. One is at the Tank Museum in Bovington, one in the Royal Australian Armoured Corps Tank Museum at Puckapunyal, and the third is in store at the U.S. Army Center for Military History in Anniston, Alabama.

DIMENSIONS AND WEIGHT:
Length 17ft 6in, width 9ft 1in, height 9ft 3in. Weight 11.7 tons.

FURTHER READING:
Mediums Marks I–II, NW Duncan; *The Vickers Tanks, from Landships to Challenger 2*, Christopher Foss & Peter McKenzie.

VICKERS MEDIUM MARK II

The Medium Mark III was an unsuccessful Vickers design of which just three examples were built. It followed directly from the company's unsuccessful A6 design, and was really a heavily improved version of that with the same 180bhp Armstrong-Siddeley V8 engine. Design began in 1928.

Two prototypes were built in 1930 by the Royal Ordnance Factory at Woolwich, and a third by Vickers themselves in 1931. This was another multi-turreted design, but this time the rear turret was deleted and the two front machine-gun turrets were moved forwards to improve the weight distribution. The armour and brakes were both improved, and there was a new main turret with a bustle at the rear to accommodate radio equipment. In trials, the tank provided a more stable gun platform than its A6 predecessor and promised both a 120-mile range and a 30mph top speed, but the suspension proved weak in cross-country use. The third prototype had suspension improvements, but overall the design was not good enough to prompt an order.

In 1933, the three prototypes were purchased by the Royal Tank Corps and became HQ tanks. One took part in the 1934 Salisbury Plain exercises (where it was used by Brigadier Sir Percy Hobart) but was written off soon afterwards; the second prototype was destroyed by fire; and the remaining vehicle was withdrawn in 1938 and scrapped.

Information about the Vickers Mark III design was sold to the Soviet Union by a British officer in 1933, and it is sometimes suggested that it influenced the design of the Soviet T-28 Medium Tank.

There are no survivors of the Vickers Medium Mk III tank.

DIMENSIONS AND WEIGHT:
Length 21ft 6in, width 8ft 9in, height 9ft 2in. Weight 16 tons.

FURTHER READING:
Mechanised Force, David Fletcher.

VICKERS NO 1 TANK

During 1921, the Master General of the Ordnance worked with Vickers on the design of a new tank, which became known as the Vickers no 1. Three prototypes were ordered, the first being completed in November that year.

Visually similar to the existing rhomboid tanks, the Vickers no 1 had a domed turret with three equally spaced barbettes that contained ball mounts for Hotchkiss machine guns. There was a fourth ball mount in the roof of the turret for a machine gun to protect against air attack, and the tank had a five-man crew. The engine was a six-cylinder Wolseley type (probably a 24hp 3.9-litre), mounted at the rear and driving very basic tracks through a Williams-Jenney hydraulic transmission of the type used in the Mk VIII tank.

Vickers themselves considered their prototype too noisy and lacking in reliability. They

Just three Vickers Medium Mk III prototypes were built, and their design followed the vogue for multiple turrets on tanks. (Imperial War Museum, KID 4625)

nevertheless delivered it to the War Office's tank testing section at Farnborough, where the transmission overheated badly. In tests against the Light Infantry Tank and a Vickers Medium D, the Vickers no 1 came a resounding last. It was returned to Vickers in 1922 and was given a more powerful engine and improved tracks. The War Office accepted it back but carried out no more testing, and by March 1923 the tank had been consigned to the stores.

DIMENSIONS AND WEIGHT:
No details available. Weight 8.75 tons.

FURTHER READING:
Mechanised Force, David Fletcher; *Forgotten Tanks and Guns of the 1920s, 1930s and 1940s*, David Lister.

VICKERS NO 2 TANK

Following on from the Vickers no 1 tank, work began in July 1922 on the second of the three prototypes that the Master General of the Ordnance had ordered in 1921. Unsurprisingly known as the Vickers no 2 tank, this one was again designed for a five-man crew. Its design incorporated new direction from the Director General of Artillery that all future tanks should have a quick-firing gun. The gun chosen was a 3pdr, a weapon with a higher velocity than was normal in tanks of the time and one which therefore also met the General Staff policy about an ability to counter other tanks. A single Hotchkiss machine gun provided the secondary armament.

The tank was completed in July 1923, and was powered by an 80hp Lanchester six-cylinder car engine. Unfortunately nothing is known about the trials to which the prototype was subjected. Certainly, the project led nowhere, and the Vickers no 2 prototype was scrapped in 1927.

The third prototype for the MGO was not built as a tank but rather as a tracked field gun carrier. There is an unproven theory that it was early evidence of the thinking that led to the later Dragon gun tractors.

DIMENSIONS AND WEIGHT:
No information available. Weight 10 tons.

FURTHER READING:
Mechanised Force, David Fletcher; *Forgotten Tanks and Guns of the 1920s, 1930s and 1940s*, David Lister.

VICKERS SIX-TON TANK
See the entry for the Vickers Mark E.

VICKERS T-15 LIGHT TANK
The T-15 was a hybrid of Vickers Commercial and Vickers Light Tank designs, built for the Belgian Army to replace earlier Renault FT tanks. It entered service in 1934-1935.

Like the standard Light Tank Mk III, the T-15 had a Horstmann suspension and Wilson preselector gearbox, but the Belgians chose the 88bhp Meadows engine that was standard on the Vickers Commercial models. They also took a special conical turret with a cast gun mantle to suit armament of their own manufacture. There was an electric turret traverse but no provision for a radio. The main gun was a 13.2mm Hotchkiss type that was already in use for anti-aircraft duties, and this was supplemented by a single pintle-mounted 7.65mm Browning automatic rifle that was intended for anti-aircraft defence. The whole tank was much lighter

The Vickers no 1 tank was an abject failure, but its revolving-turret design represented a stage in the move away from rhomboid tanks with their armament carried in side sponsons. (Imperial War Museum)

The Vickers T-15 was a version of the company's Light Tank Mk III for the Belgian Army. This one was pictured at a review in 1940, with King Leopold III and General Denis, the Belgian Minister for War. (Public Domain)

than the standard Vickers Mk III thanks to a much lower level of armour, which was 7-9mm thick rather than the standard 12-14mm. As a result, these tanks were very fast, with a top speed of 40mph and a range of 140 miles.

For political reasons (mainly a fear of provoking their neighbours in Germany), the Belgians decided to describe these tanks as reconnaissance vehicles, the full official description becoming Char Léger de Reconnaissance Vickers-Carden-Loyd Mod.1934 T.15 (1934 model Light Reconnaissance Tank type T-15 by Vickers-Carden-Loyd). Budgetary constraints caused the order to be split into two, and the first 18 were ordered in March 1934, a further 24 being ordered in April 1935 after these had been delivered. Final deliveries were in November-December 1935. In the later 1930s, the tanks were modified with an extra FN Herstal machine gun on the turret roof for air defence.

The tanks showed some problems in service. Notably, the soft suspension caused pitching which hindered accurate gunlaying, and the vehicles suffered from mechanical unreliability. They were still in service at the start of the Second World War, when they were captured by the Germans and used in France until spares supplies ran out.

There are no known survivors of the Vickers T-15 tank.

DIMENSIONS AND WEIGHT:
Length 11ft 11in, width 6ft 2in, height 6ft 3in. Weight 3.74 tons.

FURTHER READING:
The Vickers Tanks from Landships to Challenger 2, Christopher Foss & Peter McKenzie.

VICKERS VALIANT

The Valiant (not to be confused with the wartime A38 Valiant tank) was a late 1970s Vickers design that never entered production but its development programme did provide valuable experience in the production of an aluminium-hulled tank with Chobham armour.

The tank was known to Vickers as the Mk 4 MBT when development began in 1976. Early trials used a 915bhp GM Detroit Diesel 12V-71T engine but the focus then switched to a 1000bhp Rolls-Royce CV12 TCA Condor diesel (detuned from the 1200bhp Challenger engine in the interests of greater longevity). The fully automatic transmission was derived from

the Chieftain's six-speed TN12 type. The tank's torsion bar suspension was similar to that on Vickers' Mk 1 and Mk 3 MBTs but incorporated secondary torsion bars at some wheel stations.

The Mk 4 MBT was initially designed to mount the L7 105mm rifled gun, and in this guise, it was shown as a prototype at BAEE in June 1980. Secondary armament could be either 7.62mm or 12.7mm (.50 cal) MG mounted coaxially and on the commander's cupola. There was to be a Marconi fire control system, but observation and sighting equipment could be specified to suit the customer.

At that same show, Vickers also showed the prototype of a new welded steel universal turret fitted with the Chieftain's 120mm L11 gun. The turret's design allowed for a variety of main weapons to be fitted, and also made it possible for the main gun to be removed without first separating the turret from the hull. By BAEE June 82, the Mk 4 MBT had been extensively tested with this new turret, which incorporated several state-of-the-art components, and had been renamed the Valiant. A 7.62mm Hughes Chain Gun was now available as the co-axial MG. The Valiant was also tested with a 120mm Rheinmetall smooth bore gun.

In early 1983 the tank was tested in the Middle East, where it showed excellent fire-power and fire control; it had a top speed of 38mph and a range of more than 370 miles, but its mobility proved disappointing. Vickers decided to cease development in January 1984 although marketing effort continued until July 1985. A further development of the Valiant's turret was later used for the Vickers Mk 7 MBT.

DIMENSIONS AND WEIGHT:
Length 24ft 8in (34ft 10in with gun forward), width 10ft 10in 11ft 10in with appliqué armour), height 8ft 1 2/3in. Weight 43.6 tonnes (Mk4 MBT) or 47 tonnes (Valiant).

FURTHER READING:
The Vickers Tanks from Landships to Challenger 2, Christopher Foss & Peter McKenzie.

VIJAYANTA

During 1961, while Vickers was developing its MBT Mk1, the company reached agreement with the Indian armed forces to deliver a tank design and help set up a factory in India to build it. One of the MBT prototypes was sent to India in 1963, and the Indian tank was developed

The Vijayanta that was sold to India in the 1960s was a derivative of the Vickers MBT Mk 1. Large numbers were built under licence in India. This is one of three preserved at the National War Memorial, Southern Command, at Pune. (Mohit S/ WikiMedia Commons, CC by 2.0)

from this. It was given the name of Vijayanta, which translates as "victorious".

The first 90 Vijayanta tanks were built by Vickers in the UK, and the first examples entered service in December 1965, just too late for the war with Pakistan. The remainder were built in India, at the Heavy Vehicles Factory in Avadi (a suburb of Chennai, the former Madras). Some sources claim that as many as 2200 were built before production was halted in 1983, but this figure is disputed and other sources claim that there were no more than 1800 Indian-built tanks. The Vijayanta tanks were first used in battle during the Bangladesh Liberation War in 1971.

The Vijayanta tanks had a crew of four. They had six equally-spaced road wheels, each with independent torsion bar suspension, and were powered by a 535bhp Leyland L60 diesel engine driving through a David Brown TH12 semi-automatic gearbox. They had a maximum speed of 31mph with a range of 330 miles. The turret was similar to that of the Centurion but smaller, and the main gun was an L7 105mm type. Later models had the L7AS2 variant. A 12.7mm heavy machine gun and a 7.7mm machine gun were both mounted co-axially, and some tanks also had a second 12.7mm machine gun on a roof pintle mount.

These tanks had less armour than the Centurions already in Indian service, with no more than 80mm on the glacis plate and the turret, but this was enough to counter the elderly Patton tanks of the Pakistani forces, especially as the range of the L7 gun gave the Vijayanta a stand-off capability.

There were three basic Marks of Vijayanta. The Mk 1 types had a Marconi SFCS 600 fire control system, but on the Mk 1A the fire control system was a Bharat Electronics AL4420 type with improved sight mounts. The Mk 1B then had an AL4421 system that incorporated a laser sight by Barr & Stroud in Britain and a computer to improve first-round hit probability. There were two upgrades, known as Mk 1C and Mk 2. The Indian forces also conducted trials with a Vickers GBT 155 turret and an ROF 39-calibre gun but did not adopt these.

In the mean time, increasing Russian influence persuaded the Indians to turn in that direction for military equipment. There was a plan in 1997 to re-engine about half the fleet, probably with the 780hp V-84 engine used in the Russian T-72 tank, but this was shelved and the intention was to replace the Vijayanta completely by 2008. Its replacement, unsurprisingly, was a licence-built version of the T-72 itself.

There were also variants of the Vijayanta: an armoured bridgelayer, an assault tank designed to tackle canal embankments, and an ARV. After withdrawal from front-line service, some tanks were converted to Self-Propelled Guns that mounted a Russian weapon.

Several Viajayanta tanks have been preserved. There are examples at Port Blair on South Andaman island in the Bay of Bengal and at the National War Museum in New Delhi, while the National War Memorial at Pune has three.

DIMENSIONS AND WEIGHT:
Length 32ft 1in, width 10ft 5in, height 8ft 11in. Weight 43 short tons.

FURTHER READING:
The Vickers Tanks from Landships to Challenger 2, Christopher Foss & Peter McKenzie.

WHIPPET
See Medium Mark A.

Chapter 3
TANK ENGINES

It should come as no surprise that the choice of the engine for the first tanks in 1916 was entirely dependent on what was already in production – or that the choice was not great. At that stage, no British manufacturer was making an engine capable of moving a 27-ton road vehicle, and the engine that came nearest to meeting the requirement was the 105bhp, 13.5-litre six-cylinder built by Daimler and intended for heavy haulage tractors. Although it made its contribution to the success of those first tanks, it must have been clear from very early on that it could be little better than a stop-gap solution: something better was needed. There was also a certain irony in the fact that it had been designed by a German company and was now to be used against Germany in Britain's war with that country.

Before 1916 was out, some of the best engineers of the day were working on improvements, both to reduce the engine's smoke (which instantly revealed the tank's position on the battlefield) and increase its power. None other than WO Bentley got the power up to 125bhp, but his suggested improvements were not carried forward, perhaps because they were linked with to an experimental electric drive system. A good look at the existing engine convinced Harry Ricardo that the only solution was a completely new design, and during 1917 he came up with a tank engine that delivered 150bhp and made a much better job of moving these heavy machines around.

Meanwhile, the War Office had begun to think in terms of an alternative type of tank, one that would be lighter and faster and could to some extent emulate the traditional cavalry role of exploiting breakthroughs made by the infantry. This would not need such a large and heavy engine, but to achieve the necessary speed it would need plenty of power. Once again, the choices were limited, and for the Medium Mark A or Whippet that appeared in late 1917 the desired result was achieved by harnessing two 45bhp 7.7-litre Tylor lorry engines together to deliver 90bhp. That was enough to propel the 14-ton tank at just over 8mph or about four times as fast as the original rhomboid tanks could manage.

Experts in the field now began to look around for more powerful engines that were readily available, and it was Philip Johnson, later head of the British Department of Tank Design, who decided to try using an aero engine for the job. His choice fell on the Rolls-Royce Eagle, a 20-litre V12 with 300bhp that had been created by mounting two enlarged and modified Silver Ghost car engines on a common crankcase and was used in the Handley Page bomber aircraft of the time. Although his trial with one in a Whippet tank in 1918 did not lead on to any production changes or an upgrade programme, Johnson persevered with the idea and used the aero engine again in later experimental tanks.

The huge strides made in aero engine design during the Great War led others to follow Johnson's example, perhaps without even knowing of his experiments. The American-made Liberty aero engine had entered production in 1917, and was an obvious candidate for the US contribution to the joint Mk VIII or International tank design that was ready just after the war had ended in 1919. This was another 300bhp engine, and it set a power benchmark for tank engines for the next few years. Even so, 300bhp did not make a radical difference to tank speeds, and the Mk VIII could only just exceed 5mph.

With that 300bhp benchmark in view, Harry Ricardo was commissioned to design an alternative to the Liberty engine that could be made in Britain, and this was an engine specifically intended for tank use. However, the demise of the Mk VIII tank project ensured that few of these engines were actually built. Philip Johnson was meanwhile looking at the Armstrong-Siddeley Puma aero engine from another bomber aircraft, and tried one in his Medium D tank prototype in 1919. Uprated to the magical 300bhp for the 1920 Medium D**, it was also favoured by Vickers (who were part of the same group of engineering companies as Armstrong-

There was a constant search for the "right" tank engine before the Rolls-Royce Meteor became available. Here, a Matilda II called Horace receives an engine upgrade at the MG car works in Abingdon; the photograph is dated 9th January 1941. The original AEC engine set has been removed and stands on trestles, and on the floor is a new set of Leyland engines. (British Motor Industry Heritage Trust)

Siddeley) throughout the following decade for several experimental designs.

Aero engines certainly looked like the way ahead for British tanks in the 1920s, and at a time when the War Office had given a relatively low priority to tanks as a whole there was no chance that they would fund development of any dedicated tank engines. The idea of using diesel engines briefly gained some enthusiasm, a key benefit being seen as the lower flammability of the fuel, but although a Beardmore four-cylinder diesel was tried in a Mk V tank during 1923, the project went no further at this stage.

Meanwhile, as the idea of the smaller and lighter Medium tank took hold, so designers realised that smaller, less powerful and, above all, readily available car engines might be adapted as their power units. In 1921-1922, Vickers proposed first a Wolseley and then a Lanchester car engine in their experimental tanks for the Master General of the Ordnance. Three years later, Carden-Loyd (who would later be absorbed into Vickers) used a 40bhp 2.9-litre Ford Model T car engine for their small Tankette, which attracted both British Army orders and plenty of export business. Another area of the automotive industry provided the engine for the Royal Ordnance Factories' abor-

tive A3 or Three-man Light Tank in 1926, when AEC were asked to provide the 5.1-litre engine from their buses and lorries. Whether this provided the 52bhp claimed in tank documentation is debatable; AEC never claimed more than 40bhp for their production engines.

Then at the other end of the automotive scale, Vickers planned to use Rolls-Royce car engines in their designs. In 1931, they favoured a 66bhp version of that maker's Goshawk car engine for their Light Tank Mk II, and in 1933 proposed the much-admired 120bhp engine from the Phantom II for their Mark F design. The company also planned to use a pair of these 7.7-litre engines working in tandem to give 240bhp in their proposal for the A8 Medium tank. However, neither of these later designs reached production. Specialist engine maker Meadows provided their 4.5-litre six-cylinder car engine for several Vickers-designed tanks from 1933, offering around 85bhp, and car engines were still favoured as late as 1936, when the little Matilda I appeared with a 70bhp 3.6-litre Ford V8 engine.

It was during 1936 that the British Government began to take the threat of war with Nazi Germany seriously, and to reinforce the country's war readiness. That there would be a need for tanks was not in doubt, and Meadows were "invited" to prepare two dedicated tank engine designs. Both were drawn up as flat-12 types, the first being an 8.8-litre with just under 150bhp that went into the Tetrarch light tank of 1938 and the second a 16-litre size that delivered that magic figure of 300bhp and was commissioned especially for the 1939 Covenanter, although other uses were also envisaged. Lord Nuffield was determined to get in on the re-armament act and in 1937 took out a licence to manufacture the American Liberty engine, which by this stage was delivering as much as 340bhp. He used his industrial strength to get this engine into several British wartime tanks, although the Liberty by then was not only an elderly design but bulky by more modern standards.

Meanwhile, that brush with AEC commercial-vehicle engines in the mid-1920s had also led on to new things, and the idea of pairing automotive engines to achieve a higher power output gained further ground. When the first versions of the ROF-designed A7 Medium tank proved unsuccessful, it was re-engined. The revised 1934 version replaced its single Armstrong-Siddeley aero engine by a pair of AEC diesel engines that delivered a respectable power output. The A7 went no further, but the use of AEC commercial-vehicle engines did. In 1938, the company's new 9.6-litre diesel engine, originally drawn up for London Transport's buses, appeared in the A9 and A10 Cruiser tank designs, and a year later detuned versions of the engine appeared in the Matilda II's twin-engine set-up, delivering a total of 174bhp.

Increasing reliance on AEC for tank engines soon led to that company's manufacturing capacity being reached, but in the mean time the Army called for a petrol-powered version of the 9.6-litre engine, which from 1940 delivered a rather feeble 135bhp in the Valentine. Later that year, it was again AEC who provided Valentine engines, in this case paired versions of the latest 9.6-litre diesel that delivered 262bhp between them. Partly to relieve the pressure on AEC, the focus now switched to Bedford, who rapidly designed their 350bhp Twin-Six engine of 21.2 litres for the Churchill tank by mounting two of their existing lorry engines on a single crankcase. When Leyland were asked to join the tank engine programme, they provided paired diesel bus engines to replace the AEC petrol engines in the early Matildas.

As an aside, it is worth noting that the Americans were not in a much better position, even if they were able to manufacture tank engines more quickly and in greater quantities. Their 400bhp Continental R-975 tank engine was another design derived from an aero engine but this had its shortcomings and, in any case, there was a huge demand for the Wright Whirlwind aero engine that was its basis at the time. As in Britain, engines were harnessed together (the 1941 Chrysler multi-bank type being the prime example), and the Americans also turned to big diesel engines from their commercial vehicle industry, such as the 210bhp GM 6004 type that was used in some versions of the Valentine.

The next important development was already in the offing, when Rolls-Royce reacted to a suggestion from Leyland that their highly respected Merlin aero engine might make a good basis for a tank engine. It did. Suitably modified, it emerged in 1942 as the power unit of the Cromwell tank, with the name of Meteor and a massive 540bhp that finally gave Britain the tank it needed. The engine went on to power other British tanks of the Second World War and would remain the country's primary tank engine until the middle of the 1950s. It also sired a V8 derivative called the Meteorite, which was planned for various experimental tanks as early as 1944 and became a successful heavy commercial and military vehicle engine.

By the mid-1950s, Britain had finally recognised the need for a dedicated tank engine and now committed the resources to design and build it. When NATO called for all military vehicle engines to be multi-fuel types designed to run on whatever fuel might be available, Leyland Motors abandoned plans to use a Rolls-Royce diesel V8 in their new tank and drew up their own design called the L60. Introduced with the Chieftain tank in 1965, the new engine initially proved troublesome (and NATO eventually abandoned its multi-fuel policy) but by the late 1970s was producing 840bhp and was considered reliable.

When the time came for a Chieftain replacement, there could be no question that the new tank would need a dedicated engine. The one chosen for Challenger, which entered service in 1983, was a 1200bhp turbocharged diesel V12 known as the Condor. That engine, more recently manufactured by Perkins who bought out the Rolls-Royce diesel interests, has been developed further to deliver a reliable 1500bhp for the Challenger 3 upgrade that is planned to enter service from 2027.

Each of these engines, and some others too, has its own entry in the alphabetical list that follows. It is worth noting that many otherwise excellent books about tanks have tended to skip over the details of their engines, and one result of this is that there are wide variations in the power and torque outputs quoted, and even in the detail specification of some engines. The figures given here are the ones that appear most accurate.

AEC DIESEL ENGINES
AEC was a major manufacturer of buses and trucks and during the Second World War became a major supplier of heavy vehicles to the British armed forces. However, its first tank engine did not appear until the late 1930s, and was in fact derived from a bus engine.

A179
The London Passenger Transport Board asked AEC for a diesel bus engine of larger capacity than the existing 8.8-litre type in the belief that it would be less stressed and would give better fuel economy. AEC enlarged the bore of their 8.8-litre production engine to give a 9.6-litre capacity, thus creating an engine much larger and more powerful than any earlier British bus engine from any manufacturer. It had a swept volume of 9636cc (588 cu in) from a 120mm bore and a 142mm stroke.

The first version of this engine was the A179, which had indirect injection. It appears not to have been put into production for any buses (which used later developments of it) but did enter production for the A9 and A10 Cruiser tanks. In the A9, it was chosen by Leslie Little to replace the unsatisfactory Rolls-Royce car engine that had powered the prototype.

The A179 version of the AEC 9.6-litre diesel was built with a dry sump lubrication system and is usually quoted as delivering 150bhp, although its actual power output in tank form was probably rather less. It was in production in 1939-1940 and was replaced by the further-developed A190.

A183 and A184
These were special versions of the AEC 6.75-litre diesel engine that were used in pairs in the Matilda tank. They had a bore of 105mm, a stroke of 130mm, and seven main bearings.

Each engine delivered 87bhp at 2000rpm (the commercial-vehicle versions had 95bhp) and they drove the transmission through a special linking unit. These engines were handed, an A183 type being installed on the left of the hull and an A184 on the right; the main differences between them were in the position of the auxiliaries.

A190
The A190 engine was a direct-injection derivative of AEC's A179 six-cylinder diesel that became available in 1940. In its bus form, for the first 151 examples of the London Transport RT class (always known as the "pre-war" RTs, although they were built in 1939-1942) it developed 125bhp at 1800rpm and 430 lb ft of torque at 1000rpm. The further-developed tank version of the engine had 131bhp at 1800rpm and 498 lb ft at 1250rpm.

The power pack installation in the Matilda II consisted of two essentially identical engines side by side. These pictures show the AEC A183 and A184 diesel engines; at the top, the installation is viewed from the right-hand rear of the tank, while the lower picture shows the view from the front of the tank. The two engine designations resulted from minor differences in ancillaries that distinguished the left-hand engine from the right-hand one.

This engine replaced the unreliable A189 petrol version of the 9.6-litre AEC six-cylinder in the Valentine tank in late 1940, and this now became an Infantry Tank Mk III* (known from summer 1941 as a Valentine II). It also went into the Bishop self-propelled gun that was based on the Valentine. However, its success was relatively short-lived, not least because by 1941 AEC was swamped with military orders for engines. For this reason alone, the engine was replaced in the Valentine by the General Motors 6004 diesel, and the tank became a Valentine IV.

AEC PETROL ENGINES
A118
The engine used in the unsuccessful A3 or Three-man Light Tank of 1926 was a commercially-available AEC four-cylinder type that was claimed to deliver 52bhp in tank form. The most likely candidate for this engine is the A118 5.1-litre that was then used in both buses and lorries, although AEC never claimed more than 40bhp for it.

A189
The War Office was unhappy about using a diesel engine (in the shape of the AEC A179) and insisted on a petrol engine for the new Valentine tank. AEC obligingly developed a petrol version of their still-new 9.6-litre A179 diesel engine, which is claimed to have developed 135bhp at 1900rpm and 492 lb ft of torque at 1200rpm.

The first deliveries of the A189-engined Valentine Mk I were made in May 1940, but the

This demonstration cutaway unit of the Bedford Twin Six engine survives at the Bovington Tank Museum. The two engines were horizontally opposed to minimise height, and powered a common crankshaft.

engine soon proved to be chronically unreliable – perhaps unsurprisingly as it had not initially been designed as a petrol unit at all. As a result, the War Office admitted defeat and specified the latest diesel version of the 9.6-litre, the A190, for the Valentine Mk II.

ARMSTRONG-SIDDELEY
The Armstrong-Siddeley engine used in the Vickers Medium tanks, beginning with the Mk I in 1924 and ending in the early 1930s, has usually been described as a version of the company's RAF 1a aero engine that was derived from the French Renault 70/80hp in the BE2c aircraft. However, it now appears that it was actually a different engine that merely drew on the design of the RAF 1a. It had a smaller capacity than the aero engine, of 7826cc (rather than 8.8 litres), with a 4in (102mm) bore and a 4¾in (121mm) stroke.

Like the aero engine, it was a 90-degree V8. Air cooling was adopted because it was considered to be best for a slow-moving vehicle operating in tropical conditions. The first versions were designed in 1923 for the Supply Carrier, and a lightly modified version was then used for the tanks. The tank engine delivered 90bhp at 3500rpm, and was last used in the seven experimental Birch Gun derivatives of the Medium Mark II.

Armstrong-Siddeley also continued production of the Siddeley Puma engine (qv) after Armstrong Whitworth bought the Siddeley company and changed its name to Armstrong-Siddeley.

BEDFORD TWIN SIX
The Bedford Twin-Six engine was developed initially for the aborted A20 tank, to fit into an engine compartment designed for the 300bhp Meadows engine that was proving underpowered. A prototype A20 was sent to Vauxhall Motors at Luton, and their response was to create an engine based on two existing production six-cylinder Bedford lorry engines (Bedford was the commercial-vehicles arm of Vauxhall); the first engine ran less than three months after the design had begun on the drawing-board. After the A20 was cancelled, the engine was used for the A22 Churchill tank built by Vauxhall.

The engine was designed as a flat-12, the two six-cylinder engines being horizontally opposed and powering a common crankshaft. This configuration led to its name of Twin Six, and it was also known as a Bedford Type 120 engine. The total swept volume was 21,238cc (1296 cubic inches), and the power output was typically 350bhp at 2200rpm, with 960 lb ft (1300Nm) of torque between 800 rpm and 1600rpm. Each group of six cylinders had two cylinder heads serving three cylinders each, and a single Solex 46 FNHE carburettor fed each group of three cylinders. There were high-squish pistons, a dual ignition system, and sodium-cooled exhaust valves in Stellite seats.

The outputs of the Twin Six were considerably greater than those available from any other British tank engine at the time, but provided the heavy Churchill with relatively poor performance, even for an Infantry tank.

CADILLAC TWIN V8

When a shortage of Continental radial engines threatened to disrupt production of the M3 tank (known in Britain as the Stuart) in the USA, a substitute power pack was developed by harnessing two Cadillac V8 engines together. The Cadillac-powered tank was reclassified an M5, and in Britain was a Stuart Mk VI.

The engines were side-valve (flathead) types with monobloc construction and a 5670cc (346 cubic inch) capacity; they had an 89mm bore and a 110mm stroke. Each one delivered 110bhp at 4000rpm and 244 lb ft at 1200rpm, and each drove through a separate GM Hydra-Matic automatic gearbox to a common transfer box. The combined power pack gave the tank 220bhp and 488 lb ft of torque.

CHRYSLER MULTI-BANK

The Chrysler A-57 multi-bank engine was installed in the M4A4 Sherman tanks used by the British Army. It was designed in response to the chronic shortage of tank engine options in America as that country entered the Second World War.

It consisted of five existing commercially-available engines harnessed together mechanically so that the outputs of all five crankshafts (and no fewer than 30 cylinders) were geared to a common output. The result was a surprisingly compact package, although this all-iron engine was heavy. Its typical power output was 370bhp at 2400rpm.

CONTINENTAL RADIAL

Air-cooled Continental radial engines were used in American-built tanks supplied to the British Army. These were derivatives of aero engines. There were two types, the R-670 used in the

Stuart, and the R-975 used in the larger Grant, Lee and Sherman tanks.

The Continental R-670 was a seven-cylinder radial engine that was known to its makers as a W670 type and had a capacity of 10,946cc (668 cubic inches). Its output was approximately 225bhp at 2200rpm.

The R-975 was a nine-cylinder engine derived from the Wright Whirlwind aero engine. It was adapted in some haste, and as a result had some major shortcomings, notably limited accessibility for maintenance and excessive oil consumption caused by cooling problems. The standard power output was 400bhp.

The cylinder heads of two of the five engines arranged radially to create the Chrysler A57 engine can be clearly seen here. The engine was usually known as the "multi-bank" type, and this example was pictured at the Imperial War Museum in Duxford. (Geni/ WikiMedia Commons, CC-by-SA 4.0)

RAOC engineers change the Continental R-975 engine of a Grant tank in North Africa during 1942. (IWM E13233, Public Domain)

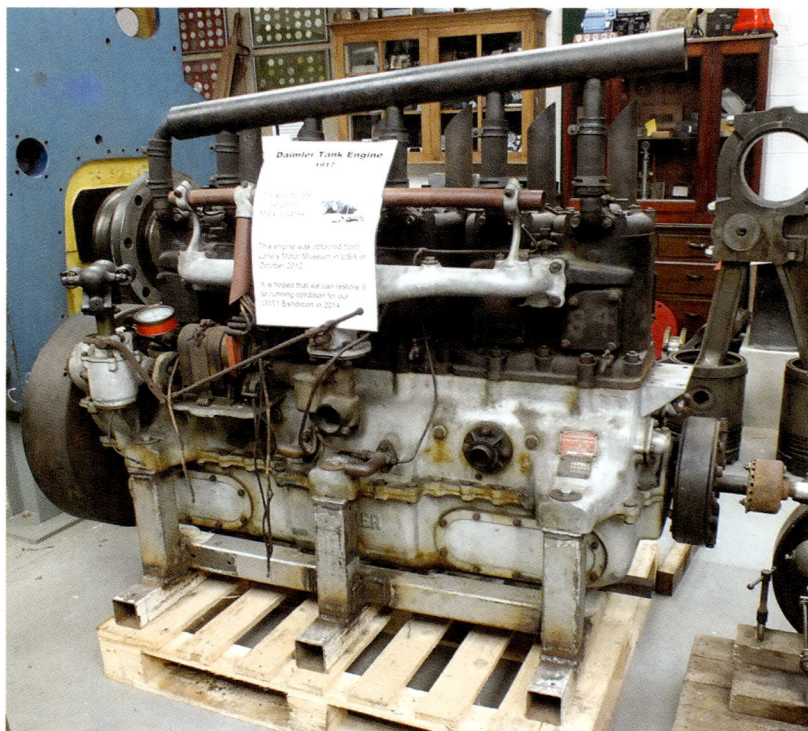

Preserved at the Anson Engine Museum at Poynton in Cheshire is this 1917 Daimler-Knight engine as used in the Mk IV rhomboid tanks. This one was supposedly taken to the USA for evaluation and was never actually mounted in a tank. (Clem Rutter/WikiMedia Commons, CC-by-SA 3.0)

CUMMINS

The US-built Cummins BTA 5.9-litre diesel engine was used to replace the Jaguar J60 petrol engine in the Life Enhancement Programme of the CVR(T) light tanks that began in 2011. It was a turbocharged six-cylinder engine with a bore of 102mm and a stroke of 119mm and delivered the same 190bhp as the engine it replaced. The engine was also built for marine applications.

DAIMLER-KNIGHT

When the War Office wanted an engine to power its first tanks in 1916, there was little choice available. The one chosen was manufactured by Daimler in Britain and was a huge six-cylinder petrol type with a 13.5-litre swept volume (150mm bore and 150mm stroke) and a power output of 105bhp at 1000rpm. Daimler had developed it, using the Knight sleeve-valve patents, for heavy tractors and for the road trains that they built after 1908 using Renard patents. It was designed to handle 15-ton road trains, and was clearly underpowered for the job of moving a 28-ton tank from the start – but it was the best that could be found.

Like all sleeve-valve engines, it burned a lot of its lubricating oil and created a distinctive cloud of smoke that quickly gave away the position of the tank fitted with it. The engine fell far short of the ideal but was fitted to all early Marks of tank until the new Ricardo engine became available in 1917. An improved version of the Daimler-Knight engine was developed during 1916 by WO Bentley, who was then serving as an officer in the Royal Navy. He achieved 125bhp at 1400rpm by increasing the compression ratio, adding twin Zenith carburettors, and fitting aluminium pistons and a lightened flywheel. However, the 125bhp engine was harnessed to an electric motor as part of another experiment with petrol-electric drive, and nothing further came of it.

FORD MODEL T

The simple and robust four-cylinder petrol engine from the Ford Model T car was pressed into service as the power unit of the Carden-Loyd Tankette in 1925. This was a 2.9-litre all-iron engine with a 95.25mm bore and a 101.6mm stroke. It had side valves and three main bearings, and a low compression ratio of 3.98:1. Although the car versions of the engine were rated at just 20bhp, the tank version of the engine was claimed to deliver 40bhp at 2500rpm.

FORD V8

Ford's original Flathead V8 engine was introduced for cars and light trucks in 1932 and was a remarkably robust petrol engine that remained in production until 1953. It powered several wartime vehicles and was built on both sides of the Atlantic, the first one from the Dagenham plant in Britain being introduced in 1935.

The engine was the first mass-produced V8, and was revolutionary in design with its single-piece cast-iron block and crankcase. The design was simple, with a three-bearing crankshaft, and a single central camshaft operating side valves. However, a compromise of the design was that the exhaust was routed through the water jacket, and in hard use the engine could therefore overheat.

The Ford V8 typically developed 85bhp for car and light truck use, but for the Matilda A11 tank it was de-rated to give just 70bhp. It had a displacement of 3622cc and in Matilda guise was known as the Model 79.

A much larger Ford V8 with different origins became the power unit of the M4A3 versions of the Sherman tank. This was the GAA derivative of a V12 engine originally designed for

The 3.6-litre Ford V8 car engine is almost invisible within the engine bay of an A11 Matilda Mk I tank. (Vickers-Armstrongs, via Tank Museum)

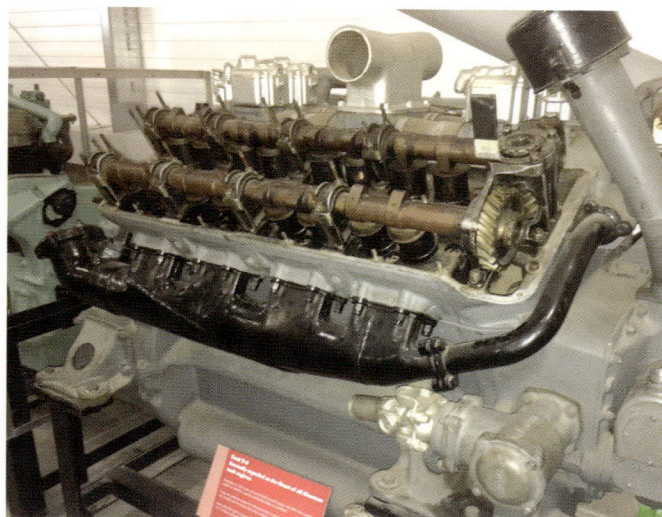

In this case seen as a cutaway demonstration unit, this is the larger of the two Ford V8 engines – the GAA type that powered the Sherman tank. It was pictured at the Tank Museum in Bovington.

aircraft but never put into production. It had an 18,025cc (1100 cubic inches) swept volume and outputs of 450bhp at 2600rpm and 1050 lb ft at 2200rpm.

GENERAL MOTORS 6-71 DIESEL

As the demand for Wright radial aero engines increased to power military aircraft in the USA, pressure was put on supplies of the Continental tank engine based on it. The military manufacturers therefore sought a readily-available alternative, and the one they found was a six-cylinder two-stroke diesel built by General Motors. This was known as the 6-71 type and had started life in 1938 as the flagship product of GM's Detroit Diesel Engine Division. It was used in several US military vehicles.

The GMC 6-71 was an iron-block pushrod engine with a blower to provide air for combustion and scavenge exhaust gases. It had a bore of 108mm and a stroke of 127mm, giving a displacement of 6.96 litres. Its name of 6-71 nevertheless came from its six cylinders and the 71 cubic inches nominal displacement of each cylinder (the displacement was actually 70.93 cubic inches or 1.2 litres). This engine had been designed to be as adaptable as possible, and the blower, starter, exhaust and other ancillaries could be mounted on either side of the block to suit the application.

In Britain, the Directorate of Mechanisation (later DTD) persuaded AEC to try a GMC

diesel in the Valentine tank early in 1940, and the experiment was a success. The first order was placed in September 1940, and the adapted version was known as the General Motors 6004S diesel. The initial versions of the engine in the Valentine Mk IV had 130bhp at 1900rpm and 786 lb ft of torque at 900rpm, and this engine also went into the Valentine V, VI and VII, and some Valentine IX tanks. A later version, with bigger injectors and a higher governed speed, was known as the A type, and was used in the remaining 783 Valentine IXs, the Valentine

The GM 6-71 diesel became the 6004S model when used in Valentine tanks. This one was pictured at the Tank Museum in Bovington.

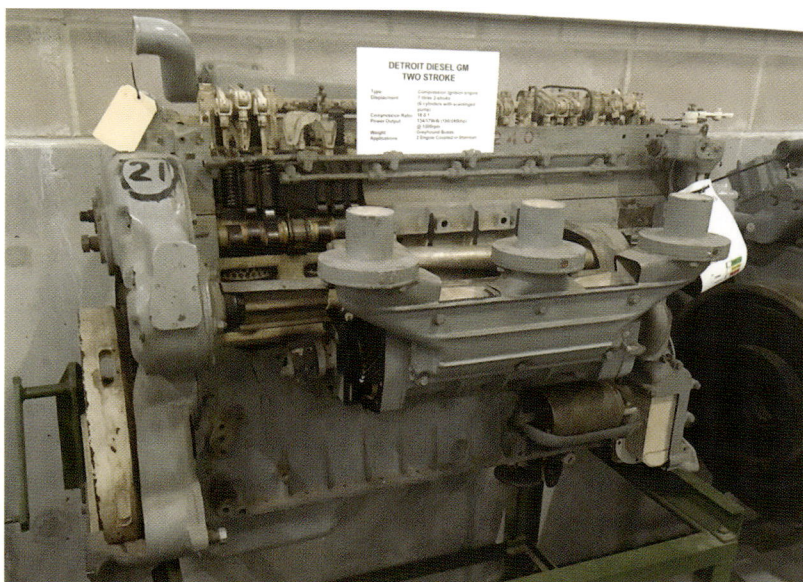

Yet another tank power pack created by twinning engines was the GM 6046 diesel. This demonstration cutaway example has been preserved at the Bovington Tank Museum. (Nilfanion/ WikiMedia Commons, CC-by-SA 4.0)

X and the Valentine XI. This had 165bhp at 1900rpm with 907 lb ft of torque at 1000rpm.

The GMC two-stroke diesel was also used in the sole Valiant prototype and, with a claimed 192bhp, in the Archer self-propelled gun that was based on the Valentine. The M4A2 versions of the Sherman tank, used by both the Americans and by the British Army, had paired 6-71 diesel engines mounted side by side and sharing an output shaft. This installation was known as the 6046 engine and is claimed to have delivered 375bhp with up to 1000 lb ft of torque.

GENERAL MOTORS V12 DIESEL

Distantly related to the GM 6-71 diesel that was introduced in 1938 was the Detroit Diesel 12V-71T engine used in the Vickers MBT Mk 3 nearly 40 years later. The link was in the bore and stroke dimensions (108mm x 127mm) and in the fact that this was a two-stroke engine. This 14-litre 720bhp V12 diesel was one of a very large family of engines, both inline and vee types and all dependent on a Roots-type scavenger blower; in this case it was turbocharged as well.

GUIBERSON T-1020

To counter a manufacturing shortage of Continental R-670 petrol radial engines for the Stuart tank in 1942-1943, the US authorities arranged for a Guiberson nine-cylinder radial engine to be adapted for the job. Originally developed in the early 1930s, this four-stroke diesel was rated at 310bhp in its original aero engine guise (when it was called an A-1020) but was de-rated to 250bhp as a T-1020 for tank

use. These engines had a swept volume of 16.73 litres, with a bore of 130.18mm and a stroke of 139.7mm.

JAGUAR

Limited space and the need for high performance persuaded Alvis to choose the 4.2-litre Jaguar six-cylinder petrol engine as the power unit of the CVR(T) family in the late 1960s. This twin-overhead camshaft engine had been designed in the late 1940s but had been progressively updated for Jaguar cars and promised as much as 260bhp. In practice, as re-worked for its new military application, it had 190bhp at 4750rpm and 250 lb ft of torque at 3000rpm. The military version was known as a J60 No.1 Mark 100B type.

LANCHESTER

The Lanchester was a prestigious make of car in the early 1920s, and the engine of its Forty model was chosen to power the experimental Vickers no 2 tank in 1922. It was a six-cylinder type with an advanced overhead-camshaft design, two spark plugs for each cylinder and a swept volume of 6178cc. The engine delivered 80bhp, which was a high output for the time and was clearly the main attraction to Vickers.

LEYLAND ENGINES

Leyland commercial-vehicle engines were pressed into service for tanks at the outbreak of the Second World War. In the 1950s, the company was then called on to design a brand-new dedicated tank engine from scratch.

L series

The Leyland diesel engines used in the Matilda II tank were developed from a new bus engine that had appeared in 1939 as the L series but whose production had been interrupted by the outbreak of war. This was a 6.2-litre six-cylinder direct-injection type with pushrod-operated overhead valves that had been used in a small number of Leyland Tiger TS8 single-deck chassis during 1940.

There is little hard evidence about what happened, but it is likely that Leyland were called on as a matter of urgency to provide diesel engines to replace the twin AEC petrol units in the first Matildas. The physical constraints of the Matilda's engine bay and the power and torque requirements probably led the Leyland engineers to focus on an enlarged version of their new diesel. Their solution was to retain the original 5in stroke but to increase the bore to 4.375in from 4in to deliver a swept volume of 7.4 litres and a power output of 95bhp at 2000rpm. Records show that the Leyland unit also took two hours less to fit than the original AEC type, which was a boon when an engine needed to be replaced in the field.

The Leyland engines were installed in pairs, as their AEC predecessors had been, beginning on production with the Matilda Mk III; from 1941, a retro-fit programme carried out by MG Cars at Abingdon saw many earlier Matildas re-engined with these Leyland units. The engines were produced as left-hand and right-hand units, and there were three different sets: E148 and E149 types were used first, in the Mk III, Mk IIICS and uprated Mk II tanks; these gave way to E164 and E165 types later in the programme, which differed mainly in having cast-iron crankcases instead of the original aluminium type. For the Matilda Mk IV, Mk IVCS and Mk V, the engines were further-developed E170 and E171 types, still with 95bhp each.

In each case the lower of a pair of numbers indicated the left-hand engine. All types were distinguished by cylinder blocks cast as two three-cylinder units, with distinctive separate top covers, but there were differences among the three sets in the location of auxiliaries, in particular of the oil tank.

The Leyland L series diesel was also used in the Mk II Hippo heavy cargo truck from 1943 and, according to *Commercial Motor* magazine, Leyland built 6888 military engines during the Second World War. After the war the engine was further developed to provide the E181 7.4-litre engine that powered the company's post-war bus chassis, the Titan PD1 double-deck type and the Tiger PS1 single-deck type.

The L60 engine

The L60 was a 19-litre six-cylinder multi-fuel engine drawn up in the late 1950s and early 1960s and primarily associated with the Chieftain tank. It was also used in the Vickers MBT and its Indian-built Vijayanta relative.

The programme for the Chieftain was originally planned around a Rolls-Royce diesel V8, but in 1957, while design was still in progress, NATO policy changed to require a multi-fuel capability. So FVRDE was asked to design a suitable replacement engine, and handed the job to Leyland. Unusually, this was to be an opposed-

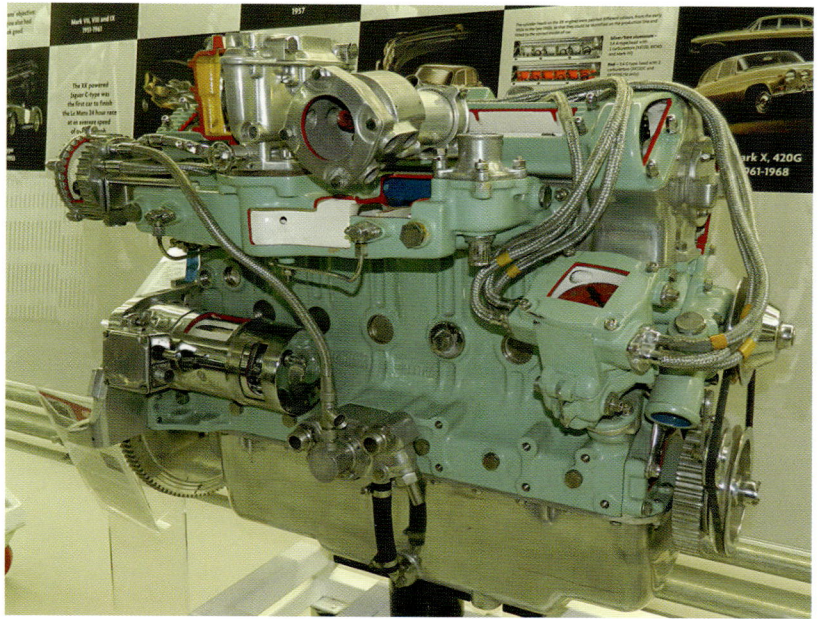

piston two-stroke diesel, a configuration chosen because of its suitability for multi-fuel use, its good fuel economy, and its ability to fit the low profile that was a Chieftain aim. Both Rolls-Royce and Tilling-Stevens (makers of the TS3 two-stroke commercial-vehicle diesel) had some input to the development process.

The Jaguar J60 was a derivative of the car maker's legendary six-cylinder twin-overhead camshaft engine for the CVR(T) family of light tanks.

Twinned Leyland diesel engines were used in later Matilda II tanks, and fitted into the engine bay originally designed for twin AEC engines.

LEYLAND POWER UNIT.

VIEW OF POWER UNIT FROM REAR OF TANK

VIEW OF POWER UNIT FROM FRONT OF TANK

123

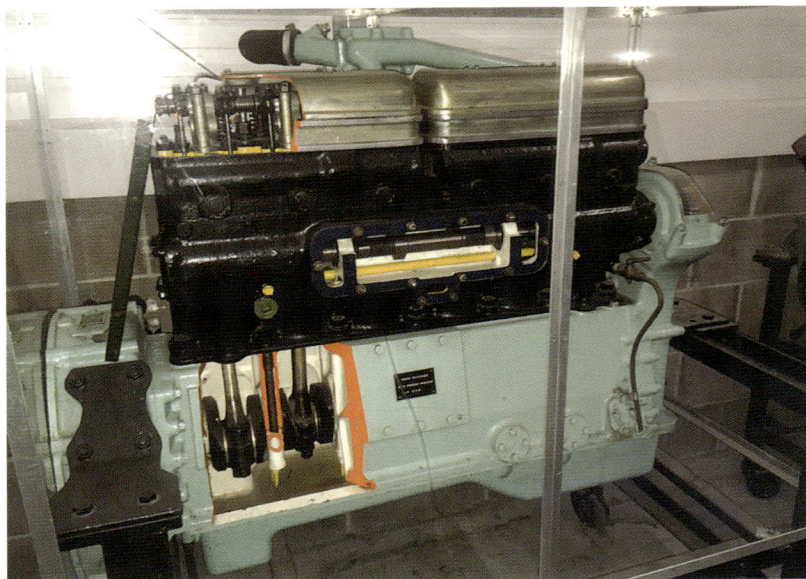

Now preserved at the Bovington Tank Museum, this is a demonstration cutaway of one of the Leyland engines for the Matilda. This would appear to be a right-hand engine, probably an E149 type.

A further aim of the programme was that the entire power pack should be easily changed, as the thinking of the time was that this was preferable to attempting repairs in the field. So the engine and its cooling system were packaged integrally, allowing a complete engine change in between one and a half and two hours; the failed engine was to be taken back to base workshops for repair.

Prototype engines were running by 1959, and the engine went through four Marks before the first production variant (the Mk 4A) was ready in January 1965. With a disappointing 585bhp – the design target had been 600bhp – this was fitted only to early Chieftains used for training. By November 1965, further development had produced the 650bhp Mk4A2. A de-rated 540bhp variant of the engine was used for the Vijayanta and Vickers MBT tanks derived from the Chieftain.

The L60's whole production history was characterised by progressive upgrades and, in the early days at least, by poor reliability. A major problem was failure of the cylinder liners, which allowed water into the bores. However, this was eventually cured, but not until the cylinder block had been redesigned for the Mk 7A engines in October 1971. This coincided with a power increase to 720bhp, and the final production engines, for the Mk 5A Chieftain in 1975, were Mk 8A types with 750bhp. In-service upgrades continued, and from March 1978 the L60 achieved 840bhp. In December 1978 it also achieved its target 4000-mile engine life – 11

years after entering service in 1967. All variants of the L60 were deliberately made interchangeable, and earlier engines that had been removed were normally rebuilt to the latest standard wherever possible.

LIBERTY ENGINE

The American-designed Liberty engine first ran in approximately 1917, after the USA had entered the Great War. It was designed to meet a call for an aero engine that would exceed the capabilities of any then in use on either side of the conflict, and was deliberately drawn up to be easily mass produced. It was manufactured by a consortium of car makers in the USA, and was originally known as the United States Standard 12-cylinder Aviation Engine.

This was a 27-litre V12 engine, with a 45-degree angle between the cylinder banks. Each cylinder bank had a single overhead camshaft, and the valvegear design was very closely based on that used in German six-cylinder aero engines during the war. The engine had a 127mm bore and a 177.8mm stroke, giving a swept volume of 27,040cc.

An American-built Liberty engine with 300bhp was fitted into the American version of the Mk VIII International or Liberty tank in 1919. However, the engine became far better known in tanks when it was built under licence by Nuffield Mechanisations & Aero Ltd in Britain as the Nuffield Liberty engine *(qv)*.

MEADOWS ENGINES

Henry Meadows Ltd was a specialist maker of engines and transmissions based in Wolverhampton. The company produced its own engine designs for tanks and also participated in production of the Rolls-Royce Meteor tank engine during the Second World War.

Flat-12 types

In the later 1930s, Meadows developed two flat (horizontally opposed) 12-cylinder engines specifically for tank use.

The earlier of the two was known as the MAT type and had a swept volume of 8858cc. It was used in the 1937 Tetrarch light tank and in its planned but unsuccessful 1941 replacement, the Harry Hopkins. This engine is variously quoted as having a power output of 148bhp at 2200rpm or 165bhp.

The second was a larger 16-litre type called the DAV that developed 300bhp at a governed

The Leyland L60 was a dedicated tank engine design, designed to meet NATO requirements for multi-fuel power units. The twin radiators normally lay flat but are shown here swung upwards to give access to auxiliary engine components.

This is the view from the other end of an L60 engine, in this case an example preserved at the Tank Museum in Bovington.

A Meadows six-cylinder engine is seen here in a Light Tank Mk VI. The picture was taken in France in 1940 and shows how the engine was offset to one side of the tank. (IWM O816, Public Domain)

The larger of the two Meadows 12-cylinder engines was the 16-litre DAV type, seen here in its Covenanter guise. This was a flat 12 with two horizontally opposed banks of six cylinders.

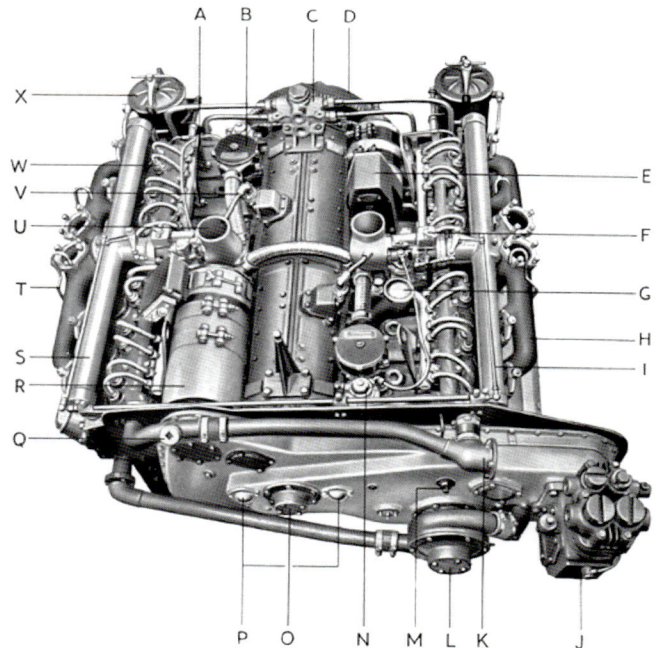

Fig. 2
FRONT END VIEW OF ENGINE

A—Lifting Eye.
B—Distributor.
C—Oil Junction and Relief Valve.
D—Clutch and Flywheel.
E—Starter Motor.
F—Carburettor.
G—Oil Filler and Dipstick.
H—Exhaust Manifold.
I—Carburettor Control Rod.
J—Compressor.
K—Water Outlet.
L—Water Inlet and Water Pump.
M—Manual Chain Tensioner.
N—Fuel Pump.
O—Crankshaft End Cover.
P—Oil Relief Valves.
Q—Cap for Topping up Water System.
R—Dynamo.
S—Inlet Manifold.
T—Rocker Box Vent.
U—Carburettor Air Inlet.
V—Crankcase Vent.
W—Sparking Plug.
X—Oil Filter.

2400rpm. Meadows were asked to design this for the 1939 Covenanter cruiser tank, for which they also supplied the four-speed crash gearbox. It was also used in the prototypes of the A20 heavy tank that was cancelled, and in the AT/1 amphibious tank prototype. This engine was an overhead-valve type with a 115mm bore and a 130mm stroke that gave a swept volume of 16,204cc.

Four-cylinder

Vickers used the four-cylinder Meadows ELA engine in its early Light Tank models in the 1930s. The ELA was an overhead-valve type that delivered between 55bhp and 60bhp over the years and was initially designed as a marine engine. It had a swept volume of 3686cc. Later versions of it were used in the Guy Ant military truck during the Second World War.

Six-cylinder

The Meadows 4.5-litre OHV six-cylinder engine was used in several Vickers light tanks in the 1930s. It was originally introduced as a car engine in 1933 and was developed from an earlier 3-litre type. As first seen in the Lagonda M45 model, it had a swept volume of 4453cc and a twin-plug design for greater reliability. It was well known as a robust engine.

The tank version of the engine was first used in the "Indian pattern" Light Tank Mk IIA in 1933, when it was detuned from the 108bhp at 3100rpm of the car engine to 85bhp at 2800rpm and was known as the EST type. In the Light Tank Mk IV, the ETS type had 88bhp. The same power output was quoted for the ESTE in the Light Tank Mk V, the ESTB in the Mk VIA, and the ESTB/A and ESTB/B variants in the Light Tank Mk VIB. The final version was uprated with triple carburettors for the Light Tank Mk VIC.

NUFFIELD LIBERTY ENGINE

As the threat of war became ever larger in the 1930s, Nuffield Mechanisations & Aero Ltd took out a licence to build the American-designed Liberty aero engine (qv) for use in the tanks it was building. Appropriately re-engineered, the Nuffield Liberty engine was used in several early cruiser tanks before being succeeded by the Rolls-Royce Meteor engine of similar 27-litre capacity but considerably more power. The Nuffield Liberty engine suffered from reliability problems that were mainly asso-ciated with its cooling system and despite several revisions its power output was unable to keep pace with the increasing weight of tanks in the early 1940s.

There were five principal variants of the Nuffield Liberty engine, with some sub-variants. The Mk I engines were actually built in the USA and modified in Britain with a different induction system, Solex carburettors, new timing gear, and changes to the crankcase breather and crankshaft end thrust. These engines produced 340bhp at 1500rpm and were used in the Nuffield-built A13 Cruiser Mk III tank of 1939. They were followed by the British-built Mk II, which had only minor differences and went into Nuffield's A13 Mk II or Cruiser Mk IV later the same year.

The Mk III Nuffield Liberty engine was designed for the A15 Crusader tank, again a Nuffield product. Minor redesign gave a lower overall height and an air compressor was added to power the pneumatically-operated brakes and steering systems. However, the Mk III engine revealed major problems in the desert conditions of the North Africa campaign, and multiple revisions (none entirely successful) resulted in Mk IIIA and Mk IIIB types.

The Mk IV engine incorporated a shaft drive instead of a chain drive for the cooling fans, plus a modified air compressor, and went into the final Crusader tanks. Then a higher-revving Mk IVA followed in 1942 for the A24 Cavalier, now delivering 410bhp and with a new inlet manifold and carburettor. The Mk V was a further redesign that Nuffield intended for the A27 Cromwell tank, with the same power but a revised lubrication system. However, with the introduction of the Rolls-Royce Meteor engine, the requirement for the Nuffield Liberty engine was reduced and the Mk V engines went only into the A27L Centaur variant.

RICARDO ENGINES

Consultant engineer Harry Ricardo was asked in autumn 1916 to look at ways of reducing the smoke emitted by the original Daimler-Knight tank engines, and he quickly decided that the best solution was a completely new engine. The War Office approved his proposal, and Ricardo went ahead, assisted by draughtsmen from some of the companies that had been selected to take part in the programme. The brief called for an engine that could be fitted in place of the existing Daimler-Knight type, and had to be made

These two views of the Nuffield-built Liberty aero engine were found in the archives of Nuffield Mechanisations. This engine was destined for use in a Cavalier tank in 1942 – by which time its basic design was a quarter of a century old. (British Motor Industry Heritage Trust)

The 1917 Ricardo engine shows its distinctive side plates in this view of an example preserved in the Tank Museum at Bovington.

without the aluminium or the high-tensile steel that were in demand for aircraft production.

Six-cylinder

The engine he designed was a six-cylinder with an overall capacity of 18.3 litres from a 143mm (5 5/8in) bore and a 190mm (7½ in) stroke. The longer stroke made it taller than the existing Daimler engine but there was room in the tank's hull. It used standard poppet valves instead of the Knight-patent sleeve valves and Ricardo also chose an unusual crosshead piston design. A pair of scavenger pumps in the oil system kept the sump dry and prevented the smoke that came with full throttle as oil was burned after a period of idling. There were also large removable side panels to ease maintenance.

Ricardo initially aimed for 200bhp but Walter Wilson did not think his gearbox would be strong enough to cope and so production engines were limited to 150bhp. There was a 4.3:1 compression ratio to allow for 45-octane petrol. On test by March 1917, the Ricardo engine entered full production in April, manufactured by several former gas engine companies in the Manchester area and by others in Grantham and Peterborough.

The engine became standard in the Mk V tank, but a planned retro-fit programme to uprate Mk IV tanks with it to Mk IVA standard did not go ahead. Around 8000 Ricardo engines were built, of which probably only 50% went into tanks;

the rest were pressed into use as stationary units to drive generators providing lighting for hospitals, workshops and other military centres in France.

Ricardo went on to develop a 225bhp version of this engine with a larger (171mm, 6¾in) bore, four valves per cylinder, and an overall capacity of 26.3 litres. This was used in the 25 Mk V** tanks that were completed after the Armistice.

Four-cylinder

A four-cylinder derivative of the Ricardo tank engine was designed for the Medium Mark B tank in 1917. This developed 100bhp and was used in all 700 production examples of the Medium Mark B, but was not seen in any other production tanks. It was successful enough to kill off plans for Ricardo to develop a new 100bhp six-cylinder type.

V12

In 1917, Ricardo was asked to design a V12 engine as a contingency plan for building the Mk VIII or International tank in British factories. It was required to have the same 300bhp output as the American Liberty engine that was planned for the tank. The design was rushed through in record time and Ricardo himself described it as a 300bhp V12 version of his 150bhp six-cylinder. However, it is not clear how many were actually built. Several were shipped to the USA but nothing more was heard of them; just 31 examples of the Mk VIII tank were built in Britain, and it may be that not all of these had the Ricardo engine.

ROLLS-ROYCE ENGINES

Rolls-Royce provided tank engines that were derived from designs originally produced for both cars and aircraft. The most well-known of these engines was the Meteor, which in turn sired the specially-developed Meteorite. Rolls-Royce also developed the CV12 or Condor diesel engine of the Challenger tank, and after the company's Shrewsbury diesel engine factory was sold to Perkins in 1984, its manufacture was continued by the new owners.

CV8

The Rolls-Royce CV8 engine was an 800bhp V8 derivative of the CV12 Condor tank engine (*see below*) and was planned for the Shir 2 tank that was ordered by the Iranians. That contract was not fulfilled for political reasons, but under

Perkins ownership the engine has had a further life as a marine power plant.

CV12

The CV12 TCA or Condor was a four-stroke twin-turbocharged V12 diesel engine, designed specifically for tanks and originally intended for use in the Shir tanks ordered for Iran. It became the power unit of the Challenger tank in the early 1980s. This was a pushrod engine with a swept volume of 26.1 litres (135mm bore and 152mm stroke), four valves per cylinder and direct injection. Its outputs in the Challenger were 1200bhp at 2300rpm and 3039 lb ft of torque at 1700rpm. A detuned 1000bhp version was planned for the Vickers Valiant tank that did not enter production.

Further development of this engine under Perkins ownership included replacement of the original direct-injection fuel system by a common-rail system. For the Challenger 3 tank, the engine was to be a CV12-8A type with 1500bhp at 2400rpm and 3922 lb ft of torque at 1500rpm.

Eagle

The Rolls-Royce Eagle was the company's first aero engine and was introduced in 1915. It was used in a number of military aircraft, including the Handley Page Type O bomber.

This was a 20-litre V12 (the swept volume was actually 2032cc) that had been derived from the company's own 7.4-litre straight six that was used in the 40/50 Silver Ghost car. Some design features were derived from a Daimler DF80 aero engine that had been used in a Grand Prix Mercedes car. Rolls-Royce doubled the number of cylinders, effectively mounting two six-cylinder engines on a common crankcase, lengthened the stroke, and changed from side valves to a single overhead camshaft configuration. The first production versions had 225bhp, which was increased to 300bhp during 1917 for the Eagle VIII. There were later versions for civilian aircraft with 360bhp.

When Major Philip Johnson made experimental improvements to a Whippet (Medium A) tank in France during 1918, he fitted it with an Eagle V12 engine – with which he would have been familiar from its use in aircraft at the time. This has been claimed as a 360bhp type but more probably had the 300bhp tune that was then standard. The Rolls-Royce V12 engine used to make the mild-steel prototype of the Mark VIII tank mobile in 1918 may also have been a Rolls-Royce Eagle. After the war, a Rolls-Royce Eagle engine was again tried experimentally in a Medium D** and subsequently in Johnson's experimental Mark DM, when it supposedly developed 370bhp.

Goshawk car engine

Rolls-Royce supplied a version of its small six-cylinder car engine (known internally as the Goshawk) for the Vickers-built Light Tank Mk II in 1931. The engine had a swept volume of 3669cc and was a large-bore development of the one that Royce had designed some ten years earlier for the Rolls-Royce Twenty. It had push-rod-operated overhead valves and had been standard in the company's 20/25 model since 1929.

As supplied for tank use, the engine had a dry-sump lubrication system with pressure and scavenge pumps. It was claimed to have a maximum power of 66bhp, although the Rolls-Royce claims of 50bhp (silenced) and 57bhp (unsilenced) for the car version were characteristically more modest. These engines were used in the 16 Light Tank Mk II and then in the 21 Mk IIB models built by Vickers, in each case driving through a Wilson pre-selector gearbox. They were said to wear badly in desert use, although it is not clear whether this was because of excessive stresses from the weight of the tank or from inadequate filtration. Nevertheless, the

Looking particularly neat and purposeful in this publicity picture is the late Perkins version of the Rolls-Royce Condor CV12 engine. This one has common-rail direct injection.

The Rolls-Royce Eagle aero engine was adapted to become an early tank engine. This one is a MkVIII type preserved at the South African National Museum of Military History. (NJR ZA/WikiMedia Commons, CC-by-SA 3.0)

Rolls-Royce engine was also used to replace the Meadows EST type in the Light Tank Mk IIA from about 1934.

Meteor

The Rolls-Royce Meteor was Britain's most successful tank engine of the Second World War and remained in production until 1964. It brought solid reliability and a huge power increase to British tanks, and ultimately led to the thinking that combined the heavy armour of an Infantry tank with the high mobility of a Cruiser tank to produce the "universal" Centurion and later designs.

The Meteor was derived from the Rolls-Royce Merlin aero engine that first ran in the 1930s and went on to become a staple of the Royal Air Force. The idea of turning it into a tank engine came from Leyland Motors in 1940, when that company was co-operating with Rolls-Royce on tank design. Rolls-Royce developed the first one using reconditioned parts taken from crashed Merlin engines. They removed the supercharger (which was primarily needed to ensure adequate fuelling at high altitudes), changed the direction of rotation to suit automotive practice, and redeveloped some components to use steel instead of the aluminium needed to save weight in the Merlin engine. The first Merlin was tested at Aldershot in April 1941 in a modified Leyland-built Crusader tank. It delivered about 600bhp when running on Pool petrol.

The prototype showed enormous promise and production engines were ordered for the Cromwell tank, in which application it was governed to 540bhp at 2250rpm. Rolls-Royce did not have the capacity to meet demand, although they did build many early engines, often using refurbished components from crashed aero engines as they had for the prototype. Meadows was then contracted to build the engine, but again their capacity was not enough and from 1943 production was split between the Rover and Morris car companies at Acocks Green and Coventry respectively. From January 1944, Rover took over primary responsibility for the Meteor and later types were known as Rover Meteor engines; in all, Rover built about 9000 Meteor engines, and also developed and produced the V8 Meteorite derivative (qv).

Further development of the engine led to the Meteor Mk 4B that became the powerplant of the Centurion in 1946. This had 650bhp at 2250rpm. The final version of the Meteor was the M120 for the Conqueror tank in 1955, with 810bhp at 2800rpm.

Phantom II car engine

The six-cylinder engine used in the Rolls-Royce Phantom II chassis from 1929 was one of the most admired car engines of its day, and delivered about 120bhp from 7.7 litres. It must have been this power output rather than its legendary silent operation that attracted the Belgian armed forces to it, and when discussing a potential order with Vickers for their Mark E Six-ton tank they requested this engine in preference to the 95bhp Armstrong-Siddeley type that was standard. This required a major redesign of the hull (which Vickers later put to good use), but only the one trials example was built (as the Mark F) and the Belgians did not place an order for more.

A pair of these engines harnessed together were in the plans for the A6 tank in 1928 and for the A8 Medium tank in the mid-1930s, but neither project progressed to production.

ROVER ENGINES

Strictly speaking, the post-1946 Meteor engine was always a Rover unit, even though it had been designed by Rolls-Royce. Rover were also responsible for later developments of the engine, which was built at the company's Acocks Green plant. This was a former wartime "shadow" factory that Rover continued to manage on behalf of the Ministry of Supply.

The Meteorite V8 engine was derived from the Meteor, sharing its 60-degree vee configuration; it was, in effect, two-thirds of a Meteor engine, with a swept volume of 18.01 litres. It was included in plans for experimental tanks as early as 1944, but became better known in 250bhp guise as the power plant of the Thornycroft Mighty Antar, a tractor unit intended for Middle East oilfield use. In the early 1950s the British Army adopted the Antar as a tank transporter tractor, and familiarity with the Meteorite

engine led to its specification in at least one further tank project.

This was the Tank Medium No 2, a research vehicle built by Leyland in 1955-1956 to enable FVRDE to test the layout of the proposed Chieftain MBT. In Mk202B form for this tank, the Meteorite developed 520bhp at 2700rpm. A later version used in the experimental-only TV1000 six-wheel skid-steer prototype was supposedly rated at 535bhp.

The Rolls-Royce Meteor V12 was derived from the legendary Merlin aero engine. This example is a MkIII type for a late-model Cromwell tank, and was pictured on display at the Tank Museum in Bovington. (Geni/ WikiMedia Commons, CC-by-SA 4.0)

This cutaway display Meteor engine and transmission from a Centurion tank were photographed in the Netherlands. (Alf van Beem/WikiMedia Commons)

The Siddeley Puma was another aero engine adapted for use in tanks. Its manufacture was continued by Armstrong-Siddeley after a change in the ownership of the company. (Public Domain)

SIDDELEY ENGINES

Siddeley-Deasy was a Coventry maker of cars and aero engines that was bought by Armstrong Whitworth in 1919. After that date, its products were continued under the Armstrong-Siddeley name *(qv)*.

Puma

The Siddeley Puma engine was an 18.8-litre (18,832cc) inline six-cylinder aero engine that was used in the Airco DH9 bomber during the First World War. It was not a great success and was built for this application only between 1917 and 1918, when it developed a maximum 265bhp at 1500rpm for take-off.

It was first adapted for tank use in 1919, when it appeared in the Medium D prototype as a 240bhp engine. For the 1920 Medium D** it was uprated to 300bhp. The engine continued to be favoured for further designs from Vickers, including the A1 in 1924, the A6 in 1926 and the Medium Mk III in 1930, by which time it was developing 370bhp at 1500rpm. However, none of these designs entered volume production.

SUNBEAM ENGINES

The Sunbeam Motor Car Company was based in Wolverhampton and branched out into aero engine manufacture in 1912. None of its early engines were successful but the increased demand for aero engines during the First World War created new opportunities.

Amazon

The Sunbeam Amazon was a six-cylinder aero engine that was used in "Amazon II" form in the Vickers Medium Mark C and Medium Mark D export tanks of the late 1920s.

In 1915, Sunbeam's chief designer Louis Coatalen had responded to an Admiralty demand for a more powerful aero engine with the Cossack V12, which had four valves per cylinder. The Amazon was a 9.2-litre six-cylinder derivative of it, retaining its 110mm bore, 130mm stroke, four-valve configuration and cylinders cast in groups of three. It was rated at 160bhp at 2000rpm. Few examples of the Amazon were actually used for aviation applications.

THORNYCROFT ENGINE

The Thornycroft RY12 engine was favoured for a time in the late 1920s and 1930s, and figured in plans for the A6 and A19 tanks. Neither entered production. Originally drawn up as a marine engine for naval motor launches, it was a V12 design which promised 500bhp in A6 form and 650bhp in later A19 guise.

TYLOR ENGINE

The Tylor engine that was used in pairs in the Medium Mark A or Whippet tank was a four-cylinder side-valve type that was also used in the AEC Y type military truck from 1917. Philip Johnson also planned to use a single Tylor engine in his Tropical Tank for India.

J Tylor & Sons Ltd was an old-established London firm that had been sanitary engineers, brass founders, pump makers and latterly petrol engine manufacturers. The engine used in the Whippet was the JB4 model, introduced in the autumn of 1913 and apparently designed to meet the requirements of the 1911 War Office subsidy scheme. Its cylinders were cast in pairs, with a 5in (127mm) bore and a 6in (152.4mm) stroke that gave an overall swept volume variously quoted as 7.7 litres or 7722cc. Power output was 45bhp at 1300rpm.

Chapter 4
TANK GUNS

From the beginning, tanks were armed as well as armoured, but in the early years the choice of weaponry was dictated by the purpose of the tank. Light, fast tanks did not need and could not carry the large-calibre guns of the heavy tanks, and for many years relied entirely on machine guns.

The choice of weaponry for the first tanks in 1916 was influenced, like so many other aspects of the design, by what was readily available. The choice fell on a naval gun that fired a 6pdr shell, but constraints on the availability of these guns led to some tanks being completed with a complement of machine guns only. On tanks equipped with the 6pdr main guns (one on each side, in sponsons similar to naval practice), machine guns were also added as secondary armament at least partly to protect the tank itself. Such secondary armament would become a standard feature of later tanks.

The main problem with the 6pdr was its size and weight. A redesign produced a short-barrelled "6cwt" version in 1917 but the gun was not what was needed for the fast, light Whippet Medium tank of that year. A complement of four .303 machine guns was considered adequate, not least because this tank was designed for very different duties from the heavy rhomboid tanks of the original design.

When Vickers came to design a range of tanks for export in the early 1920s, they naturally turned to a gun of their own manufacture and selected a 3pdr type derived from another naval gun. Although it had its limitations, it was a useful high-velocity gun and remained the weapon of choice at a time when the General Staff was not placing a high degree of urgency on tank design. It was not until Britain began to re-arm to counter the threat of war with Germany in the middle 1930s that a new candidate entered the picture. Meanwhile, smaller tanks such as the A11 Matilda I continued to field nothing more than machine guns.

From 1936, General Staff policy focused on a heavier and more effective tank gun, this time

firing a lighter 2pdr shell. The Ordnance QF 2pdr became the main armament of the Matilda II and Valentine tanks and was the most effective tank gun available to the British in the period up to 1942. Its limitations had been apparent from an early stage, and by 1938 work had begun on a new 6pdr gun. However, production was delayed for a variety of reasons and as a result the gun was not ready until 1942, when it was introduced in the A24 Cavalier tank.

Although the Cavalier was not a great success, the 6pdr was used wherever possible to replace the 2pdr in existing designs, and later versions of the Churchill, Valentine and Crusader all received it. The Cromwell and Centaur were designed from the start to take it. Meanwhile, further developments influenced the choice of guns for British tanks.

On the one hand, the latest German tank and anti-tank guns had a range far superior to that of their British equivalents, with the result that the British tanks were extremely vulnerable. On the other hand, the arrival of Sherman tanks from

British tank guns have traditionally had rifled barrels, as seen in this demonstration cutaway of an L7 105mm at the Deutsches Panzermuseum in Minster, Germany. (baku13/CC-by-SA 3.0)

the USA introduced the British to the 75mm gun which was the first tank gun they had used that could fire both AP (Armour Piercing) rounds for destroying armoured vehicles and HE (High Explosive) shells against unarmoured targets and field fortifications.

Two developments followed. The 17pdr gun then under development as an anti-tank type was identified as necessary for tanks, and from 1943 it became available in the Challenger conversion of the Cromwell and as a conversion of the Sherman (known as the Sherman Firefly). Its use was initially limited, however, as it was too big for the hulls of the existing A27 family of tanks. Meanwhile, it became clear that the existing 6pdr could be bored out to take American 75mm ammunition, and the Ordnance QF 75mm gun so created allowed the use of HE rounds as well as AP types. The 17pdr now became the main British tank gun, supplemented from late 1944 by a Vickers development of the 17pdr that was compact enough to fit the A27 tank hull and created the A34 Comet tank. This new gun was known as the 77mm type.

The 17pdr was chosen for the new A41 Centurion tank that was under development at the end of the 1939-1945 war, but it was fitted only to early production versions of that tank and from 1946 gave way to an improved 20pdr type with a larger bore that could fire both AP

and HE rounds. Excellent though it was, this gun was almost immediately outclassed by the 120mm gun of the Soviet IS-3 tank that it seemed likely to have to face as the Cold War intensified.

The answer was a somewhat unsatisfactory compromise, as the new heavy Conqueror tank of 1955 took on a US-made 120mm gun. The Conqueror lacked the mobility of the Centurion but was intended to provide Centurion units with a stand-off capability. Unsurprisingly, the next development – again ten years in the making – was a British-designed 120mm long-range gun that appeared in the Chieftain tank in 1965.

Meanwhile, Britain had pressed ahead with the design of a replacement for the 20pdr gun and from 1959 Centurion tanks could field the L7 105mm type. This proved to be an excellent tank gun and remained in service until the Chieftain was introduced as the Centurion's replacement in 1965. By then, the 120mm size had been adopted as a NATO standard, and in the years that followed there was a renewed focus on ammunition design and fire control systems, as well as on improved armour such as the Chobham type. The next new gun hardware appeared in 1995 as the L30A1 rifled 120mm type for the Challenger tank, and its replacement has been chosen as the German-designed

At the start of the Second World War, the heaviest British tank gun was the 2pdr, which is seen here on a Matilda II tank. (Sean O'Flaherty, CC-by-SA 3.0)

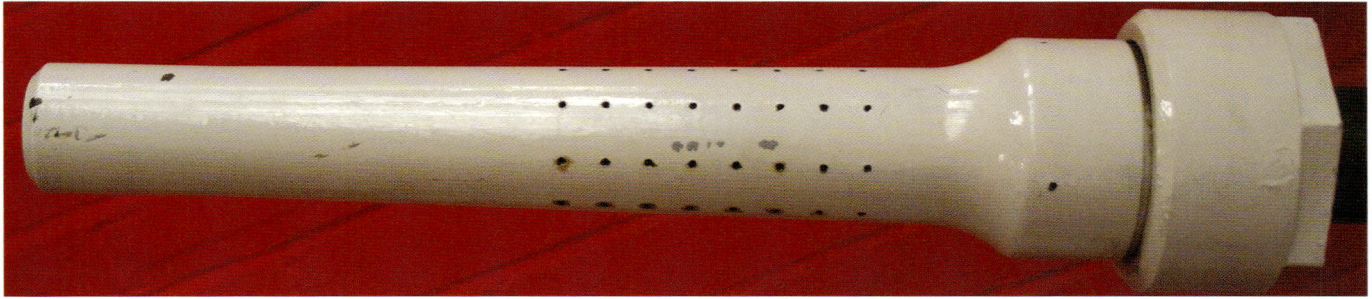

Rheinmetall 120mm smooth-bore type that is to be used for the Challenger 3 upgrade in the late 2020s.

What follows is a catalogue of the main guns used in British tanks since 1916.

2PDR GUN

The 2pdr Ordnance Quick Firing Gun was a high-velocity type that was adopted for both tank and anti-tank use in January 1935 and was the primary British tank gun in the early years of the Second World War. Its replacement began in 1942 when the 6pdr became available.

By 1941, the 2pdr was proving inadequate because of the superior range of German tank and anti-tank guns. It also had limitations because no HE ammunition was available, with the result that special Close Support tanks equipped with howitzers were needed for the destruction of field fortifications. Nevertheless, it could not be replaced at a stroke by the more capable 6pdr, and modifications increased its effectiveness in the later years of the war. From September 1942, an APCBC (Armour-piercing, Capped, Ballistic Capped) round increased its effectiveness against hardened armour, and a further late modification in January 1943 was the Littlejohn adaptor. Designed by a Czech engineer, Janecec, this increased the muzzle velocity of the gun but by the time it was intro-duced the 6pdr was taking over as the primary British tank gun.

The 2pdr gun was used in the A9, A10 and A13 tanks, in the Matilda and Valentine, in the Tetrarch and Harry Hopkins types, and in the Covenanter, Crusader and Churchill as well as in the Canadian-built Ram and the Australian Sentinel AC1.

3PDR GUN

The 3pdr gun that Vickers used in a number of the tanks they designed in the 1920s and 1930s was based on a naval gun of their own

The Littlejohn sleeve for the 2pdr was a squeeze-bore device that improved the gun's muzzle velocity. (Turbothy, CC-by-2.0)

Space to lo ad the gun and for its recoil was always an issue. This view shows the 2pdr in a Valentine being loaded. (IWM E 9766, Public Domain)

design, known as the Ordnance QF 3pdr. The Vickers Medium Mk I had the Ordnance QF Mark I version of the gun, but beginning with the Vickers Medium Mk II a Mark II type was favoured. These guns all had a 47mm bore.

The 3pdr gun had a relatively low muzzle velocity, which was the main reason why it was considered obsolete before the start of the Second World War. It could also fire only solid shot. By 1937, it was being replaced by the Ordnance QF 2pdr gun in new British tank designs.

The 3pdr gun is seen mounted in the turret of a Medium Mk II tank preserved at the Puckpunyal museum in Australia. (Bukvoed, CC-by-2.5)

The original long-barrelled 6pdr gun is seen here in the sponson of a Mk II make tank that has become ditched at Arras on 13 April 1917. (IWM Q6427, Public Domain)

6PDR GUN (HOTCHKISS)

The main gun used in the Mks I to III male tanks started life as a naval weapon in 1885. It was originally known as the Ordnance QF Hotchkiss 6pdr and was introduced to defend large warships against small and fast vessels such as torpedo boats. Larger guns were beginning to replace them by the time of the Great War, but the 6pdr was still in production for the Admiralty by Vickers Armstrong at Elswick.

The gun met the tank requirement for a compact weapon firing a high-explosive shell, although in use it became clear that the length of the barrel was a liability; the muzzle could hit the ground and dig into the mud as the tank crossed trenches. The expedient solution was to shorten the barrel, and the revised gun became the QF 6pdr 6cwt, which was used in the Mk IV tanks from 1917.

The 6cwt or "short" version of the 6pdr gun was developed to prevent the long barrel of the original digging into uneven terrain.

6PDR GUN (HOTCHKISS 6CWT)

The Ordnance QF 6pdr 6 cwt Hotchkiss gun can be considered the first gun specifically designed for tank use. It was a development of the Hotchkiss 6pdr naval gun that was used in the 1916 Mk I tanks, with a barrel shortened by a massive 47in to reduce the risk of the muzzle digging into the ground during trench-crossing operations. The shorter barrel inevitably reduced the muzzle velocity, but this was not seen as a disadvantage at the time.

The gun was introduced for the Mk IV tank in January 1917.

6PDR GUN (ORDNANCE)

The limitations of the 2pdr Ordnance QF gun were apparent from the start, and the Woolwich Arsenal began developing a new gun with a 57mm calibre in April 1938. Once again, there were naval precedents: such guns had been used by the Royal Navy since the late 19th century and the equipment to make them already existed. Delays in development were compounded by a decision to continue making the 2pdr rather than risk a disruptive delay in changing over to the new gun after Dunkirk. As a result the new gun did not enter service until May 1942. It was formally known as the Ordnance QF 6pdr 7cwt type, although the name was usually abbreviated simply to 6pdr.

As a first stage, the 6pdr replaced the 2pdr in existing tank designs, and modified Churchill, Valentine and Crusader tanks were the first beneficiaries. All three required modified turrets. These were followed by tanks specifically designed for the gun, the Cavalier, Cromwell and Centaur. There were two main types of the 6pdr, the Mk 3 and the Mk5, which had a longer barrel and usually a muzzle counterweight as well.

This was a good, accurate gun that was also adopted by the US Army as their standard anti-tank gun (when it was known as the 57mm gun M1) and was manufactured in the USA between 1942 and 1945. However, it was yet another British tank gun that lacked HE ammunition, and was further developed as the Ordnance QF 75mm type to enable it to use US 75mm ammunition that did include an HE round.

17PDR GUN

The 17pdr (76.2mm) Ordnance Quick Firing gun was initially developed as an anti-tank gun for use by infantry units. Design began in late 1940, the earliest production examples appeared in spring 1942, and the gun first saw action in North Africa in February 1943. It quickly demonstrated the ability to defeat the armour of the latest German tanks.

By late 1941, the gun was identified as ideal for use in tanks as well, but no existing British tank was big enough to accommodate it. The Cromwell was therefore adapted, first as the A29 Clan (which did not make production) and then as the A30 Challenger, to take the gun.

While the Challenger was under development, work began on a conversion to enable the US-built Sherman tank to mount the 17pdr gun. This involved modifying the gun, laying it on its side, and moving the tank's radios to a new box welded to the back of the turret to make room for the recoil. This highly successful conversion was known as the Sherman Firefly. Although only limited numbers were available at D-Day, eventually around 50% of British Shermans were modified to the Firefly specification.

The 17pdr was also fitted to a number of US-built M10 tank destroyers in British service, where it replaced the American 3-inch (76mm) type and provided greater ammunition compatibility with the tanks. The converted tank destroyers were known as Achilles. It was also used in the Valentine-based Archer self-propelled gun.

The gun was further developed by Vickers as the 77mm HV, which became standard for the Comet tank. It was also in the initial specification for the Centurion as the war drew to a close.

20PDR GUN

The Ordnance QF 20pdr gun was developed by the Royal Ordnance Factories to replace the 17pdr in the mid-1940s and first appeared in

The 17pdr gun became the primary British tank weapon in the later years of the Second World War. Here it is in an A30 Challenger tank. (IWM MH4105 Public Domain)

1948. It was an 84mm calibre gun (the figure is sometimes quoted as 83.4mm) designed to fire both armour-piercing and high-explosive rounds, and in particular was intended to counter the 85mm gun of the contemporary Soviet T-44 tanks.

The 20pdr gun was used in the Centurion, in the early-1950s Charioteer conversion of the Cromwell, and in the Caernarvon that was developed as a stop-gap for the Conqueror heavy gun tank. Early versions of the gun had no fume extractor, but later examples did. The 20pdr was considered adequate until examination of a Soviet T-54 tank captured during the Hungarian uprising in 1956 made clear that its armour would defeat the British gun. As a result, British tanks moved to the newer 105mm L7 gun.

30MM L21 RARDEN CANNON

This high-velocity gun took its name from the Royal Armament Research and Development Establishment at Fort Halstead that developed

This 20pdr gun has a fume extractor mid-way along its barrel. It is on a preserved Charioteer tank at the Latrun museum in Israel. (Bukvoed, CC-by-SA 2.5)

The 30mm Rarden cannon was fitted to the Scimitar light reconnaissance tank, and is seen here on a preserved vehicle at a display day. (Alf van Beem, Public Domain)

The huge 32pdr gun was mounted in the Tortoise with limited traverse to create a heavy assault tank. The sheer size of the gun is apparent from this picture, which shows the first prototype of the tank, numbered P1. (IWM MH 9865, Public Domain)

it in the later 1960s. The weapon was designed with minimum inboard length to allow more space in the turret or a smaller turret overall, and as a result had a long barrel. The typical range was around 2000 yards, which was of course far less than that of a full-size tank gun.

Manufacture began in 1970 and the Rarden cannon became the primary weapon of the Scimitar reconnaissance vehicle, but was also used in the Fox armoured car and the FV510 Warrior infantry fighting vehicle and some of its variants. Transferring Fox turrets to FV101 Scorpion reconnaissance vehicles created the Sabre.

32PDR GUN

As early as October 1942, the General Staff gave instructions for an improved tank gun to replace the still-new 17pdr. Several proposals came and went but in September 1943 development settled on a derivative of the Ordnance QF 3.7-inch heavy anti-aircraft gun. Later in development the decision was taken to give this

a 32 lb shell; both armour piercing and HE types were planned. The gun was also known by its calibre of 94mm.

The 32pdr was mounted in the A39 Tortoise heavy assault tank in 1944, and in June 1945 firing trials showed that it could penetrate the frontal armour of a German Tiger II tank, which was then considered its best-armoured adversary. However, development was halted at the end of the war and thoughts about a new tank gun focused on the 20pdr.

75MM GUN (ORDNANCE QF)

British experience with the 75mm gun in the American Sherman tank made clear that a dual-purpose tank gun firing both armour-piercing and high-explosive shells was feasible. As a first step, Vickers began work on a new gun that could use American 75mm ammunition, but this project encountered problems when it became clear that the gun would not fit into any turret that would fit the turret ring of the latest A27 family of tanks.

However, it then became clear that the existing 6pdr gun could be bored out to 75mm and used to fire unmodified US ammunition. This solution would make a dual-purpose tank gun available quickly and relatively cheaply, and the weapon was given the name of Ordnance QF 75mm. From November 1943, Cromwell production switched to the 75mm gun.

76MM L23 GUN

The 76mm L23A1 low-velocity gun was developed by the Royal Ordnance from the similar but heavier L5A1 76mm type. Despite its familiar name, its bore was actually 76.2mm. This was a rifled-barrel gun capable of firing a range of ammunition types including HESH (High Explosive Squash Head), HEAT (High Explosive Anti-Tank) and APFSDS (Armour-Piercing Fin-Stabilized Discarding Sabot). Its maximum rate of fire was six rounds per minute, and the typical range was 2200 yards.

The gun was used in the Scorpion reconnaissance vehicle and also in the Cougar six-wheel mine resistant vehicle that entered service with the Canadian Army in the late 1970s.

77MM GUN

The British 17pdr gun proved an excellent anti-tank weapon, but was too large to fit the turrets of existing tanks. Expensive and time-consuming work to develop tank hulls capable of taking a larger turret followed, but in the mean time Vickers-Armstrongs set about creating a shorter and lighter version of the gun that could use the same ammunition.

The reduction in length allowed the gun to be mounted on a Cromwell-sized turret ring, although the turret itself had to be redesigned. Known as the 77mm to distinguish it from the 17pdr (although it had the same 76.2mm bore), the new gun became the standard weapon of the "improved Cromwell" or A34 Comet that was

The British 75mm gun was developed by modifying the existing 6pdr to take American ammunition. This one is on a preserved Cromwell tank at the Overloon museum in the Netherlands. (Alf van Beem, Public Domain)

This short-barrelled gun is the 76mm L23 type on a Scorpion belonging to the Irish Defence Forces. Although equal in its bore dimension to some wartime guns, it was completely outclassed by the guns on contemporary MBTs and was designed to do a different job. (Irish Defence Forces, CC-by-2.0)

The late-war 77mm gun is seen here on an A34 Comet tank preserved by the Tank Museum at Bovington.

introduced in late 1944. Although its performance was slightly inferior to that of the 17pdr, it was to all intents and purposes the equal of that gun.

105MM L7 GUN

The 105mm L7 gun was an excellent weapon that was not only used in British tanks but for a while was the standard tank gun within NATO. It was used by many armies around the world that bought western tanks and was made under licence in Argentina, China, Israel and the USA.

Design of the gun began in the early 1950s at RARDE in Fort Halstead. It was first trialled in July 1956, and met a wave of official enthusiasm for a new gun after it had become clear that the then-current 20pdr was not capable of knocking out the latest Soviet tanks. User trials began in July 1959 and the gun entered service later the same year.

This was a rifled gun that had been specifically designed to fit into the turret mountings of the 20pdr so that existing Centurions with that gun could be up-gunned as quickly as possible. It was used both to upgrade older tanks and as original equipment on new Centurions from 1959. In Britain, it also became the primary weapon of the Vickers MBTs and the Vijayanta for India. In the USA it was fitted to some variants of the M48 Patton and M60 tanks, and in West Germany it became the main armament of the Leopard 1. There were three main versions, which were the basic L7A1, the L7A2 with thermal sleeve, and the L7A3 with special features to suit the Leopard.

120MM L1 GUN

The British strategy to counter the Soviet heavy tanks in the early years of the Cold War was to supplement its Centurion tanks with heavy gun tanks that would provide a stand-off capability. The gun selected for what would eventually become the Conqueror tank in 1955 was a new long-range 120mm rifled type that was being developed in the USA for its own heavy tanks and was known as the M58 type.

In British use, it was renamed the L1 gun and was manufactured both with a fume extractor (as the L1A1) and without (as the L1A2). It was capable of firing both APDS and HESH rounds but its use of a separate shell and propellant charge required two loaders in the tank.

120MM L11 GUN

In 1957, RARDE began work on a new 120mm tank gun that would replace the US-designed L1 type used in the Conqueror tank. The 120mm calibre had been adopted as the NATO standard, and so this gun would eventually also replace the L7 105mm type that was used in the Centurion from 1959. The new tank that was in design in the late 1950s would enter service as the Chieftain in 1965, and the new L11 gun was designed specifically for it.

The barrel was rifled, with a thermal sleeve and a fume extractor and, like the L1 gun that preceded it, the L11 used separate shells and propellant charges. The gun went for firing trials in 1961 and was accepted for service on the Chieftain tank. It was fully stabilised with an integrated computerised control system, and could fire a wide variety of ammunition types. Key among these were of course APDS armour-piercing rounds and HESH rounds designed to incapacitate the crew of an enemy tank.

The basic L11 deign was developed into a series of production variants, of which the most numerous was the L11A5, as used in the Chieftain.

120MM L30 GUN

A third-generation 120mm gun was developed for the Challenger 2 that replaced the first Challenger tanks from 1998. Known as the Gun, 120mm Tk L30 (Tk is for Tank), it was an improved version of the earlier L11 gun, featuring among other things a barrel made of electro-slag remelted steel with chromium electro-plating for the bore and chamber. These features gave an extended barrel life of up to 400 firings before unacceptable inaccuracy set in. Uniquely among NATO's 120mm guns of the time, it was a rifled gun, because the British Army considered this best suited their use of HESH and APFSDS rounds.

Like earlier British 120mm tank guns, the barrel was insulated with a thermal sleeve and

The angle of this shot taken at Bovington emphasises the long barrel of the L1 main gun on a Conqueror tank. (Hugh Llewellyn, CC-by-SA 2.0)

a fume extractor. Also fitted was a muzzle reference system to counter bending of the barrel, and the gun had its own electric control and stabilisation system. Again like earlier British 120mm guns, the L30 used separate projectiles and propellant charges.

Barrels grew longer and longer as greater range was needed. This is the 120mm L11A5 gun on a Challenger I tank at the Bovington Tank Museum. (David Holt, CC-by-SA 2.0)

The next stage in 120mm gun designs was the L30, pictured here on a Challenger 2 tank in Iraq. (Public Domain)

The first smooth-bore main gun to be specified for a British tank was the 120mm design by Rheinmetall, pictured on a Challenger 3 pilot model. (RBSL)

120MM RHEINMETALL GUN

The first of the 120mm smooth-bore tank guns produced by Rheinmetall in West Germany was the RH-20 L/44 type that was introduced in 1974 for the Leopard tank. It was developed further with a longer barrel and increased muzzle velocity as the L/55 type, and in this guise was chosen for the British Challenger 3 upgrade programme. For that, it will be manufactured in Britain by a joint British and German company.

The L/55 gun is compatible with a wide variety of ammunition and has a chromium-lined barrel that increases the barrel life to over 1500 rounds. The barrel has both a thermal sleeve and a fume extractor.

183MM L4 GUN

The search for a tank gun to counter the threat of the Soviet IS-3 tank in the late 1940s led to the development of a huge 183mm type that became known as the Ordnance QF 183mm Tank L4 gun. Work to find a new gun had begun in mid-1949 and an early option had been a development of the US 155mm gun, but this did not meet the extremely stringent British requirement. The 183mm size was approved in December 1952.

The L4 gun was one of the largest and most powerful tank guns ever built at the time. It had a rifled barrel with a fume extractor placed at roughly the mid-point, and its enormous weight of 3.7 tons promised all manner of practical problems in use. The tank to carry this gun had to be designed around it, and was planned as the FV215, which would have become a successor to the FV214 Conqueror.

In practice, the tank was never built, and probably no more than a dozen examples of the gun were manufactured. As an interim measure, an L4 gun was mounted in a special turret on a Centurion chassis, resulting in an impractical-looking vehicle called the FV4005 that remained experimental.

The largest-bore British tank gun was the 183mm that was planned for the FV215, among others. Its huge barrel and the ungainly turret needed to go with it can be seen here on the FV4005 Conway exhibit at the Bovington Tank Museum.